CONTEMPLATION:

Only the Crucified are Truly Alive

Gary Michael Hassig

Dedication:

To the One who dwells in unapproachable Light,
and yet calls us in love
to boldly approach His throne of grace,
the Way Who showed us
all the many facets of the way
to die in order to live:
to Him be all glory forever.

And

To all the mystics of this generation
and those who follow,
the dancers of light
drawn as moths to the One Flame:
dance on forever
in love
with the Master Dancer!

Contents

Only the crucified

are truly alive

There's no resurrection till

we've been to the Cross

Only the crucified

abundantly live

God is our everything

and all else is loss

Acknowledgements: My Gratefulness List

I am truly grateful for:

The kind hope, gracious love, constant guidance, blessed truth and eternal wisdom of God, the Lover of my Soul, the Strength of my Life, the Fountain that flows eternal, the Light that never dies.

My wonderful wife Diane, for her encouragement, for putting up with me through my contemplative journeyings and the writing of this book, and for her help with the proofreading and computer issues. Her sister Kay, for pointing me in the right direction and lighting the spark.

Jim Graven, Kate Roach, and all the people of the Sophia Group who have contributed so richly to my contemplative experience over the past seven years—Carrie, Skip, Gary K, Rick, Patty, Joe, Charlotte, Vic, Emma, Thomas and Jacy, Jay, and so many others whose names I've forgotten (sorry), and for contemplativejourney.com, the delightful fruit of which this group is the seed.

Sister Therese, Sister Ana, Sister Ann, and all the other blessed sisters of Benet Hill Monastery/Benet Pines Retreat Center, whose gracious generosity and patience with this poor Protestant pilgrim have been such an encouragement. Mike, Linda, Leslie, Rob, Heli, Steve, Helen, Monika, Peter, Alicia, Marilyn, Kathleen, the late Sally Lawson, and all the other great people I've met and spent time with, waiting on God at the Benet Hill and Benet Pines centering prayer sessions. You have blessed me more than you'll ever know.

Sister Therese for her knowledge, expertise and guidance in regard to the history and practice of contemplative spirituality.

All the Christian mystics across the centuries, known and unknown, from Origen and the Cappadocian Fathers, to the Desert Fathers and Mothers, to Augustine and Dionysius, to Bernard of Clairvaux and Thomas Aquinas, to Julian of Norwich and Hadewijch of Antwerp and Mechthild of Magdeburg, to John of Ruysbroeck and the great Meister Eckhart, to John of the Cross and Teresa of Avila, to Thomas Merton who provided my first exposure to contemplative thought, to Thomas Keating, Basil Pennington, and William Meninger for developing and introducing centering prayer to the 20th and 21st centuries.

Jay Heinlein for his continuing support and encouragement and patience, and his great expertise in the crazily changing world of publishing.

The Christian contemplative writers of the 20th and 21st centuries who have nurtured the flame and fanned the fire of the modern contemplative movement: Thomas Merton, Thomas Keating, William Johnston, Richard Foster, Bernard McGinn, Cynthia Bourgeault, James Finley, Martin Laird, Macrina Wiederkehr, Richard Rohr, and all the writers and the editor of *The Inner Journey: Views from the Christian Tradition* (Parabola anthology series).

To all, my humble, heartfelt thanks and appreciation.

A note on Bible passages: all scriptures cited in this book are my own paraphrases, based on comparisons of many translations, especially the New English Translation, New Living Translation, New International Version, New American Standard Bible, and New King James Version, as well as studies in the original Hebrew and Greek lexicons. My thanks to Strong's Concordance for decades of insight into hundreds of Bible passages, and to Bible Hub (biblehub.com) for their great treasury of Bible information and commentary.

Preface

There's a hunger way down deep inside of me
It's a hunger I know only you can feed
I will cry out to you like a lost child
Till you come and meet my need
For more of you
I can hear my heart crying out
    for more of you
People all around me
    and they're longing for the truth
I can hear the whole creation groaning
    and crying out in pain
For more and more of you...

I want to say at the outset that, although contemplative spirituality is a gift of God that can help set a lukewarm, compromising Christian on fire for God and help such people (people like me) become more and more fully surrendered to God, there's one thing contemplation definitely cannot do. It cannot save you. Salvation comes through faith in Jesus Christ and the atoning work he did on the Cross, period. That's true whether you're a contemplative or not. If you trust in contemplation, it will fail you. Just as with healing, prophecy and other spiritual gifts, it's only a tool in God's toolbox, nothing more. This point cannot be emphasized too strongly.

It's all about Jesus—not about being a mystic.[1] Just as an automobile's purpose is to safely and reliably carry its owner wherever he wants to go, not to be a Nascar star, our purpose as Christians is to know, love, follow, serve and obey Christ, not to "be contemplative." Whatever a vehicle's owner chooses to use it to carry, whether dirt or diamonds, shouldn't make any difference; whatever path Christ calls each of us to

If you think contemplation just sounds cool and you want to pursue it, set aside some time— a month wouldn't be too much— for fasting, praying, for seeking God about his will for you. Even if you think God is giving you the green light to follow the contemplative path, you still need to count the cost. It's a difficult path to walk; without God's full blessing, you just can't do it.

individually shouldn't matter— only that we walk the path he leads us down. If that involves being a contemplative, well, that's a blessing for sure, but it's also a very difficult path to walk. You don't choose it for yourself. God knows what's best for each of us, and if the path God gives you isn't a contemplative one, trying to walk such a path on your own will only lead to disaster and despair.

Also, contemplation[2] is not for everyone. It's a gift of God, like hospitality or prophecy or healing. Any believer has the potential to be used by God in any of these areas, but not everyone is called to operate in them. And contemplation is time consuming; centering prayer typically takes twenty minutes, and twice a day is recommended. If you combine it with lectio divina (Scripture meditation), that adds another five to ten minutes, at least once a day. By the time you include any preparation time needed (I usually drink a little coffee or tea and use the restroom before centering, etc.), that knocks a whole hour out of your day. (Since I started centering prayer I find that I need less sleep, so it tends to balance out somewhat.) But the point is, if you think contemplation just sounds cool and you're interested in pursuing it, there's more to it than that. You need to set aside some time—a month or more wouldn't be too much—for fasting, for praying, for diligently seeking God about whether it's in his will for you. And even if you feel sure that God is giving you the green light to follow the contemplative path, you still need to count the cost. It's a difficult path to walk; you can't do it without God's full blessing. And there are potential dangers involved. If you were to just start practicing contemplation on your own without God's guidance and direction, there are possible psychological/ mental health risks.

Also, it could be easy to read this book and think contemplative prayer is a do-it-yourself thing. That's not really true; you need others. It's important to find or start a group of like-minded people to do centering prayer with once a week or as often as possible. You need others for the purpose of bouncing ideas and experiences off each other and comparing notes, as well as for mutual encouragement. It's also a good idea to have a spiritual director to meet with at least monthly—someone who is at least a little farther ahead of you on the contemplative path, who can help you with the difficulties you will encounter. In some areas, it may be hard to find such people, but make it a matter of prayer, and be open to the possibility of guidance from other Christian traditions. (I'm Protestant, so for my fellow Protestants, that means looking to Catholic or Orthodox believers for advice on contemplation. More on that below). One of the possible risks of the contemplative life is that it tends to appeal to loners; if you're one, as I tend to be, it's easy to think you can do this contemplation thing—and pretty much everything—by yourself. Take my advice: you really can't.

Contemplation is all about dying to self in ways the average Christian isn't necessarily called to. Only the crucified are truly alive—this is a truth that all Christians should experience to some degree; it's a big part of what being a follower of Jesus means. But as I said before, contemplation involves forms of surrender to God that you can't do on your own. If you think the flesh will just roll over and die for you, think again. We call the contemplative journey a path, but it's really a very wild experience, more like signing up for a roller coaster ride that will last you the rest of your life. Committing to it is like that old bumper sticker: get in, sit down, shut up, and hang on.[3]

But maybe you have come to the place in life where, despite all the blessings you've received, you really want more of God than what you've experienced; there's a hunger that can't be filled by Christian music or Bible reading or anything else. And perhaps you have started to recognize that maybe that's not a lack of thankfulness, but that it's God himself stirring up that deeper longing in you, spurring you on to find a greater depth in your relationship than you've seen before. Worship, prayer, and other spiritual activities can bring you to a point of closeness to God, but they leave you at God's doorstep, which still feels much too far away from him. And you begin to realize there's a difference between the things of God, and God himself. You cry out, God, I want more! And the more you get, the less satisfying it is, and you start to realize it's not more things or even more blessings; there's a hunger that nothing but God himself can fill; nothing but more of God will do. And again, you may recognize that this desire is coming, not from you, but from the Spirit of God.

That's exactly the place many throughout history have come to: a deep spiritual hunger. And at some point very early in history, perhaps centuries before Christ, something happened. Someone was perhaps meditating on what it means to wait on God, and realized something profoundly powerful. They found that they could just sit in God's presence and direct their longing to him, ignoring all sensory input and their own thoughts, desires and feelings—and something happened deep within. They couldn't quite put it into words, but they knew beyond the shadow of a doubt that it was from God. And they discovered that if they did this on a regular basis, God changed them.

A Bridge to Other Religious Traditions

Although I'm writing from the perspective of my evangelical Protestant background, one thing you'll notice in this book is that many of the quotes from Christians, ancient or modern, are from Catholic or Orthodox believers. This is because, from the Reformation to the late 20th Century, most Protestant denominations rejected contemplative spirituality. Notably, the founders of such denominations as the Methodists (John Wesley) and Protestant writers like C.S. Lewis, W.H. Auden and T.S. Eliot were contemplatives. The Quakers and Mennonites have long been known to embrace contemplative practices as well. If you're of the mindset that the Catholic and Orthodox churches are astray from God, I would encourage you to read the late, great evangelist Chuck Colson's thoughts on this subject.[4]

I've heard it said that much of American Protestant Christianity is like a lake a hundred miles across and one inch deep. Though there are aspects of the Christian faith as practiced by Catholic and Orthodox Christians that I don't necessarily subscribe to, they have an astonishing depth of knowledge, tradition, and Christian love-in-action that is so greatly lacking in most Protestant churches. In the past ten years my Christian walk has been tremendously blessed and enriched by friendships I have developed with both Catholic and Orthodox believers and by the writings of many in their traditions from the second century to the present time.

To Catholic, Protestant and Orthodox Christians, let me say this: The time is over for throwing out nearly everything that came out of the Church for fourteen hundred years and refusing to believe or acknowledge that anything good can come out of the Nazareth of Catholic or Orthodox Christianity, or the Damascus Road of Protestant Christ-followership. I believe that when the ancient and modern branches of the Church can learn to love, feed and receive from each other, the cause of Christ can only benefit, and the Church at large will be wonderfully strengthened. Contemplative spirituality has great potential to be a bridge between the different branches of the Church—a bridge I believe is being built behind the scenes by God, not a work of man's own doing.

Although Christian contemplatives have initiated or become involved in dialog with mystics of other faiths (Buddhist, Hindu, Muslim and others), to me the fact of who Jesus is—the sinless, eternal Son of God— and what he accomplished at Calvary and at the Resurrection is the highest wisdom, the only essential knowledge, in the world—the plumb line for all truth for all of history. On this point, for me at least, there can be no compromise. Perhaps God will choose to use contemplatives of other faiths to teach us greater devotion to our Master or how to better serve one another, and hopefully they will know we are Christians by our love and will come to know Christ, the source of that love. It is my hope that through such dialog, contemplative prayer can become a bridge to help those in other religions come to realize that Christ is the hope their faiths have all unknowingly pointed to for all these centuries.

My purpose in writing this book is to provide a fairly concise yet thorough guidebook to help other Christ-followers discover and begin to explore contemplation and the tremendous contributions of writers from all centuries of the Christian faith. However, exploring the practice of contemplative spirituality can be like walking through a minefield; there are hazards and potential problems associated with the contemplative path. So please consider this a travel guide to the journey, written in language familiar to Protestants of all stripes, but Catholic- and Orthodox-friendly as well. The chapters are written in sections, so once you've made the decision to pursue contemplation, you can use the book as a devotional. In other words, you may find it most useful if, rather than trying to absorb the whole book in a few days, you take just one section of a chapter per day as a preface for your practice of centering prayer.

The Contemplative Perspective

The point of view which contemplation develops in people comes naturally to new Christians.[5] They are always saying things like, "Wow, so, like, in worship, we give everything to God, and yet he IS our everything! That is SO cool!" New believers often instinctively, intuitively recognize the paradoxical nature of the kingdom of God and our relationship with God, and tend to be fascinated with Biblical paradoxes. They may puzzle over them, but often, they get "the last will be first and the first will be last" in a way that older believers may have a hard time with.

New believers tend to experience the miracle of the Kingdom and its paradoxes more than older believers. They actually meditate on things in the Bible without being told to; until some well-meaning older believer tells them they shouldn't do that because meditation is dangerous, they often just spontaneously turn over and over in their minds the sayings of Jesus and other parts of the Bible, one word or one phrase at a time. They understand what it means to say that we must become like little children again in order to enter the kingdom of Heaven, because they're there; they're back to a place they remember being when they were 5 years old. To a new believer, everything is amazing, and words have their own special wonder. Jesus, the Word, was history's greatest wonder-worker when it came to putting words together. And you have to get into a place of wonder, you have to give in to wonder, to see the real meaning of his words. New Christians usually get that.

So do contemplatives. Once you begin a disciplined practice of centering prayer, you start recognizing paradoxes and, like a brand new Christian, you start realizing there's so much more to this world than the average person realizes. It's not just get up, go to work, come home, do whatever. Every moment is full of depth; everything you see and hear can be utterly fascinating if you take the time to let it be, to explore it. The patterns of the wood grain in the table are so beautiful, so amazing, and they're a record of the life of the tree that they came from. The lamp cord hanging down the side of the desk has such graceful, interesting curves to it, and the shadows it casts give depth and drama to it. And it's full of electricity! The wood was full of life before being made into a table, and even now, that life speaks to you. You soon run out of words when you're in this realm, and when you come to the place where words can no longer describe the place of awe and beauty you are in, if you choose to stay in that place and adore God without words, that's the beginning of contemplation. The fear/awe/wonder of the Lord is the beginning of wisdom!

Contemplative spirituality is simply an expression of one's passion for Christ, an area of Christian growth; some believers may consider it a cancerous type of growth, but I don't see it that way at all. To me it's like waking up one morning to discover that God has added a room onto your house. The house is big, beautiful, grand; perhaps you've always felt it had everything you needed. But when you open the door that wasn't there before and walk into the room for the first time you are in awe at what you see, and you soon realize it's a God-room, a room for meeting with and knowing God in ways you always wished you could, but didn't believe it was possible. The new room is so wonderful, you're delighted with it; you love it. And it opens onto a garden you never had before, full of fresh flowers and ripening fruit, and you start realizing just how weary you are of the canned and processed stuff. But without the house—faith in Christ—the room and the garden are meaningless, useless.

In closing, I just want to say that what I'm describing in this book is really just my own feeble attempt to describe the indescribable and to outline the path that mystical Christianity tends to follow, providing information about each of the steps you will encounter along the way. I don't claim to be an expert on the subject of contemplation, just a pilgrim on the path—one I wish I'd known about decades earlier—who wishes to invite others to prayerfully check it out. There is so much more to contemplative spirituality than I can possibly convey; I consider the information in this book to be a mere drop in the bucket. But that drop, if you drink it with the right motives, leaning on the everlasting arms at all times, will lead you to the River.

Introduction

if i don't lose myself in you
i will not find myself in you
and if i am not found in you
woe is me

if i lose myself in you
i will find myself in you
and if i am found in you
i am free

I have heard so many Christians say "I've memorized a ton of scriptures but I just can't seem to really overcome my weaknesses and live victoriously." Or, "The Bible says to love God with all your heart, mind, soul and strength, but how do you do that?" Or, "I've walked with God for years—decades—but there's still something missing. I've prayed and fasted and studied the Word and worshipped and fed the homeless and supported missions, but it seems like something's stunting my spiritual growth." Or, "I have a relationship with God, I've dealt with sin and have been active in my church, but it still seems like there must be something more to being a Christian than greeting the people around you on Sunday morning and forgetting them by lunchtime. I just don't see my life changing." I'm sure we've all heard those kinds of comments; most of us have said, or at least thought, things like this ourselves.

At the end of the twentieth century, I had gone around the Christianity track for decades, doing all the things a good Christian is supposed to do and trying hard to avoid displeasing God. When I displeased him or became entangled in sin, I was quick to deal with it before him, receive forgiveness, and move on. But I couldn't escape feeling a deep, unsatisfied longing for more of God. The more dissatisfied I became, the harder it was not to believe something was wrong with the modern view of how the Christian life should be lived. Something was missing. At a conference in about 1997, I heard a worship leader named David Ruis sing U2's song "I Still Haven't Found What I'm Looking For" as a worship song, and it spoke deeply to me: "I have run, I have crawled/I have scaled these city walls/Only to be with you/...I believe in Kingdom Come/...You broke the bonds /And you loosed the chains/ Carried the cross of my shame/...You know I believe it/But I still haven't found what I'm looking for."[1]

Prior to that time, I had felt this song was reason to question U2's claim to be followers of Jesus. How could you say that stuff if you have received Christ as your savior and know God as your Father? But at that conference, I realized the song echoed what was in my own heart: I knew the Lord, I was thankful for all Christ had done for me, and I had served God to the best of my ability, yet somehow I knew there was more. At that point in my life—a real breakthrough time for me—I was able to recognize that, although we're not of this world, we are still in it. We have the Holy Spirit living in us, yet we're still flesh and blood, we still sin, and there's still a great hunger for God that never gets completely filled by worship, bible study or prayer.

"There must be more than this,"[2] we sing, yet most of us become resigned to the idea that in this life, worship and Bible study and prayer are as good as it gets. There seems to be no way to keep getting closer to God, no way to rest completely content in his bosom like the child in Psalm 131, not until eternity. But if that's true, then what was King David talking about in that Psalm? What did the Psalmist mean by "Be still and know that I am God?" How long can one be still? Is being still for a long time somehow conducive to knowing God more deeply? Does it turn into some new-age or eastern religion thing if you do that? I had so many questions, and I had no idea how to find the answers; I hardly even knew what questions to ask. But God knew my heart, and over a period of years, the answers began to come.

In the meantime, God gave me a series of dreams that I will never forget. God has spoken to me through my dreams in some very radical ways since becoming a Christian; some of the greatest turning points in my walk of faith have come because of God-given dreams. These particular dreams came from the mid-'90's to about 2002 or so. In every one of them— there must have been at least twenty such dreams—there was a mountainous area of high, beautifully sculpted rock formations not far from where I lived, and I had a great longing in my heart to climb up to these rocks and explore them. But every time I tried, I was somehow thwarted. I sometimes woke up crying because the longing was so strong, like a deep hunger that came from God. I would ask him repeatedly what these dreams meant.

A couple years after the conference mentioned above, I was part of a home fellowship group connected with my church that began studying Richard Foster's book *Celebration of Discipline*. I was surprised to learn that Foster spends an entire chapter on the subject of meditation and contemplative prayer. And,

> I read the words
> of Origen,
> Benedict of Nursia,
> Bernard of Clairvaux,
> Meister Eckhart,
> Julian of Norwich,
> John of the Cross,
> and many other
> Christian writers...
> I realized there was
> a great hunger and
> passion for Christ
> in every century.
> I began seeking God
> to see what he would
> want me to learn
> from these eminent
> men and women
> of his Church
> who lived in ages
> and cultures
> long forgotten.

come to find out later, Foster also spends a chapter on contemplation in his book *Prayer: Finding the Heart's True Home*. I knew of Hindu and Buddhist meditation and contemplation from reading about them and beginning to explore them a little in college. After coming to Christ in the early 1970's, the Christians I knew and the Christian authors I read had all warned me to steer way clear of anything more than thinking about what a passage of Scripture meant. Beyond that, you were getting into dangerous territory, I was told. Even with meditating on Scripture, if you didn't do it right, you could get demon possessed. But now, many years later, Foster's books seemed to me to have the fingerprints of God all over them, and I could tell he knew from firsthand experience what he was talking about in regard to meditation.

About this time I began to get interested in the history of Christianity and started reading a couple of books on the subject. I'd been taught that after the first century, the Church fell into great darkness and had very little of value to offer serious Christians until Martin Luther. Yet, reading quotes from the Church Fathers and Christian leaders between 100 and 1500 AD, I began to see that this was a great misunderstanding. I read the words of Origen, Benedict of Nursia, Bernard of Clairvaux, Meister Eckhart, Julian of Norwich, John of the Cross, and many other Christians of the centuries prior to and early in the Reformation period, and realized there was a great hunger and passion for Christ in every century. Yet, other than the rare quote from Augustine or Francis of Assisi, I had never heard the words or experiences of any of the great Christian leaders of those centuries mentioned in a sermon. I began seeking God to see what he would want me to learn from these eminent men and women of his Church who lived in ages and cultures long forgotten.

The last few months of 2001 were a time of national mourning over the 9-11 terrorist attacks. For me personally, there was also a sense that a change was in the air. One Saturday afternoon in October of that year, while at work I felt enveloped in the most beautiful sense of the presence of God. As far as I can recall, I hadn't been seeking him in any special way; it was pure grace. After leaving work, I went to a park in the middle of town with hills and hiking trails; there, I walked along a path to the end of a high ridge, where I sat on a rock worshiping and thanking God and feeling caught in wonder. It was as if I was sitting inside a rainbow. It was a cool, cloudy day, not the kind of sunshiny afternoon where you just naturally feel close to God. Yet rarely had I experienced the beauty and transcendence of God like that. I wasn't sure what he was saying to me, but I longed to be wrapped and rapt in his beauty like that every day, and I let him know.

I spent part of Christmas that year at the home of my wife's sister Kay, a lifelong and devoted Catholic layperson who does her best to serve God. I knew that her life was in many ways different from mine, but I had great respect for her devotion to God. She had on her bookshelf several books by Thomas Merton, whose writings I was somewhat familiar with; I had read and enjoyed two of his books as a very young Christian, then was warned away from his writings by well-meaning Christian leaders who believed Merton, a Catholic, was on a false path. I started wondering how I would view his writings through the lens of (at that time) over twenty-five years of Bible study and Christian learning, and I felt God encouraging me to pursue it.

Kay also told me about her involvement in centering prayer, a form of prayer similar to what Merton practiced, which seemed comparable to what most Christians I knew would have called meditation. My wife had mentioned to me that this was part of Kay's faith practice, but at the time I just thought of it as some weird Catholic thing. But seeing the Merton connection, I was intrigued, so she gave me one of her Merton books. In addition, Kay gave me a book on centering prayer by Father Thomas Keating called *Intimacy with God*. The title reflected an idea I had heard mentioned in connection with worship in some of the churches I had been associated with. Yet here was the head of a Catholic monastery talking about the same thing, saying this intimacy with God could be learned or developed through centering prayer. Kay explained that centering prayer was based largely on a book called *The Cloud of Unknowing*, written in the fourteenth century by an anonymous English monk. I became determined to find out what this centering prayer thing was all about; I thought it might be totally false, proof that the New Age Movement had gotten to the Catholics; if so, I wanted to expose it for the sham I expected it might turn out to be. But I also thought that perhaps there might be something to it, something from God's heart.

I spent the month of January reading Merton, Keating and the *Cloud* book, along with shorter writings or quotes by other contemplatives. I saw how they often wrote as if from a completely different dimension, one that was humble and pure, emotionally whole and psychologically rock-solid, and very much in touch with God. The more I read, the more

I realized these were people with a genuine love for God who knew of a way their hunger for him could be satisfied, at least more deeply than anything I had experienced—the way of meditation and contemplation.

I also began to realize that the Catholic and Orthodox Churches, far from being the world's largest pseudo-Christian cult as I had been taught, were a completely different culture from the Protestant one I had been immersed in, yet with the same roots and the same God. I knew I would probably never be a Catholic, yet I felt a deepening respect for these people who had kept alive the traditions that had been part of the Christian heritage for two thousand years, traditions that were completely unknown outside the Catholic and Orthodox churches. I began to realize that, far from being idol worshippers as I had been led to believe, many of these people had a genuine relationship with God.

I began in February 2002 to practice centering prayer, and discovered within a week or two that there was something profound about it. I saw little if anything happening during the time of prayer; I just laid down my life, my thoughts, my emotions, my memories and desires, before God and, for twenty minutes twice a day, loved him with a "naked intent direct to God," as *The Cloud of Unknowing* says. I discovered that for those who have ears to hear, the Word of God speaks often and powerfully of contemplative prayer, of which centering prayer is the first stage, an invitation to God which is really acceptance of God's invitation to us to go deeper with him.

And I found that in my everyday life outside of centering prayer, I could talk to people freely about Jesus—something I had often had difficulty with in the past. I could keep my mind on God, and I often found greater strength against temptation. I had greater boldness and God-given peace in everything I did. Times of worship meant something more than just a ritual. God was real in my life, in ways I had never seen before. And around this time, I finally stopped having dreams about climbing up into the beautiful rock formations. When I realized one day that I hadn't had those dreams for awhile, I again began asking God what they meant and why they had stopped. God opened my eyes to the fact that the dreams had ended not long after I began practicing centering prayer. I was finally up in those mysteriously beautiful rock castles, exploring the riches and wonders of God, not just dreaming about it! And I have had several dreams since then, where I am in those rock formations, exploring them and the beautiful caves I find inside them, but always realizing I've barely scratched the surface; there is so much more to explore.

Since then, it hasn't been easy, and I haven't always been consistent. I've never been a very disciplined person, and sitting down twice a day to die to self—well, let's just say the flesh doesn't like it. The old nature, the false self, can find all kinds of things that need to be done right then. But I've persevered. Over time I found others I could meet with weekly to practice lectio divina (Scripture meditation) and centering prayer. There have been some serious bumps in the road; sometimes it goes from a road to a faint trail that's hard to follow. I've sometimes had to deal with sin issues. But through it all, I've grown closer to God. And I don't really have all those questions any more. I've discovered what it means to truly rest in God, to abide in Christ, to be filled with the Spirit. And I'm learning, gradually, more and more about how to love as Christ loved me.

Centering prayer is the meadowlike gateway to the broad, wondrous valley of contemplative prayer. And these forms of prayer are for me the oyster in which the pearl of great price is found. The Church has had great outpourings of contemplative prayer through the ages, but the secular Age of Reason, the so-called Enlightenment, and to some extent its precursor, the Scholasticism movement of the late middle ages, all but extinguished the light of contemplation in the centuries since Columbus, Newton and Galileo. We've learned much about ourselves, our planet and our universe since then. If we're honest with ourselves, the more we learn, the less we know. And, the more we learn, the more the universe speaks to us of God and his infinite creativity, wisdom and love—for those who have ears to hear.

But we often can't see it by just looking at creation. We must look to the Creator; we must spend time being still in his presence, like a child resting against its mother (Psalm 130). We must spend time in silence with him, allowing him to work inside us in ways that are far beyond our comprehension. We must learn to spend time loving him with all our heart, soul, mind and strength—by giving our heart, soul, mind and strength to him, by turning away from every thought but our Beloved.

I believe that just as the spiritual gifts spoken of in 1 Cor. 12-14 were restored to the Church in the twentieth century, God is restoring contemplative prayer to his people in the twenty-first century. (And, yes, the Bible does speak in many places of contemplation. Chapter 3 delves more deeply into what the Bible says, from a contemplative viewpoint.) I believe that in a hundred years, these practices will be as much a part of many churches as waiting on God for prophecy, wisdom or healing are today.

God is on the move! Don't let him pass you by. Find a quiet place, as Jesus did, and spend some time in prayer and meditation on his Word. A good scripture to start with is John 12:24: "Unless a grain of wheat falls to the ground and dies, it remains alone; but if it falls and dies, it brings forth much fruit." Then, when you're finished, don't just get up and leave. Remain silently with God for awhile. Like that grain of wheat, learn to die with Christ in stillness and silence, in the places deep within you where only God can see; then watch what God brings to the light as you spend time waiting on him in this way daily. As with the germination of a seed deep in the ground, the things we can't see hold the greatest potential for transformation. "For the things we see are temporary, but the things that are unseen are eternal" (II Cor. 4:18). In that stillness and silence, you'll be able to start receiving the hidden manna (Rev. 2:17) as you begin to discover the wondrous truth that only the crucified are truly alive.

Chapter 1

Beyond Worship

The waterfall remains in the mist behind your dreams,
    calling to you from the cleft in the rock
        between high mountain peaks
           where ravens bring you bread.
Like a bridge of light between heaven and earth
    the waterfall awaits,
        ready to receive all who seek it until they find it,
Leaving them forever spellbound, stretched in the place
    where freedom takes wing from the aerie of the heart.
At night, the spaces between the stars invoke yearning,
    recalling dark places in you that hunger for truth,
        that long for the waterfall…
That boundless cascade will never cease calling you to awaken,
    and your spirit will relentlessly thirst for that living water,
Until in your search you surrender to the voice of all creation,
    resounding with the divine splendor of the Word of the Creator,
Making you once and for all time
    a child of the King of the Waterfall,
        at rest eternally
           in the ever-flowing Waters of Life.

In the past decade or so, a new set of words has entered the lexicon of evangelicals. Those words are "contemplate," "contemplation" and "contemplative." They aren't really new words; they've been a part of the English language for centuries, with roots going back to early Christianity, though rarely used among evangelicals in the past century or so. But what do they really mean? "Contemplate" is often used to convey the idea of "thinking deeply," or "having profound thoughts." But that's not the original meaning of the word; in fact, that's pretty much the opposite of the original meaning.

For most of Christian history, the word "contemplation" has been used by Christians to speak of waiting on God in wordless silence, communing deeply with El Shaddai in a form of prayer beyond what we normally think of as prayer, going beyond all human thought. This expression of worship, contemplatives believe, constitutes nothing less than absolute surrender to God, to the point that even one's thoughts are surrendered and one is simply silent in the holy presence of God, at times in a state of wonder beyond one's ability to express it in words. Since at least the fourth century A.D., many theologians, and many thousands—perhaps even millions—of common Christians as well, have considered contemplation to be the deepest possible experience of what the Psalmist meant by the words, "Be still and know that I am God." Contemplatives believe it's also at least part of what Paul meant when he said, "I have been crucified with Christ; nevertheless, I live; yet not I but Christ lives in me (Galatians 2:20)." And for well over a thousand years this form of worship was common and well-known in the Church; throughout Christendom, contemplation was among the highest of ideals to strive for.

Today, due largely to the Age of Reason and its influence on the Church, contemplation has been all but forgotten in many corners of the Christian faith; most Protestant believers in the 20th century had no idea such a thing ever existed in Christianity. In fact, we've been taught the opposite: that this is new-age spirituality, borrowed in the 1960's and '70's from Buddhism and Hinduism, and that it's as far as you can get from what being a true Christian is all about. (Christians of the fifth century—or the eighth or the thirteenth—would be quite puzzled and probably rather amused by that assessment.) And now, in the 21st century, we stand to discover the reality of the oft-quoted saying of philosopher George Santayana: "Those who cannot remember the past are condemned to repeat it"—but for Christians, in regard to contemplation, we're *blessed* to repeat it.

The False Self and the True Self

So what is this "contemplation" thing all about?[1] What does it look like in a person's life? It's simply a form of worship—the purest form there is, I believe—what earlier generations referred to as adoration, reduced to its most basic form. There are several components to contemplative spirituality, but the most important is contemplative prayer. (We'll get to the other ones in a few pages.) Many have learned the practice known today as centering prayer—a gateway into contemplation.[2] This basically means simply waiting on God in silent adoration—a wordless prayer (or a one word prayer) of just being in God's company. To the natural mind, that may sound totally pointless, but its purpose is to bring us beyond the natural mind, to the place of silent surrender where, wordlessly, we can open our heart and mind totally to God. This is contemplation: being in a place of intimacy with God beyond the realm of thoughts, concepts, desires, memories or emotions, where God can mold and shape us to become more and more like him as we learn to die to self. By yielding every thought to God until the thoughts stop coming— if only for a breath or two at first—we learn to come to the place of detachment from thoughts, watching them as they come and go, but not becoming attached to them. There, we become more deeply aware of God's abiding presence and love.

During centering prayer, you use a word to help you keep your focus on God. It can be one of the short names of God, such as "Christ" or "Abba," or "love," or whatever one- or two-syllable word God gives you to use as a reminder of God, and to help you to be present to God instead of your own thoughts—even thoughts about God.[3] You don't repeat the prayer word constantly, like a mantra; you only use it occasionally to help you refocus your mind on God and away from your train of thought (but very gently, not like a guard dog to chase thoughts away; that doesn't work). It's probably helpful to think of centering prayer not as a technique, but as steps on a path. Unlike a technique, where we are in charge, it has to come from God and from a willingness of the heart to allow God to be completely in charge. It begins with the opening of the heart, which again—like open heart surgery—is not up to us, except for the willingness, and even that we must trust God for; it has to come from Adonai Roph'ekha, the Lord our Healer.

Why is it important to get rid of thoughts? Because most of the everyday thoughts, mental images, memories, feelings and desires that float through our consciousness are either generated or used by the ego. What is the ego? It's the false self, the pretender self, the voice inside that claims to be your true self.[4] Other names for the ego are the small self or the false self. I will often be using the terms "false self" and "ego" interchangeably throughout this book. (Ego is the word psychologists use for the same thing, more or less; it's the Latin word for "I" or "me." I'll have a lot more to say about the false self in chapter 4.) The way I see it, the false self is the expression of the old nature that continues to live in us even after we're born again; it's the face of the sinful, carnal self. That's right, the same old sinful nature Paul wrote about in Romans 7:15-24, the thing in us that causes us to do what we don't want to do and hinders us from doing what we do want to do, what we know is right. We see ourselves as the good Dr. Jekyll, but there's a Mr. Hyde hiding in all of us. We can hide Mr. Hyde from others, we can deceive ourselves into thinking Mr. Hyde's gone, but we can never completely hide Mr. Hyde from ourselves or from God.[5]

Of course, if there's a false self, there must also be a true self, and thank God there is. I think of the true self as the human spirit, what Peter called "the hidden person of the heart" (1 Peter 3:3-4—which, though addressed to women, is not just for women but applies equally to men, by the way). Thomas Merton said, "Every one of us is shadowed by an illusory person: a false self…We are not very good at recognizing illusions, least of all the ones we cherish about ourselves—the ones we are born with and which feed the roots of sin."[6]

It may be helpful to picture the inner man as being like matryoshkas—Russian nested wooden dolls, one inside another (5 to 7 or more in a set), each carefully and intricately decorated. With each doll you open,[7] you find another inside, all the way down to the smallest doll which is solid, not hollow like the rest (that's important). The largest of the dolls is like the outward appearance—the false self; get inside that and you find there are several more layers, hollow but highly developed. The whole process of centering prayer and contemplation can be a many-years-long process of allowing God to reveal to us the layers of our false self—and our true self, made in his image, buried in the depths of our psyche where we seldom encounter it.

So well does the false self camouflage the true self that, prior to a practice like centering prayer, we are rarely even aware that there is such a thing as the true self. But once each layer of the false self has been revealed and opened, we come closer to recognizing the beauty, genuineness, wholeness and unselfishness of the true self which God has created in us. There's also an element of sadness (blessed are those who mourn!) at the way we have covered up this hidden treasure with so many layers of false self in order to take the focus away from God, where it belongs, and put it on *me, me, me*.

The false self is corruptible; the true self goes deep beyond the outward appearance (1 Samuel 16:7) and may be, some believe, the actual image of God inside us. In other words, we are made in the image and likeness of God (Genesis 1:27); he has placed his image inside each of us, and that's what the true self is—something like a mirror inside us that reflects the face and truth of God, that actually connects us

Gently but firmly
surrender to God
every thought
that comes to you.
Look past each thought,
keeping your focus
on the horizon—
on God—
until your thoughts
become like voices
faintly, distantly heard.
They will gradually
fade away till it's
just you and God.
Continue to notice
any thoughts
that may come,
but don't become
attached to
any idea, memory,
feeling or impulse,
except the desire
to be open to God
in humility
and poverty of spirit
by using a word
or your breath
as a reminder of
God's presence and love.

to God and enables us to know and live for him. The true self is what enables us to discern what's of God and what is not: does it look like that image of God in us, or a counterfeit?

Although our natural minds can't understand the image of God and can't recognize the false self from the true, John also tells us that when we see Jesus, we will recognize him because we will be like him (1 John 3:2). Dying to self means dying to the false self, which is what the average person lives out of every day—including Christians to a certain extent. Being resurrected with Christ means the true self is what we begin to live out of. But if we don't learn how to keep the false self dead, it always finds a way to sneak back in, like a zombie out of a B movie, and it starts taking over again. Centering prayer helps keep the false self dead by giving us at least one period of time every day when all our thoughts—the vehicle by which the false self is expressed—are laid on the altar before God, when we are dead to all but his presence.

The twelve disciples of Jesus were aware of this issue because Jesus addressed it directly with them on several occasions (Mark 14:38, for example), though they didn't recognize or understand what was going on inside them till after the Resurrection. Reading through the Gospels, the twelve—Jesus's best friends, the ones he spent most of his time with during his earthly ministry—sound like the most self-centered bunch of people in history, yet they were actually quite normal. Their favorite topic of conversation was which of them would be the greatest in the Kingdom of God. Even after Jesus had told them repeatedly that the greatest would be the least, like a servant or like a child, they still didn't get it; even on the final night of Jesus's earthly life, after being plainly told by their Master that he was soon going to suffer and die, they were still arguing this point. Jesus couldn't have made it any clearer that, as we say today, it's all about him—yet after three years of hanging out with Jesus, in the disciples' minds it was still all about them.

Peter learned a bitter lesson later that night: all his boasting about being willing to die with Jesus came not from his heart of love for the Lord, but from his false self, which was perfectly capable of denying Christ. That's the part of us that must be crucified; it can't be redeemed. But a little over a month later when the true self in Peter, resurrected with Christ, spoke to a crowd in Jerusalem, the result was that the Church went from 120 people to three thousand in one day. What had Peter been doing during the time between the Resurrection and Pentecost? Waiting on God. Dying to self. Surrendering all that was in him to Christ and letting Christ live in him.[8]

Telling the False Self to Sit Down and Shut Up

Paul's prescription for dealing with the ego/false self was quite simple: kill it. He said, "I die daily" (1 Cor. 15:31) and spoke of our old self being crucified with Christ (Rom. 6:6-7, Gal. 2:20). He talked about how we are "always carrying around in our bodies the dying of the Lord Jesus, so the life of Jesus will be manifested in us" (2 Cor. 4:10-11). Just what did he mean about our being crucified with Christ, and dying daily? Paul was talking about dying to self. Ever since the first century, Christians have asked God, "how does one accomplish this?" The answer many in the Church were led to, especially from the third century on, was contemplative prayer. It's a way to put the old nature to death by stopping the flow of thoughts the false self uses to build up itself and its kingdom. So then, centering prayer is a way of telling the false self system—the old nature—to sit down and shut up, as we might say today. Stopping the flow of thoughts actually sort of strangles the false self, causing its knees to bow and its tongue to confess Christ as Lord (Is. 45:22-23; Phil. 2:10). Over time, this dismantles the false self system so that a person's life can be rebuilt around the true self—the new nature—which is Christ in you, the hope of glory.

So when you're in centering prayer, you're constantly having thoughts. But rather than focus on them, you can sort of ignore them, or better yet, look beyond them, "over their shoulder as it were," as *The Cloud of Unknowing*'s anonymous author puts it. It's like if someone tries to get in your face or stop you when you're walking down a path, and you just keep looking over their shoulder, focus on the horizon—on God—and continue on. You keep doing this with every thought until your thoughts become like words written on paper and then ripped into tiny pieces like confetti and thrown to the wind, or like voices you can just faintly hear in another room. You'll catch a word here, part of a phrase there, but then as you continue to ignore the thoughts, they gradually fade away to the empty-mind point, where it's just you and God.[9]

Actually, a real peace begins to come even in the confetti-mind state. It's not just the thoughts; there are times when you can also recognize that the false self sort of turns into confetti and blows away. It's like the fog begins to clear and you start to see God through the mists—you can't actually see him, but you sense his presence and know he's there. You go from illusion to reality; you get your eyes off of the me-and-my-little-world-that-I've-created-in-my-head state of mind most people live in most of the time, and you find your focus is on God, and you begin to see who he really is, in ways that are hard to put into words.

So then, does contemplative prayer put you into an altered state of consciousness? No—at least not in the sense of causing hallucinations like some drugs do. (As an ex-hippie, I admit I've had drug experiences that did involve altered states of consciousness, many years ago.) Psychedelic drugs can facilitate a sort of temporary letting go of the ego to a certain extent, but are of no value in revealing God, though they can create the illusion of doing so; drugs, of course, are all about illusion. Drugs tend to also bring about a heightened awareness, which also comes eventually with contemplation, but not the exaggerated, trippy kind of awareness of drugs; it's the completely natural, normal, yet vivid awareness one begins to become used to once the focus is not on self all the time. There's little if any resemblance to any drug experiences I ever had.

On the other hand, if the false self is our normal mode of living, crucifying it brings you to a greater awareness of the true self, and a greater openness to God, a greater willingness to yield to him, to surrender. That's what the Bible refers to as "the mind of Christ" (1 Cor. 2:16, in the context of verses 9-15). If that's an altered state of consciousness, I'll take all I can get.

Fear of the Lord: An Extremely Positive Thing

> In the fear of the LORD is strong confidence: and his children shall have a place of refuge. The fear of the LORD is a fountain of life...The fear of the LORD leads

to life: and he that has it shall abide satisfied… (Proverbs 14:26-7a, 19:23, King James 2000 Bible)

There is no fear in love, but perfect love drives out fear, because fear has to do with punishment. The one who fears punishment has not been perfected in love. (I John 4:18, New English Translation [NET Bible])

"Fear of the Lord" has been the subject of many thousands of sermons; some pastors make a point of preaching on the subject whenever they feel they need to keep their flock in line. Unfortunately, there is a lot of misunderstanding about just what the fear of God is. Many people, when they read or hear this phrase, drop the book like a hot rock, or run in the opposite direction. I'll just start with this statement: the fear of the Lord is an extremely positive thing. If you see it as a negative thing, you really don't understand it at all. In the Bible, those who fear the Lord tend to be the ones who hear him say, "Fear not, for I am with you." The fact that God is so big, so awe-inspiring, so wonder-full, is the reason people tend to be afraid of him. But he's the epitome of the gentle giant; a whole book could be written (and probably has been) on that subject. The word translated "fear" in the Hebrew Bible, the source of the phrase "fear of the Lord," can mean several things: awe, reverence, wonder, and yes, fear— the natural human reaction to the Spirit of one so great and powerful.

Who is like our God?
Holy and intimate
Tender and strong
Patient and powerful
Mighty and innocent
Jealous and kind
Sovereign and merciful
Who is like our God?[10]

The first time I ever fully experienced the felt reality of God, the sense of surprise and astonishment was overwhelming: a Person who is the most powerful thing in the universe (thus the fear), yet at the same time, a Person who *is* love, whose heart is filled with all the love in the universe (amazement beyond all ability to put into words). I was working at the time, and it definitely affected my work! Fortunately, the boss was a Christian. In fact, he had more or less told me, the previous evening, that I would soon have a powerful God-encounter. I've experienced the same thing numerous times since; it's not something one easily forgets, though in our human weakness we still do. But again, my take on it is this: the felt reality of God evokes great awe in us, but the fear is our own reaction, a human emotion that comes in response to that powerful presence—not the presence itself. God's desire is not that we close off to him out of fear, but that we open to him in that sense of wide-eyed wonder. Trying to scare us is so far from what God has in mind, so totally opposite of his character!

So why am I talking about fear of the Lord in a book about centering prayer? First of all, if you're afraid of God, you don't really want to get close to him through centering prayer, or any other way. The verse, "Draw near to God and he will draw near to you" (James 4:8) could be a terrifying idea! But that's not what God is like at all. If you feel drawn to seek God through centering prayer, that "fear of the Lord" thing may be a serious obstacle. But once you see what God is really like, it will change your life. And centering prayer is a fantastic way to experience God's true character.

Thomas Keating, the Trappist monk who has been probably the main driving force behind the growth of centering prayer, says this about the fear of the Lord:

> The biblical term "fear of God" does not refer to the emotion of fear. Fear of God is a technical term in the Bible meaning the right relationship with God. The right relationship with God is to trust him...reverence and awe for God's transcendence and immanence as well as trust in his goodness and compassion. To envisage what the biblical fear of God actually means, imagine a child at Christmas time in a huge department store...filled with toys. When the child emerges from the elevator into this wonderland of desirable objects, her eyes grow bigger and bigger. She looks to the left and to the right, seeing everything her heart has ever desired...doll houses, toys,

sleds, electric trains…She is so enthralled that she does not know where to start. She wants to grasp everything and take it home. The biblical fear of God is similar. We feel ourselves invited into a mystery that contains everything our hearts could possibly desire. We experience the fascination of the Ultimate Mystery rather than fear of the unknown. We want to grasp or be grasped by the mystery of God's presence that opens endlessly in every direction.[11]

I don't know about you, but that's not the kind of "fear of the Lord" presented in some of the hellfire-and-brimstone sermons I've heard. Fortunately, for those who are open to him, God teaches directly. And I've found that waiting on God in the place of stillness and mystery is the best learning strategy there is.

The Face of Christ Reflected in a Cup of Communion Wine

In II Cor. 3:18, Paul talks about how we can behold the glory of the Lord and be changed into his likeness. (The word translated "behold" in that verse can also be translated "contemplate," by the way.)[12] Of course, this is a normal part of the Christian life, yet one that many of us rarely experience in regular prayer with words.

As a regular part of my Communion/Eucharist experience for many years now, as I take the wine (or juice) I gaze into the cup. Praying and focusing on Christ and his broken body and shed blood—broken by my sin, shed for my sin—as I continue to gaze into the cup, I imagine that I am seeing in the wine, not my own reflection, but the face of Jesus reflected back at me. (I suspect many believers have experienced this.) The point I'm making is this: in the depths of contemplative prayer, when thoughts have stopped and you know you're in the presence of God, it can be sort of like expecting to see your reflection and seeing Jesus instead of yourself, as you reflect the Lord's glory more and more.

I'm fascinated by Mother Teresa's response to a couple of questions posed by well-known CBS Evening News anchor Dan Rather when he interviewed her back in the 80's. "What do you say to God when you pray?" Rather asked. Her simple answer was, "I don't say anything; I just listen." Rather, rather nonplussed, then asked her, "Well, what does Jesus say to you?" And Mother Theresa answered, "Oh, He doesn't say anything, either. He just listens."

A rather disjointed conversation (pun intended). And the type of prayer Mother Teresa described sounds, on the surface, like the most disjointed relationship imaginable. Two beings listening to each other not talk. Two listeners listening to each other say nothing. A Zen Buddhist conundrum, like the sound of one hand clapping. I'd love to have seen the look on Dan Rather's face after that exchange. On reflection, though, what Mother Teresa was talking about sounds to me like contemplative prayer. In fact, that's exactly what it is. The love of God expressed to humans, who express it back to God. Love expressed in a way that is beyond words, beyond description, beyond rational comprehension, yet meaningful beyond imagination.

We speak of relationship with God; for Christians in America in the twenty-first century, that's what life is supposed to be all about. Well, Mother Teresa's kind of prayer is true relationship with God. The kind of relationship where you don't have to say anything, you just look in each other's eyes or listen to each other breathe. The kind where there's really nothing to say, nothing that needs to be said, nothing that can be said; the love is there, so unfathomably deep you couldn't begin to put it in words. It's prayer beyond the point of feeling like you have to say something to fill in the silence. It's the look, followed by the embrace, that breaks down the walls of nervousness, that melts the anxiety and fear and loneliness, until all is dissolved in love and everything else is forgotten. That's really what contemplative prayer is. It's being heart-to-heart with God.

Not that prayer with words is not important. There are times in any relationship where things need to be said and things need to be heard. I doubt that Mother Teresa was saying she never engaged in those kinds of prayers. But when you love someone, it's not the conversations you remember, so much as just being together, knowing there's something there between you and your beloved, something in the silence that's more powerful than all the words in all the dictionaries in the world.

It's the perfect peace that comes after everything's been said, and after the realization that some things never can be said. Like Paul expressed in Philippians 4, you make your requests to God, and then—peace that passes understanding. That peace is what keeps our hearts and minds in Christ. True prayer begins in silence and ends in silence, because we can't know God through our minds or through words that come from us, but only from the Word. He is ever speaking (Ps. 19:1-4, 14), but we have to be silent to hear that still, small voice so deep in our hearts; we can't hear him when we're full of our own thoughts. The meditations of our hearts, as well as the words of our mouths, are necessary parts of prayer and yieldedness to God.

Of course, it's important to note that centering prayer is not to be done instead of your regular prayers. It's still as important as ever to pray the Lord's Prayer and elaborate on aspects of it as needed, such as forgiveness and provision; to intercede for the saints and those in need; and to make your requests known to God. But if you're like me, you will find that once you begin centering prayer, all other prayers will tend to flow more naturally, at all times of the day. Centering prayer does not replace "regular" prayer; rather, through it, the Holy Spirit empowers and enhances your prayer life.

Other flowers in the garden of contemplative spirituality

Besides centering prayer/contemplative prayer and the daily dying to self which it teaches, there are several other aspects of contemplation which you might want to know about. Once you are firmly established in a daily centering prayer practice, you may see God beginning to incorporate some of these into your life. First, there is lectio divina[13] or sacred reading, a wonderful method for meditating on Bible verses or short passages that makes them come alive and allows you to often hear God speaking to you about what a specific verse means for you personally.

Then, there are repetitive prayers[14] such as the Jesus Prayer that has played such an important role in the history of the Orthodox Church and is still practiced today; many Christians in our time are finding these types of prayer to be very powerful in bringing about transformation in their lives. Also there is what's been called the sacrament of the present moment, or finding God in the now, an openness to the Holy Spirit's teaching through simple everyday events that we usually overlook as being too "mundane" to learn anything from. Another useful practice is meditation on paradoxes. The teachings of Jesus are full of paradox— it's one of the most important teaching tools he uses, and one of the most overlooked today. Paradox is also seen in various forms in many other parts of the Bible, especially the New Testament. Contemplatives have always known that meditation on Biblical paradoxes is useful for transforming one's thought life from the natural mind to the mind of Christ.[15]

The things listed in the previous paragraph are practices anyone can do; the ones listed below are more in the area of giftings. One of these involves dreams and visions from God. Those who have the type of prophetic gifting to receive such manifestations of the Spirit may experience more of it once they begin practicing centering prayer. Another is unitive seeing. Generally, the deeper you go with God in the contemplative realm, the more you see yourself as one with all people. Many in our churches call one another "brother" and "sister," but never really see each other as God sees us—as one. A deeper level of unitive seeing is recognizing yourself as one with all things. He's got the whole world in his hands, we sing. The entire universe is wrapped in his love, for that matter; we know this by head knowledge—but actually seeing all things as one in God is pure gift, an opening of the eyes that only his Spirit can bring—seeing as God sees.

And finally, there is union with God,[16] the crown jewel of contemplative experience, in which one becomes intimately aware of being joined to God. It's the final stage in the progression hinted at in the parable of the Prodigal Son and in the Song of Songs: from servant of God to friend of God to child of God to deeply and intimately beloved of God. (Of course, we are fully accepted and fully loved by God as soon as we receive Christ into our lives; the stages of this progression have to do with how people see themselves in God's kingdom and also the deepening of our relationship with God; they are *not* about how God sees us.) Unlike the other contemplative "flowers" mentioned above, union with God is not a practice but a wondrous gift of God which he can bestow on those who are passionate for him.

More than any of the other things mentioned in this section, union with God is not something we do or initiate; it's given by the Holy Spirit when and to whom he chooses, and there's no way we can make it happen. But in all of the above-mentioned practices we are being led slowly but surely by the Spirit, first toward being increasingly aware that through the Cross of Christ we are made one with him, which is called substantive union, and then gradually being brought to realized oneness. In this transformed-mind state we become fully, gloriously aware that in Christ we truly are one with God, as a child is adopted into a family or a branch is grafted into a vine—fully accepted, fully loved and brought near to him, to the highest degree of intimacy with God the Father, Son and Holy Spirit. On us is bestowed the unspeakable gift of loving God as he loves us, constantly pouring out our love for him and being refilled as the persons of the Trinity are continuously pouring their love out for one another and into one another, eternally.

By all of these contemplative practices and giftings, the Holy Spirit helps us to become more and more aware of the layers of illusion that surround our lives, in order to help us to get free from them so we can give our undivided attention to the work of Christ and the unfolding of the Kingdom of God on earth.

So the previous five paragraphs provide a glimpse of what it means to be a contemplative. Again, centering prayer is the start and the heart of contemplation; the other aspects of the contemplative lifestyle will flow out of centering prayer as the Holy Spirit leads. Centering prayer can be part of one's quiet time and can fit quite well into the Christ-follower lifestyle.

A Deeper Kind of Worship

That's how I eventually felt about the subject back in early 2002 when I was first learning about contemplative spirituality. I was very cautious at first because it totally went against the grain of what I'd been taught, but I increasingly recognized that it was the Holy Spirit leading me into this area and not just my own curiosity. Before beginning to practice centering prayer, I spent a couple of months checking it all out as thoroughly as possible, doing a lot of praying for God's guidance and a lot of reading, and discovering in the process that contemplation isn't something someone dreamed up in the 1970's. As I said earlier, it has been very much a part of the Christian tradition through the centuries, though less so in the past four or five hundred years. Eventually, I took the plunge and began practicing centering prayer, and it wasn't long before I saw my love for God, my passion for Christ, and my responsiveness to the Spirit growing and blossoming beyond what I'd ever known in nearly thirty years of following Christ.

To me, being a Christian is all about surrendering one's life to God through various forms of worship. When I first became a born-again Christian, back in the days of the Jesus Movement of the early 70's, worship wasn't a word I heard much. "Praise" was the thing; I was taught to spend time "praising" God by saying "Praise the Lord" and thanking God for things, and by singing songs about God, and this was how people could come into the presence of God. Reading the Bible and memorizing verses would also fill a believer with his Spirit, I was told, so I did a lot of that. (Of course, all of that is scriptural; I'm not putting it down.) The term "meditation" could mean thinking about a passage of scripture, but people were careful to point out that this "meditation" was totally different from what Buddhists and Hindus did, and you had to be careful because you could get demon-possessed by doing things the wrong way. And perhaps there's some truth to that. But in some Christian circles, it was considered best to err on the side of caution—so don't meditate on Scripture, just in case what you were doing was a bit too close to the edge of the cliff. Memorizing scripture was good, and presumably you'd be thinking about it pretty thoroughly in the process of memorization, but you didn't want to think about it to the point of getting into anything weird or mystical. That would be tempting God and teasing the devil—i.e., extremely unwise.[17]

So how did I get from there to centering prayer? Through the path of worship. Today's worship music movement is truly one of the best things to happen in Christianity in centuries, and something that, as a worshiper and a musician, I've been greatly blessed to be a part of since the mid-80's. Around that time, I experienced a shift from the old praise-chorus type of worship, which was mainly focused on singing *about* God—or even about the Christian life, with only passing references to God—to a more intimate kind of song which was usually sung *to* God.

The change in music was accompanied by a deeper sense of God's beauty and seeing the Holy Spirit at work in deeper ways. This change was a great milestone in my Christian walk. Perhaps you have experienced this kind of worship as well, in which you and those around you get caught up in singing and dancing along to a song that really speaks to the heart. You sense the love of God as you express to him your thankfulness, your joy, your longing, your love for him. In the process, you often come to a place of surrender to God and find him doing a work in your heart as you sing words like this:

> Jesus, be the center
> Be my source, be my life, Jesus…
> Be the fire in my heart
> Be the wind in these sails
> Be the reason that I live
> Jesus, Jesus…[18]

You can sing a word-prayer like this, and that's powerful. I've done it thousands of times and continue to do it constantly. But as with anything we do, when it comes to our dealings with God, self can get in the way. Especially in group worship, even on a song about asking Jesus to be the center of our life, our self-centered thoughts can take over: Can the person in front of me hear the awesome way I'm singing this? Why didn't the songwriter realize he/she should change the words on this one part? Why is the drummer playing so loud? Does the piano player know she just played the wrong chord? Why don't they do this song the way I learned it at the other church? And so on. The fact is, singing worship songs in a group setting tends toward a performance mentality. That's one of the biggest dangers for worship leaders and musicians. If you're not careful, even in the midst of worship, the self can run rampant and the whole point of worshiping God is lost.

This problem came home to me one night in 1999 when I heard, for the first time, a beautiful song called The Heart of Worship:

When the music fades
All is stripped away
And I simply come…
I'll bring you more than a song
For a song in itself
Is not what you have required
You search much deeper within
Through (beyond) the way things appear
You're looking into my heart
I'm coming back to the heart of worship
And it's all about you
All about you, Jesus
I'm sorry, Lord, for the thing I've made it
When it's all about you
All about you, Jesus…[19]

That song, its message, and the power of God that came with it, hit me like a ton of bricks, and I ended up on my knees. I didn't have the words for what was going on, but I realized that the Holy Spirit was pointing to what I now know to be the false self, and the way it tries to build its own kingdom even as we are in the midst of worshiping God. My prayers that night, and what God began to show me about how we can go beyond worship, had a lot to do with how I came to be practicing centering prayer a couple years later.

Let's take a look at what a few contemporary worship leaders/songwriters have to say. The question is: how can we develop the awareness of God in everyday life? The best way I've found is by laying our crowns at the feet of Jesus, as worship leader/songwriter Chris Tomlin says (We Fall Down); it's then we often discover that what we thought was a crown of gold is really just a Crackerjack toy that soon breaks, in comparison to the grace of God in which we can rest as we lay our thoughts down before him who loves us. We can learn to develop a deeper awareness of God's presence by trading our ashes for beauty, as Don Moen says (At the Foot of the Cross), and our sorrows and shame for the joy of the Lord, as Darrell Evans says (Trading My Sorrows).

We can find God in the mundane details of our everyday lives by spending time every day taking every thought captive, and laying all that is within us at the Cross. And there's no temptation toward a performance mentality. It's just God and you; no one else sees you, even in group centering prayer, because everyone has their eyes closed. And any notion of performing for God, he gently breaks you out of very quickly. You soon realize centering prayer isn't a matter of performance; it's very simple, and very humbling. You don't have to do anything but *be there* with God. Anything that needs doing, he does. All you do is surrender, lay down all of your agenda, and wait on him.

The Cross and all it represents is one analogy that's not a large part of our 21st century Christian culture, yet if we learn to daily let it become a part of our inner reality by surrendering everything else in life to the One who died on it, it will transform everything else in our lives into pure gold.

Centering Prayer 101

When I seek God in centering prayer, I sit in a comfortable but straight-backed chair, feet flat on the floor and sitting up straight but not rigid, with my hands on my lap or folded. Usually I start with lectio divina, although you can center without it. Then I take time to remain in a place of rest with God, in silence. I gently surrender every thought that comes to me and stay in that place for about twenty minutes, looking beyond each thought, looking to God, and finally becoming detached from every idea, concept, memory, feeling or impulse except the impulse to refocus or reopen to God, in an attitude of humility and poverty of spirit. This reopening is done by using a simple word—generally referred to as a "sacred word"—or my breath as a reminder of God's presence and love.[20] I think of this as a one-word prayer—"God"—like when saying someone's name upon greeting them, or like a child out for a walk with a parent, calling out "Daddy!" when the child briefly loses sight of the parent. God answers not with words but with his presence, which was there anyway (he's omnipresent, after all) but he lets you know he's there. And throughout each centering prayer session, I just sit with him like a calm, contented child on his parent's lap, saying nothing. "Like a weaned child rests against his mother, my soul is like a weaned child within me," says Psalm 131.

During a centering prayer session, thoughts will come and go like flies to a picnic. That's normal. Even if I find that I've been caught up in watching and responding to a whole herd of thoughts, that's okay. Whether it's one thought or a cavalcade of them, when I realize my focus has gotten away from God, I just go back to my sacred word or breath, and get my attention back on the horizon—on God and his presence. If I can't feel his presence, I know he's there anyway, so that doesn't really change anything. He is my everything, and I rest in that knowledge until all things in my heart, mind and life are absorbed into God. If I don't get to that point, well, God was still there, still loving me, still working in me although I can't say exactly what he was or is doing at any given moment. Even if it seems like I'm a total failure at centering prayer, that's just my false self judging. My true self knows that God is God and I'm his beloved child, and that's all that matters.

So that's it, that's centering prayer—a form of worship in which we can draw near to God and experience his drawing near to us, as James says. Some people prefer to start with the Lord's Prayer or another short prayer, and some don't do the scripture meditation. For me personally, I find that centering prayer helps me to be more aware of the peace of God during the rest of my day, and it also keeps me growing in Christ more than any other form of worship I've run across in over forty years of being a Christian. My heart longs for God and, through centering prayer, I find God longing for me to just be with him, often awakening me early in the morning to go spend time in silence with him. Then, traditional prayer—asking God to do stuff—often comes more naturally, and Bible study tends to be more fulfilling. I keep loving Jesus more and more. And so far, I haven't gotten demon-possessed.

Conclusion

Why is there a need for contemplation? Why isn't church, Bible reading and regular prayer enough? For many, those things really are enough; although theoretically silent prayer is for any believer, some feel called only to verbal prayer and Bible reading. But for others, there's a deeper hunger that none of their Christian activities can fill. Such people aren't better or more spiritual. But for those called to ascend the mountain of God as Moses did—for those who have a deep yearning to know God more deeply—just gathering the daily manna will never be enough. For these people—people like me, and many others, perhaps you—God has provided a way: contemplation.

In centering prayer we deny ourselves, deny our thoughts, desires, feelings and memories, to go beyond our limited view of God, thus allowing God to take us deeper—to show us, as he did with Moses, more of who he is. The more we see him as he is, the more we are transformed into his likeness; the more we become like him, which is his greatest desire for us (1 John 3:2, 2 Cor. 3:16-18). And we discover that coming to God on his terms, leaning not on our own understanding but trusting him with all our hearts, acknowledging him in all our ways, is the way to becoming like Christ. And when we do this even to the point of throwing away the very thoughts and intents of our hearts for more of Christ in us—the hope of glory!—it pleases God and enriches us in ways we could never have imagined. And we begin to discover the wondrous depths of God hinted at in scriptures like this: "Those who dwell in the secret place of the Most High abide in the shadow of the Almighty" (Psalm 91:1). As some of the ancient Christian mystics would have said, we begin to know God, not as we conceive of him, but "to know God as he is in himself."

Chapter 2

Facing Objections to Contemplative Spirituality

> Lord, take the hard ground
>   of my heart
> And grow in me
>   a garden
> I want to meet you there
>   where the roses wave in the wind...

Wait a minute, you're saying. You heard that so-called "Christian meditation" was really just an insidious New-Age plot, a scheme of the Devil to take over your mind, and it should be avoided at all costs. Besides, this guy (me) openly uses terms like "mystical" when speaking about Christ and relationship with him. That *has* to be New-Age! And aren't most people who get into that type of thing just looking for experiences, rather than seeking God?

In this chapter I will discuss misunderstandings and misconceptions about contemplation, and there are many. Yes, there are possible dangers to be avoided (I'll talk about that in Appendix 1), but there is much in the Bible and Christian history that is rich and fulfilling, that we've been taught to beware of for fear that it's "mystical," and thus out of fear we can miss out on some of the most wonder-full things God wants to give us. Contemplation is a spirituality of people encouraged by God to accept his loving, joyful invitation to "come up higher,"[1] and not to be afraid of delving into the deeper things of the Word.

In Christian circles, people are often told that if they empty or turn off their minds, they could get demon-possessed.[2] The idea is presented as a defense against Eastern religions and New-Age practices.[3] It is fully Biblical, however, to "cast down imaginings and everything that exalts itself against the knowledge of God, and to take every thought captive to the obedience of Christ" (2 Cor. 10: 5)—and that "imaginings and high things" part is a good description of much of what goes on in our minds when they are still under the influence of the ego/false self (more on that later). The Bible also speaks in many places about the vital need to be still before God (for example, Psalm 37:7, 46:10, 62:5, 131:2, Lam. 3:25-6, 1 Peter 3:4). This emptying of self to be filled with God is a way of emulating Christ (Philippians 2:5-9); it's called *kenosis* in Greek, meaning self-emptying: Jesus emptied himself (Philippians 2:7). That's exactly what centering prayer is: the way of self-emptying. Contemplatives find that emptying the mind is the way to empty the ego/false self, to let go of one's agenda, to check that desire to force life to be on one's own terms, and to fully surrender to God.

Can you get demon possessed by doing centering prayer? Well, it's a form of worship of God, sometimes called "pure prayer" because there's nothing about self in it—no false agendas, no hidden motives, just "God, I want to be with you. I want more of you. I love you"—but from the heart, without words. Jesus said, if a child asks his father for a fish or an egg to eat, will he give him a snake or a scorpion instead? Of course not. "How much more will your Father in Heaven give the Holy Spirit to those who ask him!" (Luke 11:11-12). The idea that God would allow one seeking him to get Satan instead is as foolish now as then.

So, in centering prayer, we yield to God all our thoughts as they come, as a form of worship—silently, wordlessly surrendering each thought to God with this attitude: "no, Lord, this thought is not as important as you, so I lay it on the altar. I give it up. And this thought. And this memory. And this feeling. This desire. Even this brilliant idea. All of them. All I need is you. All I want is you."[4] By surrendering every thought to God like this, to the point of letting our prayer go beyond words, face to face with God in awestruck speechless wonder, we can come to the point of actually being fully aware of God's power in such a way that the only way to honor God is by our silence. (Zechariah, the father of John the Baptist, spent several months involuntarily exploring the reality of being silent before God [Luke 1:5-25, 2:59-79]; many others in the Bible and throughout Church history had similar experiences.)

In this state, thoughts are like distant voices where you only hear a word or two here and there, like a TV on in another room, because we're turning our attention away from everything but God. For Christian contemplatives, that's the "emptying of the mind." Where this eventually leads is to recognizing that you are more than your thoughts; there's more to the real you than what goes on in your head. Once you see that, you can begin to recognize the false self for what it is, and occasionally get a glimpse of the true self—the image of God in which you are made, the face you had before you had a face[5]—"Christ in you, the hope of glory" (Colossians 1:27).[6]

The point is to come to a place in your life where the false self/ego/old nature is off the throne, and from your heart—wordlessly—you put God on the throne by faith. You look to him, you feel the hunger and longing and aching of your own spirit for him, you ignore the voice of the false self that wants to give its opinion about everything, and you sense God's response in allowing you to taste and see that the Lord is good, and your response to God is one you can't put into words. You silently, wordlessly rejoice together with God.

Of course, the false self doesn't like being kicked off the throne of your life. It will put up all kinds of resistance; it will tell you you're going astray from God, jumping off a cliff, or whatever it can come up with to deter you from its own death. In my opinion, the idea that centering prayer leads to demonic possession comes from the false self and from Satan, the god of this world, the one to whom the false self ultimately bows down. Satan is the one who twists and misuses Scripture. Satan and his kingdom are ultimately the losers, and God and his kingdom are the winners, when someone practices centering prayer.

Illusion and Reality

I have some things on my face that cause me to live in an illusion. They've been a part of my life for so long that I rarely think about them, at least not consciously. I'm talking about my eyeglasses. I'm not legally blind without them, but it would be hard to function if I lost them. The frames broke one day recently, which is what made me realize that the reality of my life is 20-70 or so vision, but my glasses provide the illusion that it's 20-20. Thank God for ol' Ben Franklin or whoever invented the things. (I've tried contacts and they always make my eyes hurt. If I could wear them, though, it would look to others like I had natural 20-20 vision, but that wouldn't be true. It would be another illusion.)

And that's just one of the many types of everyday illusions we live in. We could spend all day naming others that we unknowingly participate in. The greatest illusion in the world, one that affects all of us at times, is the idea that there is no God. After all, we can't see him, can't hear or smell or feel him with our normal senses, can't find him with any scientific equipment. But seeing a spiral galaxy through a telescope, or hearing the song of a meadowlark, or watching a pitcher stare at a runner on second base for several seconds and then, with incredible speed, turn and fire and throw a perfect strike over the corner of home plate, or any of a million other things, is a sign pointing to God in big red letters, for those who have ears to hear. The Bible says we can "taste and see that the Lord is good" (Psalm 34:8), that we can hear his still small voice (1 Kings 19:12); our worship songs proclaim that we can feel his touch, even that we can see God. I've even had people tell me they can smell God, that they know the smell of his presence, his holiness and his joy. But these kinds of awareness of God deal with the spiritual senses, which are little understood but which, like the very existence of God, science can't confirm.

Of course, the fact that we look to science as the final answer rather than to God is an illusion in itself; it's the idolatry of placing science on a pedestal and making it our be-all, end-all, our go-to source of truth, when that's really God's rightful place. But billions of people around the world are guilty of this sin; I've been there plenty of times myself, and you probably have too. In the busyness of life, between CNN in the morning, your Facebook time during lunch break, and your favorite TV show at night, it's easy to forget that there's a God whose life and beauty and love is in every cell of our bodies, every molecule of our houses, every atom of the earth, every second that ticks away.

When people awaken to the reality of God—whether they ask Jesus into their heart or just begin to respond to his reflection in creation or his kindness that leads them to repentance—they usually begin to see him in the innocent eyes of children, hear him in the lyrics of songs, feel his friendship and care in the gentle afternoon breeze, sense his hope in the darkness behind their own sighs deep in the night. In the awakening of spring, they get glimpses of the Resurrection. In the intense light of the morning sun they faintly recognize the face all the earth will someday stand before. That's mystical spirituality, and many come to Christ or are led to a deeper walk with him through such experiences. Yet, if you call it mystical, some will reject it, rebuke you, and sometimes turn away from such experiences—because they've been told that anything mystical is evil. Thus, millions in today's Church have fallen prey to an illusion that says that contemplative prayer, or anything attached to words like "mystical," can't possibly be of God.

Christianity and Mysticism

Is Christianity mystical? The standard answer many believers today would give to that question is an emphatic NO! The words "mystic" and "mystical" present a stumbling-block for many would-be contemplatives in the Church. These words have an appeal that is seemingly of the flesh, an appeal to a hunger deep within that, in reality, only God himself, in all his mystery and magnificence, can fill. The New Age movement claims to be able to fill that hunger; the words "mystic" and "mystical" have also been used by them. Most Christians today (though not in the past; see below) connect these words not to Christianity but to the New Age religions. To further confuse the issue, these words are also used by those who practice magic (both the illusion kind—from card tricks to Criss Angel, David Copperfield, etc.—and also the wiccan/"magickal" kind, which is manipulation of evil spirits, or working with evil spirits to manipulate people). So Christians are justified in their concern that "mystical" or contemplative spirituality could lead them into something rooted not in God but in Satan.

This controversy and confusion isn't new; it goes back to the early centuries of the Church. The words "mystic" and "mystical" have their roots in the mystery religions of ancient Greece and Rome. Though Christianity was not a mystery religion, there were clearly recognizable parallels between the two: salvation, resurrection, and eternal life were ideas both had in common. Christ himself is the ultimate mystery; that's one of the main themes of the New Testament. The word "mystery" was probably used by the original writers, Paul and John especially, to appeal to those involved in or drawn toward mystery cults of the first century in an effort to bring them to Christ. The word "mystical" was used in the writings of Christian leaders beginning in the Second and Third centuries,[7] and its roots are in the word "mystery," which is used in the New Testament in speaking of Christ and our relationship with him.[8] But theologians of the late 19th and early 20th centuries such as Adolf von Harnack said that the use of the words "mystic" and "mystical" in the writings of the Church Fathers show that they were overly influenced by Hellenistic (Greek) thought, and that the real roots of Christianity were solely Hebrew in origin. Harnack even rejected the Gospel of John as being too Hellenistic. Theologian Louis Bouyer and others have refuted these ideas, saying that the writers of the New Testament used these words in a way that clearly reflects back to Christ and to the Jewish roots of Christianity.[9]

The fact is, Christianity really is full of mystery and paradox, and forms of Christian belief and worship that downplay or ignore this fact miss out on an essential aspect of the Gospel. The earthly life of Christ was one big mystery, resting on some amazing paradoxes. He was the King of Kings, yet he was born in a barn (actually, a small cave)—the highest of the high beginning as the lowest of the low. He was a carpenter—a builder—who, through his death, is able to build new lives for us. He was the Light of the World, yet also a man of sorrow and grief. His life was a series of paradoxes, and his teachings were full of paradox. His death and resurrection only compounded the mysteries. (See Appendix 3 for more on paradoxes.) We shouldn't be tricked by the New Agers and occultists—or those overly fearful of them—into avoiding the mystery/mystical aspect of following Christ. Perfect love drives out fear (1 John 4:18); we should not be led by the fear of man, but by the Spirit of God, who is himself the supreme mystic. As much as some preachers would like to have us believe that being disciples of Christ is as simple and easily understandable as any marketable product on TV, it's really not that way. The Trinity, the birth and entire life of Christ, his parables and paradoxes, the Cross, the Resurrection, the Church, the Word—every chapter, every verse—it's all full of mystery; it's all mystical. We needn't be afraid or reluctant to admit this, and to enter the mystery. That's where we truly encounter God, the ultimate mystery. That's where we are transformed—and God's transformation process is in itself mystical: Christ compared it to a seed that dies in order to bring life to many more seeds (John 12:24).[10]

Lest we think contemplation turns Christianity into a mystery religion like those of ancient Greece, they're not the same at all. Basically, the mystery religions were so secretive that to this day not a whole lot is known about them. What is known is that through their secret rites of initiation, they created the illusion of being received into full acceptance by God or the gods—sort of an elite, exclusive inner circle, the chosen few. Christianity, on the other hand—including contemplative Christianity—is open to all. Jesus accepted all who came to him; his "chosen few" were and still are often the outcasts of society. Concerning initiation rites, that would basically be baptism, and virtually all baptismal ceremonies are open to the public. (However, there is a hidden quality to the Christian life. It's true that only God can open your eyes to see who Christ really is, and to recognize his great love for you. That's no illusion; that's the basic underlying reality of the universe. Trusting Christ doesn't create illusions, it removes them.)

> The Trinity,
> the entire life of Christ,
> his parables
> and paradoxes,
> the Cross,
> the Resurrection,
> the Church,
> the Word—
> it's all full of mystery;
> it's all mystical.
> We needn't be afraid
> to enter the mystery.
> That's where we truly
> encounter God,
> the ultimate mystery.
> That's where we
> are transformed—
> and God's
> transformation process
> is in itself mystical:
> Christ compared it
> to a seed that dies
> in order to bring life
> to many more seeds.

The mystery religions, tricksters, illusionists, those who follow the new-age or witchcraft or paganism—these are all counterfeits of following Christ. But as countless believers have discovered down the centuries, true mysticism—Christian mystical experience—is a matter of entering and hiding inside God, the Mystery of mysteries (Psalm 91:1); it's about the mystery of his Word, the Logos (John 1:1, 14). It's a way of participating in the mystery of godliness: "Without controversy, great is the mystery of godliness: God was manifested in the flesh, justified in the Spirit, seen by angels, preached among the Gentiles, believed on in the world, received up into glory (1 Timothy 3:16 NKJV)." Saying these things are not mystical does nothing to glorify God; in fact, it takes away from the glory of God by seeming to make him out to be on the level of the common, the ordinary, as mundane as a haircut, when he is beyond our comprehension, mystical, the hidden manna behind the facade of everyday life, the Mystery of mysteries.

What about the idea that through contemplative practice, we can become one with God or even become a god? There is much written in contemplative texts on the subject of theosis (divine union, or union with God). This needs a little exploration. When I first heard the term "union with God," I took it to mean we can become equal with God, and I said, no way—totally unbiblical. The term "union with God" is taken (indirectly) from John 14:19-21, 17:20-23, Galatians 2:20, 2 Peter 1:3-4, and others that speak of God and his people acting together as a unit, like a hand in a glove. Of course, we're just the glove; God is the hand, and the brain that makes it move. God can pick up a white-hot piece of steel without a glove; he doesn't need us to help him do anything. But he includes us, like a father letting his children help him do the dishes or set up a campsite. He could do it just fine by himself—probably better, in fact—but he lets us help. We act as a team together with him, and we are the body of Christ—each of us a cell in his body—and thus the term "union with God." It's interesting to me, and a bit humorous, that some who get very upset about this concept attend churches where the word "communion"—which literally means union with God—is what they call the Lord's Supper or Eucharist.

Cynthia Bourgeault, in her book *Centering Prayer and Inner Awakening*, deals with this issue: "...does this mean that God dwells within us, as the center of our being? Is that...our "divine awareness"? Cautiously, the answer to this question is "yes." I say "cautiously" because Christian theology makes very clear that the human being is not God and that the innermost core of our being is not itself divine. And yet theology has always upheld the reality of the "divine indwelling." As we move toward center, our own being and the divine being become more and more mysteriously interwoven."[11]

With Christ, we are crucified to self and the world, identifying with him so we can fully live in God. As Paul's words to Timothy in the previous paragraph make clear, no question about it: that's a mystery. 1 Peter 1:3-4 tells us that through Christ, God has given us a way to "partake of the divine nature" (NIV)—an opportunity for "participation in the life of God" (the Message). That's a great mystery. Real mysticism isn't a bunch of hocus-pocus stuff involving magic tricks based on illusion—it's all about getting beyond the layers of illusion in which everyday life in this world is wrapped, and coming to the One who is beyond all illusion, who reveals the truth and allows us to work with him in removing illusion from the world in which we live, by—paradoxically—entering into and becoming part of the ultimate mystery, the unfolding of God's Kingdom.

Not New-Age, but Newness of Life

The new age movement began in the late 1960's/early '70's; Christian contemplative prayer began at least 1600 years earlier, in the third century Church, with roots going back clearly to the second century Church Fathers, and with their writings being based on the New Testament writings. There's a lot of reason (though no hard evidence) for thinking that Peter, John, Paul and other first-century Church leaders, as well as Christ himself, practiced "be-still-and know-that-I-am-God" sessions similar to what we know today as centering prayer. It's important to realize that the character and nature of centering prayer and contemplation, while seeming similar in some ways to new-age and occult practices, are actually the opposite in purpose and design: rather than trying to gain spiritual power or channel a spirit, the objective of contemplation is to participate in the death of Christ by laying down one's life to God—to yield to Christ in total surrender, to submit to the

Holy Spirit—one thought at a time, one day at a time. It's not a New age thing; it's a newness-of-life thing.

I don't believe that contemplation, as I'm presenting it, has anything whatever to do with New Age practices. I will admit, however, that from an outsider's point of view centering prayer seems pretty similar to Transcendental Meditation, a Hindu form of meditation. Such forms of meditation employ a mantra, a constantly repeated word or phrase used to focus the mind for the purpose of freeing the practitioner from the everyday forms of thinking so one can enter a state of inner peace.[12] Centering prayer uses a word, a name or symbol of God, to help one come into God's presence and stay focused on God. But, rather than constantly repeat the word like a mantra, you merely think the word whenever you find your mind drifting. The Spirit of God is what you are to keep returning your focus to; for all other thoughts, you notice them but don't respond to them. Each one in turn is gently allowed to pass away, as one uses the prayer word only when needed to help refocus the attention on God.[13]

So centering prayer is a true form of prayer,[14] albeit one which could be considered meditational prayer—that is, it contains aspects of both prayer and some forms of meditation. If prayer can be defined as seeking God and waiting on God, then centering prayer is certainly more prayer than meditation, which generally (in Christian meditation at least) implies thinking about some subject or verse of scripture, prayerfully pondering it in order to understand it better. If you think of worship and prayer in general as a process analogous to the Biblical temple in Jerusalem (the outer court, inner court, holy place and Holy of Holies), contemplative prayer is entering into the Holy of Holies, where it's all God; unlike what's done in the Holy Place of regular prayer, in centering prayer nothing is left to us. It's all God's work; all we do is show up with a worshipful heart. There, we're completely silent; the blood is already placed on the altar by Christ himself, so all we have to do is be in God's presence worshiping him, loving him, becoming one with him.

New-age spirituality considers other gods besides God; the new-agers acknowledge that they channel spirits and trust in angels, but they don't know and apparently don't care if those angels are of God's kingdom or

Satan's. That's a crucial difference, because 2 Cor. 11:14 says dark angels masquerade as angels of light, and that even Satan himself, evil as he is, can fool people into thinking he's an angel of God. But in Christian contemplative prayer, we worship and bow down to the God of the Bible, his Son Jesus Christ, and his Holy Spirit, and no one and nothing else. (Like what we see in the Old Testament, a lot of what the Christian life consists of is destroying idolatry, and the main idol we all have to get rid of is self—the false self or ego, the face of the old nature that pretends to be the real you but is really an idol on the throne of your life as long as you let it be.)

Although on the surface there appear to be similarities between Eastern meditation practices and centering prayer/contemplation, there's a vast difference between the two. Hindu and Buddhist meditation aim for mental clarity through awareness by way of concentrated attention. Contemplation aims for purity of heart by a constant practice of letting go of our selfish desires, thoughts and feelings[15], to make our minds and hearts available only to God. Also, the objective of Eastern meditation is to come to the point of realizing that you are one with the universe. While this is not completely different from silent prayer, the aim of contemplation is to bring about in us what the title of 18th century writer Jean-Pierre de Caussade refers to as *Abandonment to Divine Providence*, that is, complete surrender of self and its desires, plans and goals to the will and work of God and the full flowering of relationship to God which results.

Oneness with God through Surrender

We become one with God by denying self and becoming one with his will. Our purpose is to acknowledge God as the center of all things and Christ as the one who holds all things together (Col. 1:17). Awareness of the world around us is only good if it awakens us to the God who is behind it all (Rom. 1:20). We center our lives on the one who gave his life for us, to bring us into the glorious freedom of the children of God. That freedom entails openness to the natural world around us and being able to see God in all things, to sit and learn at the feet of the God who "stands at the still point of the turning world."[16]

Yes, Christian contemplatives seek to be in the present moment, as the alternative title to de Caussade's book suggests.[17] We can find Christ in the now, in the simplest, most ordinary things of everyday life—but it's only for those who have "eyes to see and ears to hear," as Jesus himself put it. It's for those who are set apart from the world enough to consider the lilies of the field. They are the ones who can see Jesus in the face of a homeless man, a crack-addicted prostitute, a child with down's syndrome, a person on death row. Contemplation is a way of opening our eyes, not just to the natural world around us—though the heavens declare the glory of God to those who are listening—but even more, to what God wants us to see: his heart.

This gets into the larger misunderstanding, prevalent in the western Church in the past few centuries, of what prayer really is. We tend to think of prayer as asking God for stuff that we need or want, and for more mature pray-ers, just talking to him as you would talk to a best friend. And, of course, there's a lot of truth to that scenario, but it also leaves a lot out. As Pastor Bear Trillizio, former strength-training coach for the Buffalo Bills NFL football team, puts it: "The older I get, the shorter my prayers get; they're often down to just 'Help, God!' because God knows it all anyway."[18] In other words, the more you become one with God, the less you need words in prayer. Jesus's prayers were often remarkably short: "Be healed," "Be clean," and so forth.

The whole "in secret" thing is *the* main theme of Matt. 6:1-18; it's interesting to note that the true self has been referred to by some of the mystics as the *secret* self—it's where we meet with God in secret, the part of us that lays up our treasures in heaven, where the false self can't put in its two cents worth about anything, because it's crucified. Jesus's main point is that we need to pray in secret; that doesn't just mean don't blab it out on the street corners like the Pharisees. There's an element to prayer, like giving (v. 3), of not letting your left hand know what your right hand is doing; this is symbolic of not letting your false self know what your true self is doing in prayer with God.

Regarding repetitive prayer, Jesus isn't speaking against repetition, per se, but against the idea that God won't hear you unless you keep praying the same thing over and over again. For those who pray the Jesus Prayer, they know sooner than later that it's not about getting God to hear you; you know that he hears it the very first time. What the Jesus Prayer is about is the ever-increasing, ever-expanding work of humility and trust and purity of heart the Holy Spirit is working into you as you pray it; it's about the ever-deepening relationship with the Father that it brings. The words themselves are only a vehicle for the work of the Spirit to help us grow in keeping our minds on God and in the peace and freedom that accompanies praying without ceasing (Is. 26:3, 1 Thess. 5:17).

Jesus's comments here (Mt. 6:7) are in line with other times when he spoke out against the Pharisees and other religious people who made long prayers for self-aggrandizement—not for God to answer, but to make themselves look good. Jesus is really making fun of such people; it's an example of his sense of humor, as when, in speaking about the Pharisee and the tax collector, he said the Pharisee prayed to himself, or when he spoke of those who can see the speck in someone else's eye but can't see the log in their own. So he's talking about prayer that comes from the false self; from God's point of view, it's just plain goofy, worthy of mockery. Of course, the alternative, Jesus says, is prayer in secret—prayer from the secret self, the true self, which flows from God through us and back to God. Centering prayer is, paradoxically, the divine counterpart to the Pharisee's prayer: God praying to himself, through us, unhindered by our own thoughts, ideas or words.

As for those who would just be looking for a spiritual or mystical experience and not really wanting to follow God, yes, I'm sure there are those who begin with that motivation. But you can't practice centering prayer that way. Perhaps some would try to enter into centering prayer at least partly for such reasons, but such a person would soon discover there's a catch. The whole purpose of centering prayer is to help us do exactly what Christ spoke of: losing ourselves so that we can find ourselves in him. Contemplation accomplishes one main thing: it brings about the death of the false self in us. Even if you start into it with false motives, you'll soon realize that centering prayer centers us in God; it puts him on the throne and takes self off. Those who get this go forward; those who don't, well, they eventually phase out. You can't proceed very far in contemplative practice without passing through the narrow gate of dying to self. Jesus spoke of that gate, where the sheep go in and out and find rich pasture, find life in him. They—we—pass into his kingdom, out of our own little kingdom controlled by the false self, through the narrow gate of daily dying with Christ. False motives are shed there; they won't lead you there, and you can't take them with you. Only the crucified are truly alive.

Chapter 3

What the Bible Says about Contemplation

> "To you it has been given to know the mysteries of the kingdom of God."
>> Luke 8:10
>
> "For the word of God is living and powerful, and sharper than any two-edged sword, piercing even to the division of soul and spirit, and of joints and marrow, and is a discerner of the thoughts and intents of the heart."
>> Hebrews 4:12

The Bible is a very mystical book. (I'm sure some will take issue with that statement.) In Chapter 2, I spoke about the words "mystical" and "mysticism," and the misunderstandings about them that have been passed along to the Church in America. Yes, there are dangers to be avoided, but much in the Bible that is rich and fulfilling, we've been taught to beware of for fear that it's "mystical," and therefore we have missed out on some of the most wonder-full things God wants to give us. For those who have eyes to see and ears to hear, the Bible is a true treasure chest of these gems of living wisdom, with Christ himself as the Mystery of mysteries, the true pearl of great price. (We'll look more closely at that hope diamond in chapter 7.) Contemplative spirituality is a spirituality of people encouraged by God to not be afraid of delving into the deeper things of the Word. In chapters 1 and 2 I've already discussed various scriptures in light of the contemplative point of view. In this chapter we will unpack and examine a random sampling of several more of these treasures.[1]

Does the Bible talk about contemplative prayer, the sacrament of the present moment, union with God, and other aspects of contemplative spirituality? The answer is a clear, definite, resounding YES! But are the scriptures always so clear and obvious about it? No, usually not. Psalm 46:10 says, "Be still and know that I am God." That is probably the paramount scripture in the entire Bible about contemplation, but there are many interpretations; some say it's talking about something else.[2] When we read something in the Bible about being with God in silence, or about union with God, we see "through a glass, darkly"— because those who wrote it saw things that way. (To a certain extent, our knowledge of God and the things of God will always be that way in this life.)

To see these things spelled out somewhat more clearly, you have to read later writers—Augustine, Bernard of Clairvaux, Teresa of Avila, or others among the dozens of great Christian contemplative writers down through the centuries. Many of the books of the Old Testament show evidence that the writers had contemplative experiences, some deeply, but like contemplative writers of all eras of history, they met with the difficulty of trying to express the inexpressible and thus were not able to write of their experiences in clearly understood language.

The New Testament writers encountered the same problems; in addition, they were too busy building on the foundations of the Church Christ established to fully immerse themselves in contemplation, though their writings certainly touched on it.[3] But they and the next several generations, like the old testament prophets before them as well as Christ himself, had to face persecution and difficulty on all sides, while still trying to lead the Church and make a living as well. So it was not until the end of Roman persecution in the third and fourth centuries that contemplation became more fully developed as a spiritual discipline.

At that time, as Christianity became mainstream and persecution ended for the most part, an even more insidious threat began to emerge: a more worldly form of Christianity, more relaxed, more glib, more prone to take God and grace for granted.[4] Many of the most sincere believers then withdrew to the deserts to seek God with their whole hearts and to show to the world and to the rest of the Church a deeper love for Christ and a fuller living out of the Gospel than what they were seeing in the more "civilized" churches. Taking the examples of John the Baptist, Jesus during his temptation in the wilderness, and Paul in his first years after conversion (as well as Abraham, Moses, Elijah, and other Old Testament heroes of the faith), they answered the call of God to go into the wilderness to seek his face in solitude.

It was then and there that they were able to more fully explore the contemplative dimensions alluded to by Moses, David, Isaiah, Christ, John, Paul, and other Biblical authors. So the roots of the contemplative writings of these pioneers of mystical Christian faith—Pachomius, Irenaeus, Origen, Anthony, Gregory of Nyssa and his brother Basil, Dionysius—are in the Bible, especially the New Testament gospels, epistles, and the Book of Revelation. These early contemplatives were spurred on by Christ's prayers in solitude, his Sermon on the Mount and other teachings they recognized as mystical, and Paul's challenge of learning to bring Christ's death and resurrection into daily practice.

There are hundreds of Biblical texts from Genesis to Revelation, a handful of which we will explore in this chapter, that Christian mystics of all ages of the Church have considered mystical. In other words, they echo the mystery, the awesomeness, the paradoxical nature of God himself as experienced by contemplatives of all the centuries since Christ. The key to recognizing this is to see as the mystics see—to "see" or perceive God not with the eyes, not with the mind, but with an open, childlike heart—just as Jesus taught: you must become as a child again to enter the kingdom of Heaven.

This is why many contemplatives practice Lectio Divina: a way of reading the Word of God from the heart, not primarily the mind (or not just with the left brain); reading in a way that is prayerfully open to God and his inner light, not just to whatever comes through that cerebral filter the Age of Reason taught us to test everything with. Even those who say they are always listening for the still small voice of God in their Bible reading are sometimes appalled when, upon careful analysis, they find out just how much their rational mind filters out things that don't "make sense," twists them until they do, or insists that something like the Transfiguration of Christ is not mystical. Such people are often delighted when they learn how to allow God to teach them in ways that go beyond the rational mind—to take them into places the rational mind can never go.

In the next several sections, we'll look at passages of Scripture that involve great paradoxes, even paradoxes within paradoxes.

Psalm 23:1-3 - Beside Still Waters

"The Lord is my Shepherd; I'm in need of nothing [but him]. He leads me to rest in green pastures beside still waters. He restores my soul. He leads me in paths of righteousness for the sake of his name."[5] To me and many others, that is a picture of contemplation: a place of peace and refreshing, a place where we are at rest from our own agenda and awake to his goodness, his fullness, fully alive in God. In him we receive everything we need. He is both the place of rest and the Shepherd who leads us there. He is the restorer and, in some strange way, also the restoration. He is both the path and the destination.

Okay, I admit that for most people, especially in modern society and culture, the place where all our needs are met would not be a pasture next to a pond or gently flowing stream. There's not much there; most teenagers today would probably call it boring. Sitting in silence with God would be in the same category for most, including Christians. But in Christ's parable of the treasure hidden in a field, so is the field. Having nothing to do except be at rest in God's presence is exactly what contemplative prayer is all about. There's something mystical about finding God in what others call nothing, seeing Christ where others see worthlessness.

In a place of rest, it's not our work that's being done; it's God's: "In repentance and rest is your salvation; in quietness and peace is your strength" (Is. 30:15). It's not our issues or desires that are of concern there; it's all for the sake of God's name, his glory, his kingdom, his plan. It's a place where God can do in us things we have little or no awareness of at the time; we never do know in this life the full effect of our prayers, and that's even more true with contemplative prayer than regular verbal prayer. So the fact that some scripture passages are considered highly contemplative in nature is not always obvious. In the passage just discussed, all that I said is highly subjective. I can't prove to you that that's what the passage means, but I have no doubt that among the many things in the mind and heart of God that it represents, contemplative prayer is one of the foremost. If you feel called by God to pursue contemplation, you will eventually see what I mean.

Revelation 21:5 - All Things New Every Moment

"Behold, I make all things new!" declares the risen Jesus at the end of the world and the end of the Bible. We speak of having God open our eyes; we plead in worship, "Open the eyes of my heart, Lord—I want to see you!"[6] And yet, on a daily basis, not many of us—Christians included—can say with singer John Michael Talbot that we truly "Behold now the Kingdom! See with new eyes!"[7] The cares of this life come and crowd out the Word the Lord has planted in the soil of our lives, so that we see only with tired old eyes, blind to God in the world. We see bills and schedules, work and worry, pain and trouble, death and taxes. Occasionally, if we're lucky or blessed, we catch a glimpse of humor or fun or beauty; if we're really on a roll, there's a touch of joy sometimes. And those glimpses, those touches of the Master's hand for brief moments of our life, are truly all that keeps many people going; the fact that they are few and far between is the reason so many spend their lives in misery and fear, growing old before their time and dying without ever really having lived.

But there it is in black and white (or red, if you have one of those special bibles): "Behold, I make all things new!" Or in some translations, "I am making all things new!" or "I am making everything new!" Or even, perhaps, "Behold I AM, making all things new!" (In all translations, it's always present tense. Not, as some think, "I am going to make all things new." More on that a few paragraphs down.) What does this mean? There will be a day when the complete fulfillment of this passage is accomplished, when "the old order of things has passed away" (v. 4). No more crying, no more pain, no more death. Until then, and pointing to that day, God is in the business of constantly renewing the world.

Some of the *new* things God does or commands which are spoken of in the Bible: we are called to sing to him a new song (Ps. 40:3, 96:1, etc.). Isaiah says the same thing, then tells us, "Forget the former things; do not dwell on the past. See, I am doing a new thing! Now it springs up; do you not perceive it? I am making a way in the desert and streams in the wasteland" (Is. 42:10, 43:18-19). His mercies are new every morning (Lam. 3:22). He has written on our hearts and minds a new covenant (Jer. 31:31). He has given us the new wine of his Spirit and new wineskins to keep it in (Mt. 9:17). And he has given us a new commandment—love (Jn. 13:34). In Christ, we are new creations; Paul tells us that we can "behold, all things have become new" (II Cor. 5:17). So how is it that we don't see all things made new?

I submit that it's all the fault of that ridiculous voice inside our heads that keeps our eyes on us, our selfish nature, and our problems. It's the ego—the false self—that old, sinful, carnal nature we inherited from Adam and Eve. It's the impostor self, that voice in your head that claims to be the real you, that leads you to do things you know are wrong, that tells you what a wonderful person you are when you do something good and gets you to tell others what you've done, but never says a word when you sin. Or if it does, it tells you you're an absolute dirtbag that God couldn't possibly love or accept.

Both extremes are total lies. Yes, it started with that serpent in the garden, but Satan doesn't have to be at our side every moment for us to be blind to the beauty, the enchantment, the grace of life. That ongoing pack of lies inside called the false self, the old nature, does a fine job even if we aren't crackheads, sexual deviants, murderers—even if we live a godly life and never come near Satan. And in order for us to see the glorious truth that all things are continually being made new by God, every moment that we live—the truth that God himself is and has always been new every moment since before the universe began—we have to learn to silence the deadly voice of the false self.

Contemplative prayer does just that. It's a time of giving your thoughts to God, every one of them, knowing they all either come from or are filtered through the false self. So—sit down to pray, and every time you catch yourself thinking, stop and focus your mind on God and give that thought to him, and realize that by doing so you are giving him your total attention and affection and love, just for that moment. Just for that moment, you are setting your mind and heart fully on things above and not on earthly things; just for that moment you are dead to self, and your life is hidden with Christ in God (Col. 3:2). Do that for a few minutes a few times a day, or twenty minutes once or twice a day, and you'll begin to see with new eyes; you'll begin to recognize that, indeed, you are invited by God to look into the silent, turbulent, boundless mystery of creation, the beauty and wonder of all things being made new with every heartbeat, every breath, every blink of your eyes.

This glorious verse, "Behold, I make all things new!" (Rev. 21:5), isn't just a promise for the future. It's an open invitation from God to see for ourselves, in quiet amazement, that he is constantly making the world and everything in it brand spanking new, every instant. Every detail. Every second, every cell in our bodies receives fresh oxygen and other nutrients. Every molecule in the world is constantly changing; the positions of the electrons and other subatomic particles in every atom in the universe constantly shift from moment to moment. And the infinite, unchanging God sees it all, commands it all, delights in it all, in infinite love. Nothing gives him greater joy than sharing it all with us—with "those who have ears to hear."[8]

I spoke earlier of how contemplative prayer is a way of accepting the invitation, a way of entering into the process of seeing with new eyes the glory of God in the smallest things. Somehow, the prayer of gently refusing to pay attention to anything but God for a short part of the day leads, at other times in your day, to becoming aware of God directing your attention to the little things he does all around you that you never noticed.

As you begin to develop the discipline of doing this prayer of full submission moment by moment, day by day, you truly begin to see with new eyes. You begin to marvel at the most simple, mundane things. You notice that the wax on a candle has dried into the most amazing shape. In the bathroom, you see a baby spider and, instead of smashing it to death, you watch in fascination as it climbs so patiently, so nimbly, up the wall. On a chilly afternoon, you see icicles hanging from the gutter in the sunlight and find yourself in rapt attention as they slowly melt, delighting in each drop as it hits the sidewalk and splatters every which way. Preparing to make spaghetti, you catch yourself staring at the blue flame on a burner on the stove and pondering the magical, mysterious way it heats water in a pan from cold to bubbling to boiling.

You cut an apple in half and are fascinated, as you were in childhood, to see the unique arrangement of this unique apple's insides—something no one but God and you have ever seen, something you feel so privileged and grateful to have been shown by the Creator. You begin to recognize that, in fact, all things *are* being made new every moment by God. The utter unfathomable joy of being allowed to see as God sees, just leaves you speechless and silences your mind for a few moments—bringing you full circle to the silent awareness of God that you've known in centering prayer, completing one revolution in the endless spiral of contemplation. The fascination of God's presence in every moment has shown you once again, as the psalmist says, the importance of learning to be still and know that he is God.

Some would argue that this interpretation of Revelation 21:5 takes Christ's words out of context. He is talking, they say, of what he will do in the fullness of time, when he makes a new heaven and a new earth, after Satan and his servants are finally banished forever to eternal torment. And in God's continually expanding revelation of himself to man, yes, this will certainly happen—the full flowering of God's fulfillment of this astonishing promise, our eyes eternally open wide to the fullness of grace beyond imagining, as part of Christ's return, millennial reign, and the final vanquishing of evil. But as with many of the promises of God (or perhaps all of them), there are multiple fulfillments. Before the final, ultimate realization of this truth—"Behold I Am, making all things new"—comes, it begins as a seed planted in our lives that begins to take root. Slowly, gradually, as it grows it discloses to us the everlasting miracle of God, the Master of all worlds. He is truly incomprehensible, yet he's revealing himself in the most insignificant details of our own fascinating, scintillating, marvelously dazzling world, with every tick of the clock, day and night, throughout all history.

Thus, this ability to see the ongoing work of God as he constantly makes all things new isn't something we have to wait till heaven or the end of time to realize; it comes standard on all models of the human race, though few recognize it. Even fewer learn to live daily in the realm of awe, but it's part of the abundant life guaranteed by Jesus to his followers. So, the next time you sing, "Open the eyes of my heart, Lord—I want to see you," try taking a new approach. Close your eyes for twenty minutes to gaze on God and give him a chance to answer your prayer. Then open them to the glorified world everywhere in your midst.

Hebrews 4:11-12 - Laboring to Rest: the Prayer of Letting Go

Most of us in the Church—especially if we've been Christians since the '80's or longer—have heard the saying "let go and let God." It comes from the Twelve Steps of Alcoholics Anonymous (AA), and it means we must stop our own striving, stand back, and see what God can and will do. When we step away, give up on our own efforts to rescue ourselves, it's then and only then that we really give God a chance. It's not giving up or giving in to sin; it's a matter of giving up on self as an essential step toward trusting God. Some have said that the "let go and let God" philosophy is overly simplistic, that we have to do something, we can't just sit around waiting for God to move. That point of view is about the same as the old "God helps those who help themselves" attitude, which is really just a phony cover-up for the false self's idea of self-sufficiency—a deception if there ever was one. We are not self-sufficient; we are fully reliant on God from the moment of conception to our last breath, whether we realize it or not.

And yet, even in "letting go and letting God," there is something we can do. The Bible tells us in Hebrews 4:11 that we should "labor to enter (God's) rest" (KJV). The word "labor" can also be translated "strive," "make every effort," "be diligent," "endeavor," "be zealous," "make haste" to enter God's rest. In other words, it takes work to enter into God's rest. Is this like working our way to heaven—salvation by works? No, it's more like working *out* our salvation, with God working *in* us (Phil. 2:12-13). But still, one of the clear implications of Hebrews 4:11-12 is that rest requires work. That's a paradox. Well, maybe not; you have to get your work done before you can take a break, right? We work now, in this life, and then rest in heaven eternally. But I don't think that's really the main thrust of what this verse is saying. I think the writer is talking about God's rest for us in this life, not just in the next. Let me explain why I say that.

We're saved by grace, period—not by works; by God, and by nothing at all that we can do ourselves; all we can do is trust God and wait on him. Another way of looking at it is: without work, there's no such thing as

Like the "work"
of a baby
at its mother's breast—
the most intimate,
nourishing work
imaginable—
contemplative prayer
is perhaps the best way
we can labor
to enter God's rest.
One sits,
still and silent,
doing the work
of loving God
with all one's heart,
soul, mind and strength,
doing nothing else
at all—
and being nourished
by God
in ways that are
beyond our understanding.
It's a true
labor of love.

rest; rest and work follow and give meaning to each other as do night and day. However, the paradox remains: resting involves working. So, what kind of work are we talking about? Hebrews 4 gives us a clue a few verses earlier: "Now we who have believed enter that rest..." (v.3). So, faith is the work; believing God, with the obedience that goes with faith, is required for entering God's rest. As faith without work is dead (James 2:26), rest without work is meaningless. And faith works through love (Gal. 5:6); love is work—it's faith in action.

Does one enter God's rest merely by believing? To an extent, yes. The point where we stop trying to work our way to heaven is the point where we trust Christ's work on the cross to bring us to heaven. And heaven is the real place of rest. But believing is itself work; Jesus said, "The work of God is this: to believe in the one he has sent" (John 6:29). Whatever work we do for God must be done in faith; it must be based on the life, death and resurrection of Jesus, the knowledge that our work is meaningless without the work he did on the cross, and the understanding that we are working with him and that he is working in and through us. Otherwise we may as well not bother; without that perspective, our work is building our own kingdom, which will burn.

But with faith, along with the knowledge of God's will and the commitment to it, our work is building the Kingdom of God. Faith is the mustard seed that starts the work, and the work proceeds entirely from that seed, empowered by the Holy Spirit; we supply the muscle (provided by him to begin with), while God empowers and guides us in this kind of work as we trust in him. It's like the "work" of a baby at its mother's breast: yes, there's work involved—muscles are flexing, etc.—but it's the most intimate, nourishing, peaceful kind of work imaginable—a truly restful kind of work. It's not the retirement of heaven; even there, that restful work will still continue in some form or another. But it's work for the Kingdom, fed and led by faith in Christ.

So what does all this have to do with contemplative prayer? It's perhaps the best way we can labor to enter God's rest. One sits, still and silent, seemingly doing nothing, looking to Jesus the author and perfecter of our faith (Heb. 12:2) and forsaking every other "work"—thoughts about today, feelings about yesterday and fears of tomorrow—laying at his feet each thought that comes, doing the work of surrender. Doing the work of loving God with all one's heart, soul, mind and strength, doing nothing else at all—and being nourished by God in ways we can't understand, any more than a baby can understand how the nutrients in mother's milk are building its growing body. It's a true labor of love, dying to self and resting in peace, not asking for anything, just being with the Almighty. Resting for a few minutes in wordless loving relationship with God the All-in-All. The natural mind can never understand or make sense of it, but that doesn't change the reality of it one bit. That's also a paradox. And here's another one: since God is almighty and omnipotent, why does he need rest? Also, think about this: the Bible says God rests and strongly implies that when we enter his rest, that rest is ongoing, eternal. Yet it also says God has never stopped working (John 5:17; see Amplified Bible and Contemporary English Version, among others). How can he work and rest at the same time? How can we work and be in his rest at the same time?

To me, the Kingdom of God resolves the paradox. God rests on his throne, yet he's still giving orders, running the universe by his authority. The work done out of his rest, including the work we do for him, is the work of building the Kingdom—work that can't be done in the old nature, but can only be done by faith. (That does not mean there's no physical labor. Hard work is quite often part of Kingdom work. Think, for example, about missionaries who build houses for the poor or dig wells for people to have clean drinking water.) But in work done from God's rest, there's rest from our agenda, from our old nature, as we work in the power of the Spirit. Hebrews 4:10 says God rested from the work only he could do in creation; thus, he now works through us. And we rest from the work that's only human in nature, working with God to build what's a joint effort of human and divine, through service and faith and prayer—silent, wordless prayer as well as verbal and vocal—the building of the Kingdom.

Hebrews 4:12 adds a new layer to the paradox. For years, there seemed to me to be a non-sequitur between Hebrews 4:11 and 4:12. I now see that the connection is in the answer to the question, why do we enter God's rest? The answer comes in verse 12: because the Word is alive, the Word needs to act, there's work to be done, and we're invited to be part of it, but we can't do it in our own strength. It must be done from what's of God, not of man—God's agenda, not ours—in his strength, not ours—flowing out of his rest, his peace. So verse 12 tells us we need the Word to reveal the difference between what's of man—the soul—and what's of God and man together, the spirit of man. The Word also reveals the difference between what kind of spiritual food is to be thrown away as nutritionally worthless—the joints—and what kind is to be savored as nutritionally rich—the marrow.

Another thing the Word brings to light is the difference between our thoughts, and the attitudes and motivations behind those thoughts—what is of God and what is of man. The Word of God is dividing the two asunder, as the King James version of verse 12 puts it. He is teaching us to get rid of all that's merely human and to cultivate what's being built into us by God himself. And you can't learn that through any human ability. It requires putting to death the old nature, the false self—letting it rest in peace in the grave, while the new nature given by God, the resurrection life in us, is resting in God, living with God, active with God, going where God takes us and seeing what God reveals to us and doing what God gives us to do, praying as God leads us to pray. That's why we must enter God's rest—this is work that can only be done from a place of resting in God; any attempt to do this by the old nature only pollutes and corrupts the work of God. That's why contemplative prayer is so valuable. It's all about dying to self, dying outwardly and being renewed inwardly each day (II Cor. 4:16).

So, how can we know we've entered and are in God's rest? Answer: are we doing the work of the Kingdom, or mostly our own thing? Is the fruit of the Spirit growing in our lives, or primarily the works of the flesh? Those things tell the tale.

1 Cor. 1:21-25: The offense of the Cross

Why is the cross so offensive? I don't see anything in any other religion that brings such violent reactions—emotionally and sometimes physically—as the idea of Jesus on the cross, or the idea of being crucified with Christ. We just don't want to go there. It's the thing that really turns everything upside down—or right side up, really, but from the perspective of people who don't believe in Jesus Christ or relate to the world through him, the idea of becoming a Christian means their entire life gets turned upside down. In a way, it's like something in a science-fiction movie: passing through a portal into a different dimension, into the unknown. The cross is that portal, and compared to the glamorous smoky shiny mysteriousness of a Spielberg movie scene, the cross seems ugly and humiliating and way too plain, too ordinary. We want adventure, not a boring life of reading the Bible. But once you pass through that portal of the cross, you find the treasure hidden in the field—gold and diamonds sparkling in the sunlight in the middle of a dry, empty piece of land that appears to have nothing to offer but weeds and dirt clods.

Europeans and Americans picture becoming a Christian as going from being a "normal" person to some squeaky-clean religious freak who wears suits and ties and doesn't have any fun and goes around quoting Bible verses and talking about sin all the time; from a beer-drinking, joke-telling average person to a Billy Graham. For people in non-Western cultures, the idea of the cross is more a matter of leaving their own culture behind and believing in something their family and friends can't relate to at all, won't understand and will persecute them for. (That can happen to those in Western cultures too, though usually in less extreme ways.) For someone in a place where Jesus Christ is unheard of, it's hard to imagine what the cross would mean, but it's definitely what a cross looks like—a crossroads, a crossing of paths, suggesting a turning from one direction to a different one, to the unknown, leaving the old life behind.

And that's a lot of what's so offensive about the cross, no matter what a person's background is. It's accepting that Jesus is the same as the unblemished, perfect, innocent lamb or kid goat or other animal taken for a sacrifice to turn away the wrath of God or the gods or the forces of nature or fate so we don't have to suffer, or suffer as much. It's accepting that people in the midst of a plague, lost in a middle eastern desert thirty five hundred years ago, could look at a crudely fashioned brass sculpture of a snake nailed to a piece of wood and the plague would be stopped for them, and that that's the same as Jesus on the cross. How can he be both a snake and a lamb? What does this have to do with anything in my life, anyway? The mind can't reason its way through the issues of the cross; as Paul of Tarsus said nearly two thousand years ago, the cross is foolishness to the mind. For anyone and everyone, it's offensive.

Jesus on the cross is a stone that people stumble over, tumble upside down and land on their heads, heads that can't understand ultimate truth; it's a rock people fall and land on and get broken, and find out who they really are and who God really is. The mind can't handle that, either, so after pondering the cross you can get up and walk away or go back to work, or you can sit in silence with the God who is there beyond the thoughts that can't grasp the cross and its meaning, or the way it turns everything upside down. You can sit with your eyes closed and mentally gaze at the cross, and at the repulsive, naked, condemned man hanging from it, bleeding from a thousand places on his hideously torn body, a body that feels pain beyond the scale of one to ten.

You can see, in complete contradiction to everything else in that scene, the sad eyes gazing lovingly right straight into your own eyes. The mind can't fathom love, especially that kind of perfect love. So you give up trying and just rest in it; you stay in the stillness, in the presence of that perfect love, and in a way you die with him, ignoring every thought, every impulse of the self, everything that could feed the ego, until the fragments of thought are like chaff, like flower petals on the breeze. You stay in that place, dead to self, and you rest in the grave with him, and wait in hope, knowing that for such love, even death isn't the end (Ps. 16). In the words of that Man, "Blessed are those who are not offended [at him and his message] (Matt. 11:6).

The Word that Became, and Becomes, Flesh (John 1:1-5, 14)

How can we know God? Through his Word, first of all. The Word becomes alive in us as we trust God; it begins to unfold the reality of who God is, like a seed begins to germinate, puts down roots and pushes up shoots, and keeps growing and developing until it's a full grown Sequoia tree or a coral reef. So we need to know the Word; it's vital, more necessary than our physical food. Meat and potatoes and toast and salad and Hershey bars feed us for this life only. The Word feeds us for eternity.

So, is merely reading the Bible enough? I used to think so, but the longer I live and the more I study God's Word and see him working in my life, the more I realize that the Word is just the blueprint. Like a magic picture of a house in a storybook where the house jumps out of the book and becomes real, or like a wonderful character in a story being told around a fire, a character who then steps out of the fire into your life, or like a story you can enter and live in, God becomes alive to us through reading and more-than-reading the Bible. Memorizing scripture is good; meditating on it is better; prayerfully searching it out in naked humility and pure-hearted hunger, in the strength of God and in the power and wisdom of his Spirit, is better yet. The brilliant yet paradoxical interpretations of Old Testament scripture given by Jesus, Paul and others in the New Testament could not have come about by any other method (Jesus's reference to Daniel 2:34-5 in Matt. 21:42-44, for example). Such revelations of God's Word usually go beyond the basic, face-value meanings, often delving into the territory of type-and-shadow, original meanings of words, and the symbolic . Yet they can also be tremendously simple, practical and down to earth as well (a case in point is Jesus's teaching in Luke 14:8-11, based on Proverbs 25:6-7). Such Bible reading has opened the eyes of the heart for untold millions around the world; for some this is a daily occurrence.

In college years ago, around the time I became a Christian and before I knew much about the Bible or Christ, one of my professors (who was probably an unbeliever) told the class about the Logos, the ancient Greek word for "word." He told us that to the Greeks twenty-five hundred years ago, the term Logos meant a story you could actually step into and become a part of and find protection from your enemies and the outside world. Hearing this was a great little gift from God that he stored away in me until I knew what to do with it. Now, as I practice lectio divina and centering prayer, I see the reality of the Logos—Christ, the Word that became flesh and offers each of us a role in the Story of Stories. In him we live and move and have our being; in him we have abundant life; he dwells among us, full of grace and truth; within our crucified flesh, he lives the resurrected life in us. He writes history—His story—in our lives.

So merely reading the Bible is not enough. We have to receive the seed of the Word into the well-prepared, fertile ground of our hearts or it will die. Just reading the Bible doesn't accomplish much; James says people read it, glimpse themselves in the mirror of the Word, and then go away and forget what they look like, go back to their old ways of darkness. The Word that falls on the highways and byways of our lives will be stolen by Satan before it can accomplish anything; the Word planted on stony or thorny ground will die. But the Word planted in a heart prepared by God to receive it will bring forth a great harvest of fruit—including, but not limited to, bringing others to Christ. The real miracle that the Word brings forth in each of us is transformation—going from looking like a seed to looking like a stalk of wheat or a lilac bush; going from looking like our old self-absorbed life to looking and thinking and acting like Christ.

How does God prepare our heart to receive his Word? Waiting in silence makes a huge difference. In centering prayer, we allow the Holy Spirit to work behind the scenes in ways we can't understand. We surrender every thought until we come to a place of inner silence, resting in God, like a weaned child resting in the arms of its mother (Psalm 131:2). There God works in us and changes us into who he has created and called us to be, in invisible, incomprehensible ways, just like the child in the mother's arms grows emotionally in ways the child can never understand.

Resting in God prepares the ground of our hearts to receive the Word; it builds humility, the peace of God, a hunger for more of God, the desire to love as Christ loved, etc. Then, when we read the Word, rather than merely checking a passage off our to-do list, we can study and meditate on it; we are reminded by the Holy Spirit of other scriptures that echo the same truth; we see how the Word applies to life in ways that we never recognized before, but which seem so obvious once God has opened our eyes to his own way of seeing. The Word, once again, daily, becomes flesh and dwells among us and in us, full of grace and truth; the Kingdom of God is within us. You step into the story of God and become a part of it; he steps out of the fire into your life and becomes a Father, a Master, a Friend, beyond anything in any story you've ever heard.

2 Corinthians 12:1-10 - True Brokenness brings Healing

Paul speaks of having been given a gift from God, one he didn't ask for, one nobody wants. He called it his "thorn in the flesh." No one knows for sure what Paul's affliction was, but it appears to have been some kind of physical limitation, perhaps a painful one; some have theorized about it being headaches, eye problems, great temptation, epilepsy, etc. Whatever it was, Paul's ordeal in this situation—and God's word to him concerning it—turned him right-side up in ways he hadn't been, though his ministry and suffering for the Gospel prior to that point in his life had already proven him to be one of the greatest men of God of all history. He discovered more deeply than ever what it means to be crucified with Christ—by accepting his own woundedness, his own weakness, his own failings in the eyes of the world—his own brokenness. He discovered the truth that only the crucified are truly alive.

We all have a thorn in the flesh - it's called original sin. Fortunately for us, that's not the end of the story. God's strength is perfected in weakness, as shown by Christ in his death and resurrection—and through us when we emulate that death and resurrection. And that's what we do in centering prayer. It's all about becoming nothing, as Christ did (Philippians 2:7, NIV); other translations say he emptied himself, became of no reputation, etc. However you put it, Christ became a man. What was the first man? A dirt clod that God molded and shaped and then breathed into—a walking, breathing, thinking, talking dirt clod. And that's all we are as well—nothing. Isaiah 44 says those who create and worship idols create a nothing out of what's worthless—a stick of wood that could just as well be used to build a fire and end up as a bit of ash—and then they worship that nothing. To worship nothing, you have to make yourself out to be something. Why not turn that around and make yourself nothing, as Christ did, and then worship God, who is your everything? (I don't mean that in a pantheistic way; I just mean that God becomes literally the only thing that's truly real to you, the one who gives meaning to all things and without whom all things are meaningless.)

And in becoming nothing, we can often become "the least of these" (Matthew 25:31-46) to others. It's not pleasant being in that place, but as Paul discovered, it truly is a gift from God. He can then use us in ways he can't use a person who arrogantly thinks he or she is something. Once we become nothing, we can recognize others who are "the least of these." And we can reach out with true compassion to such people because we can truly see Christ in them. God can't use a puffed-up person, but a nothing he can use in many ways. One of those ways is to challenge other believers to see Christ in the least of these. Many a ministry has been built of wood, hay and stubble instead of gold, silver and precious gems (I Cor. 3:11-15) and has eventually come to ruin because the leaders hadn't learned to become nothing, so they could not recognize Christ in "the least of these" in their midst.

So God's strength, as Paul discovered, is in weakness. When we make ourselves weak, when we make ourselves nothing, when we accept our brokenness, when we become "the least of these," then we can "draw near to God with a true heart in full assurance of faith" (Hebrews 10:22 NIV/KJV). It's hard to really worship God, to make him your everything, unless you make yourself nothing first. That's what contemplation accomplishes.

The Word in the Millennium

What will Jesus be like in the Millennium? Specifically, what will he say? If God's Word, the Bible, is truly complete, then what's left for Jesus to do and be when he returns to rule the world as King of the Universe to whom every knee will bow? Will he just say the same things he said before as the Son of Man walking the dusty roads of Judea?

Of course not. The Bible we read, the Jesus we see in it, is just a seed of what Christ will be in the Millennium. And what he will say then will be fresh new words full of the life of God for all those who hear them, with power to transform people into the image of God just as the words of Christ in the Bible do now. What his words then will be, we cannot imagine, though they will not contradict his words in Matthew, Mark, Luke, John and Revelation. But just as the Messiah was eagerly anticipated yet hard to recognize by those who read the Law, Psalms and Prophets two thousand years ago, when Christ returns, his words and actions will be something men and women will recognize and understand only by the Spirit of God, not by their own understanding.

And as hard as it was two thousand years ago for those who read the Law and the Psalms and the Prophets to recognize Jesus as the Messiah, that's how hard it will be for people—Christians included—to recognize him when he returns; his words will be just as radically different and as hard for people to recognize as the true Word of God they will be. He won't fit anyone's expectations.[9] That's why it's a good idea to have no expectations. We have to learn to let God be God, to let him reveal himself to us as he is. The more we try to fit him into our expectations of who he should be or who he is, the more we go astray.

In our 20/20 hindsight, we can recognize how Christ was the fulfillment of all that was written about him under the Mosaic covenant. But when he walked the earth, only those who truly were poor in spirit, mourning over sin, meek, hungering and thirsting for righteousness, and so forth (Matt. 5:1-8), could recognize the Savior of the World in the wandering rabbi whose words and actions seemed so strange.

It wasn't those who had the Law, Psalms and Prophets memorized who recognized Jesus as the Messiah; it was those who hungered for the God behind the stories of Abraham and Moses, who thirsted for the Spirit of Life behind the words and lives of Abel and Jacob, Gideon and David, Isaiah and Obadiah. Not all those who read the word can receive the

Word. And it will be the same in the Millennium. Christ, though King of Kings and Lord of Lords, will not come in the way any of us expects; he will not appear the way any of us envision him in our human minds. And just as the world we live in will be restored and made new in the Millennium, the words Christ will speak—the word of God—will be new and different to us. The words he spoke on earth 2000 years ago will never pass away or be superseded, any more than the words of Noah or Abraham or Samuel, thousands of years old in Christ's time, could pass away. The words of Christ the Word in the Millennium will add enrichment and color and light and life to the words he spoke when he was here the first time, just as those words brought new life and meaning to the words of the Law and the Psalms and the Prophets.

How can believers during the Millennium, especially those who are alive when Christ returns, make sure they will recognize the new words of Christ in the Millennium as coming from the same Christ as the carpenter from Nazareth who died on the Cross? The same way we can today: read and hear those words not in our own authority, leaning not on our own understanding—not as those who have it all figured out— but as the poor in spirit, as those who mourn over evil, as those who are meek, as those who hunger and thirst for righteousness. The words of Christ, the Word of God, now and then, will never be just words. They will be Spirit and Life, and only those who have the life of God in their hearts will understand. Merely reading the Bible doesn't do much good; it's those who take it in, who treasure it in their hearts as Mary did (Luke 1 & 2), who meditate on it and let it change them, who will understand the new words of Christ in the Millennium. And our Bibles now, Old and New Testaments, will have a third Testament added to them: the new Millennial words of Christ. Or perhaps we won't need to read them any longer; perhaps he will speak them directly to our hearts; perhaps they will ever remain there, never to be lost. One thing is sure: no eye has seen, no ear has heard, no heart has imagined what God has prepared for those who love him.

Conclusion

This chapter is just a sampling of passages in the Bible that can be seen as contemplative. Hopefully it has given you a glimpse into seeing the Word of God from a mystic's point of view. In the chapters to follow, as in the previous parts of the book, there will be many more such passages to consider, dealing with different aspects of contemplative spirituality.

Chapter 4

True Self, False Self, and Crucifying the Ego

> You can safely assume you've created God in your own image when it turns out that God hates all the same people you do.
> — Anne Lamott

> Is the "you" that people see for real or just a mask?
> Can you truly say you're happy, or is it hard to even ask?
> ...Are you tired of feeling lost?
> Are you willing to count the cost?
> Are you ready to lay your life down and let Jesus be the boss?
> Or will you stay adrift on troubled seas,
> By wind and wave driven and tossed?
> Can you ask yourself the question if the answer is the Cross?

There are people, including a pastor or two, that I've spoken to many times but never met. I don't mean we haven't been formally introduced; in each case, we have. What I mean is, I've never met the person they really are. I've only been allowed to interact with the person they want me to think they are. They wear masks. And in all cases, they've spent years—most of their lives, in fact—refining and polishing those masks. Those masks are personas—invented personalities—created to fool everyone they encounter into thinking they are something else besides who they really are. One man I met—a Christian—actually looks, walks, talks and acts like an Old West gunslinger. That's the mask, the character, he has developed; that's how he presents himself. That's apparently who he wants you to think he is. That's his carefully crafted false self.

And who he really is deep inside—no one is ever allowed to see that self. He keeps it well hidden. He apparently thinks it's inferior. He's not willing to be vulnerable enough to let anyone see his real self. And the strange thing is, that true self is the self God knows. Somewhere deep inside, he knows that God sees right through his false self, and that he can't hide his true self from God. But he constantly hides it from people. And yet, God sees him and loves him—but as he really is, not as he pretends to be. Every day. Every moment. All the time.

The false self can take on many disguises: the leader, the hero, the victim, the lover, the teacher, the free spirit, the caregiver, the rebel, the artist, the philosopher, the clown, etc. Pretty much everyone in the world wears a mask of some sort for much of their life if not all of it; most people have a false self that consists of one dominant element—one disguise—and at least one lesser element. And becoming a Christian doesn't exempt you: there are Christian versions of all of the above categories, and more. It's amazing how the false self can weave its own story of who it thinks you are, in defiance of the Creator and in contradiction of the real you, the true self designed by the Creator long before you were born. Thomas Keating, one of the 20th/21st century pioneers of contemplative prayer, has a lot to say about the psychological development of the false self, beginning with things that happen in early childhood. We will delve more deeply into Keating's wisdom in chapter 8.

The Fast Track to Phariseeism

Are Christians exempt from ego trips?[1] We should be. We're told in the Bible, "those who belong to Christ have crucified the old nature with its passions and desires" (Gal. 5:24). And yet, have you ever been in a prayer group with someone whose vast outpouring of prayer for everything under the sun appears designed, not to address the needs of the lost or hurting, but to impress all the other people there who can't get a prayer in edgewise? Or perhaps you've known plenty of Christians who take it as a point of pride to read only the old King James Bible. Or, "we don't believe in _____" (fill in the blank. It used to be dancing, playing cards, etc.; it can also take forms like long hair or facial hair for men, wearing pants and makeup for women, and so forth.)

These things can come to define holiness for Christians, and we can get so caught up in outward appearances that it's an ego trip. We are the Christians, the mighty mighty Christians, and if you're not like us, we don't accept you. They're holier than thou, even if you're a brother or sister in the Lord, because you don't go to the same church, or because you differ slightly from them about certain fine points of doctrine. (That was me at one time in my walk; perhaps it still is at times, but I hope not. Please don't ever think I'm saying that if you don't practice centering prayer, you're not as good as us great and glorious contemplatives. If I ever convey that message, please forgive me. I'm not perfect, and I don't expect to be any time soon.)

That kind of thinking leads to a Christianity where the poor and needy and sick and homeless and hurting are ignored, forgotten, considered less than acceptable, because their outward life supposedly reveals their inward poverty. Ego-driven Christianity (what an oxymoron!) is the fast track to Phariseeism. And, of course, just about anything can become an ego trip: our church or denomination or favorite Bible translation or favorite ministry or Bible study or home group or clique—we're the best, we've got the goods, we're the real deal, we're the insiders and everyone else is second best. That's not Biblical Christianity, it's ego talking.

There's something about spending time with God in silence that eventually opens your eyes to what the ego is, and you begin to learn to crucify it. Actually, just sitting in silence with God is itself an ego-stopper; constantly refocusing attention on God slowly kills the ego, and the longer you do that, the less the ego controls you. (It's a very long process, if you think you've arrived, that proves you haven't.) Also, the more you are making a daily practice of silencing the ego, the more you recognize that there's a true self inside that loves God, that cares about the lost and the poor, the sick and the wounded. It wants to reach out and help them and love them with God's love and doesn't want anything back. Choosing to follow that impulse—to follow the leading of the Spirit—is one of the most powerful things we can do to break the ego's grip.

And what, exactly, is this ego thing? Ego is a psychological term for the false self, the face of the old nature which is the sinful self, the selfish part of you. If it isn't crucified, it remains the big "I" on the throne of your life, getting fatter, more deceptive, and more selfish by the day. And it's the part that will all burn at the end along with all its actions. The true self and its actions are what will be left, what won't burn, because it's the work of God in your life.

And, of course, we also have to guard against allowing contemplative prayer to become an ego trip.

A pastor friend of mine once said that of all the groups of people mentioned in the Bible, the group most like evangelicals were the Pharisees. It came as quite a shock to hear it put that way, but the pastor—himself an evangelical—pointed out that the Pharisees loved the Word of God; they believed in missions and did everything they could to bring people to God; they were known as people of prayer; they took care of the poor and widows and orphans; holiness and righteousness and purity were very important to them; they were scrupulous about their tithing. In other words, their values were pretty much the same as those of today's so-called Religious Right. That's scary. I've been part of that group (by church affiliation at least) for about forty years.

What was it, then, that was so wrong with the Pharisees? In a word, religion. They loved their traditions, their "old time religion," more than they loved God and more than they loved their neighbor. Their religion, their belief system, rather than love, was the standard against which they measured everything—even, as it turned out, the Messiah they so longed for. And that was what brought them to the point of "fighting against God," as Gamaliel, one of the Pharisees' most respected teachers, put it in Acts 5:34-39. Verse 40 of that chapter goes on to say they took Gamaliel's advice to leave the Christians alone, then in the next breath it says they flogged them and warned them not to speak in the name of Jesus. They valued their religion more than God; they obeyed their religion rather than the truth.

Why is religion problematic for Christians? After all, there's so much good in it; it's like a set of guidelines for living the way God would have us live, built more or less around "love God and love your neighbor." So what's the problem? Was the early Church religious? Well, that depends on how you define the term, but I would say no, for the most part at least. The early Church was loving; sometimes love and religion are diametrically opposed. That's the point; that's the issue; that's the choice.

It all comes back to the ego, the false self, the sin nature. Anything we do, actively or passively, to build up the false self is sin. That can happen even when one is attached to and prideful about things that are in themselves good. Paul discusses this in Romans 7 in regard to the Jewish Law (the first five books of the Old Testament). The same thing goes for the attributes of evangelicals as compared to the Pharisees earlier in this section. We can be attached in egotistical, selfish ways to things like tithing, "correct" doctrine, political issues as an extension of our religious identity, and so forth. Again, not that such things are wrong; it's all about motive. Is the Spirit behind such actions or positions, or is it the flesh that's leading us? If it's the latter, these things can become attachments that feed the ego. Breaking those types of prideful attachments—religious or otherwise—is a lot of what contemplative prayer is all about.

The main way such attachments are broken is through becoming more and more attached to God and nothing else. He's the one who changes us; we can't do it, but by placing our lives in his hands, we can facilitate God's work; placing all our ways in God's hands, we can help "make the crooked places straight and the rough places smooth so the glory of the Lord will be revealed" (Isaiah 40:4-5; Luke 3:5-6). Breaking attachments to things other than God—including religion—breaks down the ego and places God on the throne of one's life instead of the ego; it leads to Christ-centered rather than self-centered service and worship, and it teaches us to love. Failure to crucify the ego leads, in the religious sphere, to Phariseeism.

Retraining the Mind vs. Silencing the False Self

I recently heard someone on a Christian radio program talk about how it's important to examine the thoughts you think and the way you think, and retrain your thinking to reflect the Word of God. The person was trying to help others to become better Christians and better people, better equipped to serve Christ, by reforming the mind according to the principles established in the Bible. They were willing to send their six-DVD set to anyone who called on their 800 number (for a modest "donation") to take them through this program of retraining the mind.

That's admirable. This person's motives are good. Our minds are a mess; we think all kinds of wrong thoughts about ourselves, about who Christ is and what our relationship is with him and with others, and that's just the beginning. Idolatrous thoughts form in our heads and begin to take root in our hearts before we even realize what's going on. They can start bearing fruit much earlier than we would expect, and then we need to root them out and replace them with good thoughts, true thoughts. And for most of us, this process was well under way long before we became Christians; our minds were beginning to sprout wrong thoughts and thought patterns by age two or three. After coming to Christ we constantly have to work on thinking right thoughts and not thinking wrong thoughts. For those who follow Christ, it's a daily battle. For those who don't, their minds and consciences are defiled, polluted, what a tangled web we weave, etc.

So, a change of mind is definitely in order. The Bible tells us to be transformed by the renewing of our minds (Romans 12:2); the Message Bible puts it this way: "fix your attention on God. You'll be changed from the inside out." The problem is how to go about it. Reading and studying and meditating on Scripture is certainly part of the transformation of our lives through the renewing of our minds. But, note: true transformation is something God does, not something we do. We're participants in the process and recipients of God's grace, so it's not like we don't do anything.

But it's God who makes it all happen; he's the initiator of the process, the dispenser of grace. He's the one who transforms us and renews our minds. We can read our Bibles and examine our thoughts till we're sick of it and we still can't change *self* enough to really do much good at all or to make much difference in our lives. You can't just pave over the old, potholed road of old-nature thinking with the pavement of Bible reading and memorization; the old thinking, like old pavement, must be removed. In other words, the self can't be reformed; it must be crucified with Christ. It is Christ who changes us; we can't do it ourselves merely by reading and memorizing Scripture.

Centering prayer takes a different tack. It says, rather than study and examine your own thoughts, take twenty minutes a day, twice a day if possible, to just abandon your thoughts and, as the Message puts Romans 12:2, fix your attention on God. It's helpful to start with a short word-prayer expressing your intention to lay every thought at the foot of the Cross. Then, every time you notice that a thought has come, rather than pursue it, gently forsake it and go back to fixing your attention on God. You will learn to come to the point of stopping the ordinary thinking patterns; you'll also begin to recognize your own false self which is the source of those thoughts and which wants you occupied with responding to them, rather than to God.

By looking over the shoulder of the thought, as it were, and fixing your eyes on the horizon—on Christ—you humbly but firmly replace the false self with Christ on the throne of your life. Ignoring the pleadings, threats, and subtle lies of the flesh, "turn your eyes on Jesus; look full in his wonderful face,"[2] as the beloved old song says. You will usually do this many times in a centering prayer session, but over the days and weeks of doing this type of prayer daily, you will find your love for Christ and your closeness to him growing. If you precede the centering prayer with a five-minute meditation on a phrase, sentence, verse or short passage from Scripture, you will see God renewing your mind even more, transforming your life accordingly in his love, changing you from the inside out. And you can do all this without having to buy a single DVD.

Recognizing the True Self through Deadly Disease

Perhaps you've seen this happen to you or someone you know: a person learns they have cancer or some other incurable disease, and they recognize that their days are numbered. Upon discovering this, the person's thinking totally changes and many will focus on God as never before, as their true self is allowed to override the games and illusions of the false self. If the person was a Christian prior to the dreadful diagnosis, their prayer life and awareness of being in the presence of God increases dramatically; if not, they may become born again through this experience. A person in this position often sees what their true self has always known: that their entire life has been cradled in God's hands. And because they are so clearly able to see what's really important in life, they are able to recognize their own true self and false self.

A common response at this point is to bow down in every area of their life, surrendering it all to God. Such a person will pray and pray and pray, asking for healing, for forgiveness, for mercy, for anything and everything they can think to ask for—and when they're done, they often just remain in silence and stillness with God. Long sleepless nights, moments of waiting in doctors' offices, break times at work, commutes, all turn into times of waiting on God. They discover what "be still and know that I am God" really means, for minutes or hours at a time in which they are at a loss for words but still sense they are in God's care in ways they never realized before.

Many people in this situation find themselves spiritually transformed in the process. Perhaps they can beat the cancer and go on to live many more years, a different life than they would have lived had not the disease been a catalyst for change. For some, the disease has progressed too far; the best scenario in this case is that in the midst of a long (or short) decline they find the times of waiting to die to be times of increasing surrender and learning to rest contented in the arms of their Savior, their blessed hope.

It's a horrible, painful process, a dark night of the soul no one ever wants—and yet so many who live to tell about such an experience freely declare that their lives were truly saved, that they wouldn't trade it for the world because of the way it changed them. Near-death experiences do tend to simplify everything for us; they make us refocus on what truly matters in life, so that letting go of everything else but God becomes mandatory, not just the highest priority but the only priority. After such experiences, people often wonder why it took such drastic measures to awaken them to God and to the shallow foolishness of their normal self-pursuits. And they clearly see the hand of God in events that under ordinary circumstances they would chalk up to Satan or to great misfortune. That's a sign that one's thinking has been changed: we start seeing life from God's perspective, which is upside down from the normal human point of view (or, as I've said before, it's really right side up; it's our normal way of seeing and living that's upside down till God turns us right side up.)

Many Christians who have not experienced such dark times nevertheless recognize the parallels with their own lives: through the leading of God, whether in gentle, simple shepherding or through dire straits, disaster and desperation, we become His and see our existence changed from darkness to light, from our own weak and willful ways to God's path of grace, goodness and peace. But for those who practice contemplation, especially those who begin the contemplative path after years of living the typical Christian life, the parallels to someone diagnosed with cancer are intensified and, at the same time, sort of reversed: we begin in silence to focus on God through contemplative prayer, then learn to surrender more and more to Him, then gradually recognize ourselves as dying.

I think this final stage is what Paul was talking about when he said that he and other apostles and servants of Christ were "always carrying around in our bodies the death of Jesus, so that the life of Jesus will be revealed in us." A life which can seem so deeply spiritual, so transformed, is recognized as shallow once we are faced with the challenge of dying to self, which is what contemplative prayer is all about. Contemplation goes beyond the surface factors of going to church and reading the Bible and praying for our needs or those of others. It carries us deeper and deeper into the territory of loving God wholeheartedly, which can only be done through increasing depths of surrender, of offering our lives up as living sacrifices in order to receive more and more of Christ.

It's often said in churches that you can't crucify yourself, that it takes others, and that's why we need to be in relationship, in church. That's true, but contemplative prayer is a way of surrendering ourselves to Christ on the cross, becoming one with him in his suffering so that we may become one with him in every aspect of life. It's crucifixion, not by other believers—who can be brutal—but by God himself, gently loving us even to the point of joining us with Christ in his death. It's the ultimate relationship, one that brings us beyond death and into the resurrection life.

The real victors over cancer are those who come to see Christ as victorious over death—whether they survive their bout with cancer or not. His victory goes far beyond the issue of whether or not they survive the disease, to the complete surrender of their lives to Christ and thus sharing fully in the resurrection with Him. They are overcomers not just in regard to physical cancer but over the more insidious spiritual cancer that eats away at all of Adam's children: the cancer of the fallen, false self.

True Self and "The Least of These"

"I tell you the truth, whatever you did for one of the least of these brothers of mine, you did for me...Whatever you did not do for one of the least of these, you did not do for me." (Matthew 25:40, 45)

How we treat the least of those among us—the overlooked and ignored, the "different," the unwanted, the pushed-aside, the forgotten—is the standard for judging transformation, both personal and as a society. This has everything to do with contemplation. Through the centering prayer practice of laying every thought down at the Cross, we learn surrender to God. It's a way of bowing down before him to say with our whole life and everything in it, "here, Lord, it's yours." In this daily emptying of ourselves, we learn to constantly take out the trash of the false self, dumping out all that's worthless. Through this means we become "the least of these" in a sense: humbling ourselves, recognizing as worthless before God all the treasures we've stored up for ourselves on earth, and pouring them out before him as an offering, our life as a living sacrifice. We can then more readily recognize the least of these among us and love them as Christ loves them.

That's what Paul is describing in Philippians 3:7-8: what he considered gain, he came to count as loss, and to rejoice in it. So we become, at least once a day, as much as possible, empty of thoughts. The point is, empty of thoughts means empty of self, that is, of the false self. (Of course, once you think you've emptied out that bag, you find there are other things in there—they just keep popping up! There is truly an endless supply of thoughts, of self, so this is a constant endeavor that will keep you busy till the day you die!)

Becoming empty of thoughts/ empty of self enables God rather than self to be the center of our world. That takes self off the throne, helping us to see that we're not such a big deal after all. From that perspective we can identify with the weak, the sick, the misfits, the also-rans, the poor, the lost, the mentally ill, the handicapped, the homeless, the riffraff, the pariahs, the outcasts, the refuse of the world, just as Paul did (1 Cor. 4:13). Just as Christ himself did (Matt. 8:1-4, Mark 10:13-16, Luke 19: 1-10, Jn. 8:2-11).

In humbling ourselves this way, in taking every thought captive to the obedience of Christ, we make room for God to change our perspective, to see others and the world around us not as the false self does but as God does. Once self is out of the way, we can see more clearly, from the perspective of the true self—sometimes referred to as the "no-self." Self blinds and must be removed—like bricks in a wall—one thought at a time, in order to see what God wants us to see. (That's a long process, not something that happens in a day or a week or a month; it's a journey that takes many years.)

Through the centering prayer practice of laying down every thought at the Cross, we learn surrender to God and we become "the least of these" in a sense: humbling ourselves, recognizing as worthless before God all the treasures we've stored up for ourselves on earth, and pouring them out before him as an offering, our life as a living sacrifice. We can then more readily recognize the least of these among us and love them as Christ loves them.

So once self is at least in the process of being whittled down, we can begin to see "the least of these" among us, and to pray with true compassion rather than mere obligatory, perfunctory, check-it-off-the-to-do-list prayer. We can both see and begin to be "the least of these"—which is what having the mind of Christ, the true self, is all about—and we can pray and befriend and serve others with the heart of Christ.

Here's an example of this from many years ago in my own life: God challenged me, at one point in my life years ago, to try to understand what it would like to be a certain person I'll call Chris. Chris had had a very difficult life, with some measure of minor physical deformity and a slight degree of mental deficiency which may have resulted from rejection and abuse, and which continued to cause more rejection and abuse. To me, Chris's life looked pretty ugly and messed up, and just being around Chris made me rather nervous. So when God asked if I could try to get inside Chris's mind and emotions enough to know and feel at least some of what it would be like to be Chris, the thought of even trying to do this made me feel very uncomfortable and a little scared; I just didn't feel like I was ready to go there.

I'm ashamed to admit that although I'd been a practicing Christian for over 20 years at that point, my level of compassion and my recognition of the importance of seeing Christ in "the least of these"—in Chris—was pretty low. That changed over time, and I truly came to see Jesus in Chris; God used him to change me in ways I still don't fully understand. I'm not exactly a saint now either, but since beginning contemplation practices, I'm much more comfortable with being around and trying to befriend "the least of these;" seeing Christ in some of them has truly changed my life. And getting inside their heads and hearts to try to understand what it's like to be them—well, that has become just a normal part of intercessory prayer now.

Larry was another example of "the least of these" in my life. He came to my house and knocked on my door one day with a bucket in his hand; in it there was a bottle of Windex and a roll of paper towels. Larry appeared to be homeless, and he smelled like it too. But he smiled and asked if I would let him wash my windows for a few dollars—whatever I felt it was worth. I said sure, go ahead, and I agreed to pay him five bucks to wash the outsides of my front picture window and two smaller windows that faced the street. He was dutifully washing them when I distinctly heard God say something to me: "Go tell him I want to clean *his* windows." I wasn't sure I wanted to get into a theological conversation with a homeless guy right then; I was in the middle of a project and wanted to get it finished. But I went outside and told him what God had said. We did indeed have a theological conversation that lasted over a half hour, and I gave him some lunch and a few extra bucks beyond what we'd agreed on. Most importantly, Larry prayed to receive Christ that day. Over the next decade or so, I found him to be one of the most colorful and interesting people I've ever met, and we became close friends up until his death in 2011.

Larry had anger issues, as well as problems with mental illness and substance abuse. He remained homeless for much of the time I knew him, usually by his own preference. But occasionally when he had a little money, he insisted on taking me out to lunch. Whenever he had a place of his own, we had some great times together, listening to his beloved Deep Purple and Blackmore's Rainbow and discussing music. I helped him in every way I could, and I prayed with him and for him many times. It was amazing to see his anger at someone's insult (real or imagined) just melt away in God's presence as Larry chose to forgive and to pray for his enemies, and to put his problems in God's hands and rejoice in his salvation. I truly miss him. As with Chris, I learned to see Jesus in him, and God used him greatly in my life.

Deny your (False) Self, Take Up your Cross, Follow Me

One way to understand centering prayer is by comparing it to a basic pattern set forth by Jesus himself. No, he didn't say to sit in a corner and focus on a sacred word or the breath, though he did say to go into your inner room and pray in secret (some believe this refers to our innermost being, since very few people in his culture had houses with "inner rooms"). But Jesus also told us, "If anyone would come after me, he must deny himself and take up his cross daily and follow me" (Luke 9:23). This is a hard word; the Greek word translated "deny" in this passage can also mean "disown." As a basic blueprint for centering prayer, it speaks of disowning your false self—the self you've lived out of for most of your life, your inner home, the place you feel most comfortable in. Let's look at each of the three parts.

Deny yourself – Each time you sit down to do centering prayer, you make the choice to walk the path of self-denial that is centering prayer. You make a commitment to deny the self-building, narcissistic thoughts that come out of your own ego/false self. Say no to them when they arise, choosing Christ instead by gently redirecting your attention to him. If you can't feel his presence, take it on faith that he is always there (Deuteronomy 31:6, Psalm 23:1, Matthew 28:20) and, in faith, go on being attentive to him. The false self will try to deceive you by getting you to focus on a religious thought or a scripture, not for true spiritual edification, but for the purpose of building itself up about how spiritual it is. Ignore those thoughts, even the scriptures, for the time being; this is a time to deny yourself, to be in a place where there's nothing but God on the throne, where you and all your thoughts, all your treasures, are laid before his throne.

Take up your cross – remain in that place and learn what it means to die to self, to rest in the peace of being dead to self, and alive to God's wholeness in you and in the world around you. Only the true self can do this. The false self can't travel that road to Calvary; it can't carry a cross; it can't see God at all. It can only deceive you and turn your focus on itself, not on God, so it has to be crucified.

Follow me – keep refocusing your attention on Jesus; once you're done with centering prayer, live like Jesus and continue refocusing your attention on Jesus throughout the day. Remember, only the true self can follow him, so live out of the true self and continue denying the false self.

Jesus follows this warning by saying that "whoever wants to save his life will lose it, and whoever loses his life for me will find it." That's exactly the issue with centering prayer: will you give up yourself—your false self—to God, one thought at a time? If so, you'll find yourself—your true self, the one that loves and follows Jesus—and you'll begin to walk with Jesus in refreshing newness of life, even if you've been a Christian for years.

The contemplative view of this passage (Luke 9:23-24) also involves what is known as detachment or non-attachment. I spoke of the importance of breaking attachments a few pages back, so non-attachment is the condition of a soul who has let go of all attachments except God. Non-attachment simply means living a life of letting go of everything except God—in other words, self-denial in daily life, a life of choosing the Cross over all our attachments, every day, even every hour. We are attached to so many things, from food and physical comfort, to money and all it buys, to the attention and respect of others, to being in control and getting our way. The Bible has a lot to say on the subject of non-attachment,[3] although you probably haven't heard too many sermons on it—at least, not using that term.

Note: attachments are not necessarily sin. You can be attached to your home, your job, your family, your hobbies, your favorite TV shows, in ways that aren't necessarily sinful but aren't always spiritually healthy either. It's about keeping versus losing your life, according to Jesus. Can you hold lightly to the things of earth—even family? Can you lose things, or just lose, without falling apart? Is Jesus truly more important to you than anything this world can give? Can you walk the Calvary road with Jesus on a daily basis? Centering prayer helps.[4]

Now, there's a great paradox that goes with non-attachment. The paradox is this: by practicing non-attachment to things—letting go of all things—we gradually become aware that we are one with all things through Christ. We can't know that oneness as long as we are attached to things, but once we let go of everything, we discover that we have everything. This letting go is just losing what the ego thinks it has, which is all just illusion; once the soul is freed from that illusion, it discovers the real possessing of all things in the oneness of all things that we have in God, in love.

I think that's at least part of what Jesus meant about taking up our cross and following him. Again, he follows this admonition with, "For whoever wants to save his life will lose it, but whoever loses his life for me will find it. What good will it be for a man if he gains the whole world, yet forfeits his soul?" (Matthew 16:25-26). From the contemplative point of view, it's all about letting go of things in the mind, letting go of everything but

God. Non-attachment is also partly what Jesus was talking about when he said, "Those who have will be given more, and they will have all they need. But those who do not have, even what they have will be taken away from them" (Matt. 13:12). This "having" is about having all things in non-attachment, knowing it's all God's; what we are attached to is what we think we have when we really have nothing. Also, consider 1 Cor. 3:22-23: "All things are yours…and you are Christ's, and Christ is God's."

Keeping our Eyes on the Prize

I've noticed something. If the television or the radio is on and I decide to turn it off and just be in silence instead, it seems like I'm going to be losing something. But once I switch it off, I find that I've actually gained something. Don't ask me to explain that, except to say that silence isn't loss, and that the decision to turn off the radio or the TV usually involves saying no to self. There's a richness behind the silence, and it feeds you if you attend to it, far more than a radio or TV ever can. That's at least partly because silence tends to feed the true self, not the false self. (It doesn't do any good if you just let your imagination do its own thing in the silence.)

God can't be experienced by the mind, the emotions or the senses, yet he's there and makes himself known; he's personal. The Word spoken in silence before creation becomes flesh to us here and now in creation, but on his terms, not on ours—in spirit, not in flesh. You can't turn him on and off like a radio. He speaks and we listen. That requires silence, at least inner silence. We keep our eyes on the prize of our high calling (Philippians 3:13b-14); the prize is God himself and our relationship with him, and for this we are willing to tune out the world, once we've tasted of his goodness (Psalm 34:8). We also must bear in mind that God can present himself to us in the form of "the least of these," someone we wouldn't have noticed or paid attention to, or someone we would have avoided. So we must love the world in the John 3:16 sense, though in the 1 John 2:15-16 sense we sort of tune it out as we tune in to God Radio, and he becomes our focus.

Even Jesus when he was in human form was a mystery; he was and is the Word. And this Mystery, this Christ, couldn't and can't be figured out.

He reveals himself in a different way to every person who encounters him, according to their need. (Even to those who don't know him, I'm convinced that he reveals himself; a few of them recognize it, and a relationship with God begins, but most of them are completely unaware of God because they're tuned in to the world, not to God.) To Thomas after the resurrection, Christ came in a way that proved he was living flesh and blood (and so much more, of course)—even after death. But that revelation to Thomas fed Thomas's spirit—his faith—not his flesh. It wasn't so that he could go around boasting that he had put his finger in the nail holes of Jesus's hands. It was so he could be made alive again in his spirit, so he could be tuned in to God completely and get his focus away from the world and himself. God knew what Thomas needed. He knows what we need, too, and it's not anything flesh and blood can give. He makes us alive in our spirits, alive to his presence, day by day, hour by hour, minute by minute, second by second. But he won't compete with the world. God feeds us in silence. Without it you can't hear that still, small voice.

I've also noticed something similar to the radio thing in regard to the ancient scripture-meditation practice known as lectio divina: often I'll read a passage of scripture a few times and feel like I'm not getting anything out of it; it isn't really speaking to me. But once I close the Bible, close my eyes and begin going over it just a little in my mind, I usually begin to see that there's something there that merely reading the Bible can't bring out: the personal nature of God. A hundred people can read the same passage, then meditate on it, and what each one gets out of it will be slightly different than all the others. That's because God feeds us all individually. He's a personal God. He knows what we need and he feeds our spirits.

The Word became flesh. Jesus, the Living Word, speaks to us, and we live it out in flesh crucified, surrendered to God and dead to the world. The Word is alive in the silence before we ever hear it spoken, and no scientist will ever be able to examine it under a microscope. Yet it's the most powerful, beautiful, intelligent, kind sound in the universe: the voice of God himself. Our flesh can't apprehend God, so we must go to him in silence to find out that he's so much more than all the noise around us. We read the Word but it's revealed to us in silence—that still small voice of God that is sometimes just a sigh. We can't comprehend God with our minds, so we forsake thought—which is another way of saying we come to the end of ourselves—and sensing our hunger and loving desire for God, for more of God, for oneness with God, we let it point us toward God and ignore everything else but God. We keep our eyes on the prize, on God, and remain dead, revel in being dead, to everything else but God. There we find the silence is alive with God—and in that silence we find that we, too, are filled with the life of God.

Eyes for Only One

Imagine that you're going to meet your real father or mother for the first time (or a person on the way to meet the person they will marry). You don't know what he looks like, but you just know that you'll know him when you see him. Your heart longs for her. You can't wait to see him, to hear her voice, to hold him in your arms, to tell her how much you love her. The mind can't make sense of this, because it says you can't love someone you haven't met. But your heart is intensely in love with this person already, as if your heart and theirs were intertwined from eternity, destined for each other, and you're just approaching the moment in time when the two of you will begin to explore a reality that has always existed. Even though the two of you have never met, it's as if you know and have always known each other. So you intently watch the road ahead for your beloved.

Things happen along the road; you pass other people and they try to talk to you, but you ignore them and keep going. Animals appear in the trees and grass beside the road, and you pass beautiful mountain landscapes, rushing rivers, fields of wildflowers—but you barely notice any of that. Your eyes are fixed on the road ahead and everything else is just a tiny blip on the radar; things momentarily appear in your mind and then disappear, because you are focused on your Beloved, and nothing can take you away from the joyful purpose in your heart: to be with her, to love him with a pure love and to receive his pure love for you. You don't try to imagine what she will be like or anticipate what your relationship with him will be like. You just look forward with joy to a joyful meeting. You have the promise that it will happen and that's all you focus on. And there's more joy in the hope, the soon-to-be-reality, than in all the imaginings you could ever experience; you know that your fantasies are just phony pseudo-realities that will take away from your joy in the true reality of your Beloved, which exists even though you haven't experienced it yet. You know that when the two of you finally meet, you will be perfect for each other in every way; he will be your perfect soulmate and friend, and you will be his, or hers.

Now, recognize that the "him" or "her" above is God. That's contemplation.

The late Coach Dan Stavely of the University of Colorado football team used to tell a story that went something like this: A great medieval warrior chieftain, patriarch of a clan of great warriors, ruled wisely over many towns and villages, until one day his land was attacked by an army from a large, wealthy neighboring country. He and his men fought valiantly, but they were no match for the invaders' catapults and crossbows, and they were greatly outnumbered. Defeated at last, the enemy general captured the chieftain and the leaders under him, shackled them, and took them to the king of the conquering country. In chains they entered the castle, and there they saw and heard many things they had never even imagined, things of great splendor and the finest craftsmanship. The walls were bedecked with beautiful tapestries, its halls revealing the most amazing furniture of ornately carved wood. Gold, silver and precious stones were everywhere, and musicians were playing the most wondrous music they had ever heard. Brought before the throne, the man marveled at the luxury and splendor all around him and at the lavish opulence of the king's throne, his robes, his scepter and his crown.

As the chieftain knelt down before the throne, the king spoke. "You and your warriors fought bravely and well, my good man, but my armies conquered your little fiefdom." He then ordered one of the captured men, a brave soldier and good friend of the chieftain, to be led forward. The king commanded one of his own soldiers to raise his sword in readiness to strike the man down. "Here is one of your lieutenants. I can order his life to be taken at my whim, and he will be dead in a second. What would you give to spare him?" The great man replied, "For his life I would give all my land." The king thought a moment, then said, "And what of this man over here, your greatest captain? What would you give to spare him?" The captain, second in command to the chieftain, was his brother and dearest friend. "For his life, I would give my home and all my cattle, all I own." The king then nodded to a guard and the man's wife was brought in, blindfolded; the king ordered her to be placed next to her husband and the blindfold removed. The chieftain was delighted to see her unharmed, yet fearful of what might befall her. "And what of this lovely woman, your wife?" said the king. "What if I were to order her death? What would you give in exchange for her life?" The great man didn't hesitate or falter, but spoke boldly and quickly: "For her I would give my life. Take my life and let her live."

Deeply moved at such love, the king soon freed the man, his wife and his leaders, swearing them to cooperation and peace, then sending them home again. After being led out of the castle, brought to the border and released, the chieftain and his wife were together again at last. Following much hugging and kissing, the chieftain said to his wife, "Did you see the tapestries on the walls? I have never seen such beautiful handiwork, such dazzling colors!" His wife responded, "I really didn't notice." "What? How could you miss them? What about the hand-carved furniture? A brilliantly skilled craftsman it would take to create such masterpieces!" "I didn't notice those either." "My darling, surely you were greatly impressed with the gold, silver and gemstones all around." "I wasn't aware of them." "How?" he asked her. "How could you miss such beauty as all that?" Gazing at her husband, she replied, "I could not take my eyes off the one who would give his life for me."

This sounds like a fairy tale, but for the Christian it's a reality. "Dear friends, now we are children of God, and what we will be has not yet been made known. But we know that when he appears, we shall be like him…" (1 John 3:2). The contemplative experience is one of exploring that reality, not with the mind, but as a journey of the heart, going where the mind can't go, to meet the One you have always known in your innermost being. The hidden man of your heart has eyes only for the one who gave his life for you.

Chapter 5

Being Alone with God

You brought it to my attention
That everything was made in God
Down through centuries of great writings and paintings
Everything lives in God
Seen through architecture of great cathedrals
Down through the history of time
Is and was in the beginning
And evermore shall be

When will I ever learn to live in God?
When will I ever learn?
He gives me everything I need and more
When will I ever learn?

- Van Morrison
  When Will I Ever Learn to Live in God?

He who dwells in the secret place of the Most High
Shall abide under the shadow of the Almighty.

- Psalm 91:1

We live in a world today, in developed countries at least, where most people have lots of light. It's not like the old days, where you had to read by candlelight or lamplight. Before Thomas Edison's invention of the light bulb, if you wanted to see things outside at night, you had to carry a torch or a lantern (unless there was enough moonlight, of course). Even torches and lanterns didn't provide very much light; the night was a time of deep darkness, and there was just no getting around that. But one thing they could do that we can't: on any clear night they could see the stars. They knew what the Milky Way looked like. They were familiar with the constellations, the planets, and how the sky looked at different times of the year. They knew the night sky, like a million eyes winking down at them from heaven through the darkness of this life. We can find a thousand different recordings of "Twinkle Twinkle Little Star," or listen to the Beatles sing "Bright are the stars that shine, dark is the sky/I know this love of mine will never die."[1] We can travel to see the Grand Canyon, the Himalayas or the Great Barrier Reef. Yet we can't see the dazzling splendor and majestic beauty of something in our own back yards that's greater than the Seven Wonders of the World combined—the night sky.[2]

With all our streetlights and vehicle headlamps and motion-sensor home security lights, we think we've conquered our fear of darkness, but inside our hearts, many of us in this world are as dark and lonely and empty as a cave. All our man-made light doesn't bring us warmth or make our lives more beautiful. It appears to be a blessing, when really, in a way, we're cursing ourselves with it. Even the idea that it makes the world safer is somewhat of an illusion; there's as much crime, even in well-lighted areas, as ever—perhaps more. The overwhelming pervasiveness of artificial light in our world appears to be a good thing. But the truth is, all that man-made light is a sad reflection on our human sickness and fear, our selfishness and greed. "This little light of mine," we sing, "I'm gonna let it shine..." (notice the emphasis on personal pronouns, not on God), but by our own lights we are lost. We need to get back to God's light—which shines in the darkness—rather than extinguish the darkness with the light of human reason, human intelligence, human wisdom, human foolishness.

We try to kill the silence as well. And yet, we live in a world of noise—traffic, the TV on in the next room with no one watching, the radio churning out opinions and rhythms in our cars, I-pods in our ears; even our refrigerators and vehicles speak to us. The beauty of silence is a luxury most people today can't afford; it's very hard to find. We can be hiking or camping in a wilderness area many miles from civilization, and still hear planes fly overhead and other sounds of civilization. Why all this noise? Because silence scares us to death; Bob Dylan said it's the thing we're most terrified of. Are we conquering our fear of silence? No—we're just shutting out God.

Removing the night sky and silence from our lives is a parable of much of today's Christian religion. We have the Bible on our cell phones and home computers, but not in our hearts. Christ, the Light of the World, is tattooed on our arms but not enthroned in our lives. We go through the motions of going to church if we feel like it; if not, we can always listen to Pastor Charlie on the radio or watch him on TV, with a thousand-voice choir or state-of-the-art worship band backing him up in living stereo. We demand that God submit to our ways, not we to him. We cover up our inner darkness and silence with our own light, our own opinions. By our technology we delude ourselves into thinking we don't really need God.

And God is still there, waiting, knocking, calling our names as with Adam and Eve in Eden. And we're still busy stitching fig leaves together. Remember, also, that not all light is of God. Satan's original name was Lucifer, which means Light-Bringer. Is the light in our world coming from Jesus, the Light of the World, or is it more like Lucy in the Sky with Diamonds?[3] It's time we embrace our silence and invite God into it, like the stars in the night sky. It's time we shut off the TV and the lights and sit in darkness, feel it resonate with our own inner darkness, and begin to call on the One whose light shines in darkness, who whispers to us in the silence of the prayer closet, who waves and smiles at us in the twinkling of the stars.

The Lord is Gracious and Compassionate

The title of this chapter could be quite intimidating for some people, and downright terrifying for others. Let's face it: God can be scary. First of all, he's bigger and older than the universe. Second, the Bible talks a lot about "the *fear* of the Lord," and although usually a better translation would be "reverence," no matter how you parse it, sometimes it just plain means fear. Also, there are some pretty terrifying passages in the Bible (much of the book of Revelation, for example). Often when the Bible records people's direct encounters with God, it speaks of them trembling violently or just falling flat on their faces, terrified. And God isn't exactly

Removing the night sky
from our lives
is a parable of
today's Christianity.
We have the Bible
on our cell phones
and home computers,
but not in our hearts.
Christ, the Light
of the World,
is tattooed on our arms
but not enthroned
in our lives.
By our technology
we delude ourselves
into thinking
we don't really
need God.
And God is still there,
calling our names
as with Adam and Eve
in Eden.
And we're still busy
stitching fig leaves
together.

lax about how we live; when we do something wrong (which is, like, a few times every day, at least)—well, as people said in the '60's, we're afraid of getting busted. So, the idea of just hanging out with God may remind you of the kid in the Jack and the Beanstalk story: the giant is one nasty dude, and he doesn't play games.

But God isn't a giant (well, not exactly). Not a fairytale giant, anyway. And more important than his size (which could never be measured anyway), the first thing to know about him is what it says in 1 John 4:7-8: God is love. Just like a human father, he loves all of his children and wants the best for them. But unlike human fathers, he doesn't make mistakes. He doesn't get drunk, violent, or vindictive. He doesn't wound us with words, not even accidentally. He is more than capable of loving us perfectly, much more so than any human father. One of my favorite worship songs—based on Psalm 103:8 and other passages—says, "The Lord is gracious and compassionate, slow to anger and rich in love. And the Lord is good to all; he has compassion on all that he has made."[4] He loves his enemies, and is kind and generous even to those who are evil (Matt. 5:44-45, Luke 6:35). Even those who turn away from him discover, the moment they turn back to God, that he comes running, filled with compassion (Luke 15:20).

And because something deep inside all of us recognizes the loving nature of God, there's a deep longing to just be with him, a hunger to connect with the Source of all life. We bury it with work and play; we camouflage ourselves behind our own human love or hate. We hide behind our prayers, firing off requests so fast that we can't hear what God is saying to us, because we're afraid, like Adam and Eve in the garden. We can pretend that the hunger isn't really there, and then we manage to forget about it. But in moments of great sorrow or trouble, we can't deny that he's there, standing at the door, knocking (Rev. 3:20)—whether we've known him for years or have never even believed in him at all. And that's often what happens when we get in complete silence, inside as well as out: you're by yourself, you're completely alone, and yet...he's there. And once we get past the fear, we want to embrace him! And then we realize that's what he wants as well.

So what actually happens when we get alone with God? The tendency for many people would be to say, not much. But that's not true. God works in amazing ways inside us all the time if we ask him to. We can't comprehend most of what he does, but as with Moses on Mt. Sinai, he shows us enough—at times, anyway—to shake us way down deep. On that occasion, what God spoke to Moses is a lot like what the song referred to in a previous paragraph says: the Lord is gracious and compassionate! Or you could just sum it all up by saying, as the late, great Rich Mullins sang, "Our God is an awesome God!" Better yet, spend some time waiting on God in silence, ask him to reveal his awesomeness to you, surrender every thought to him, and discover for yourself the truth of what Mullins sang.

The Image of God in Us

God created us in his own image. Many believe something within us—the human spirit, or the true self, perhaps—is the actual image of God in us. The more we yield to God, the more who we are mentally, emotionally, physically and spiritually becomes like the image of God in us, like God himself. The more time we spend in God's presence, the more we lose our heritage of sin and sickness passed down to us from the first Adam, and the more we take on the nature of Christ, the second Adam.

Part of that process, however, has to do with allowing God to change our understanding of him. Who we think he is and what we think he's like tends to be flawed, sometimes greatly, even for those who have spent a lifetime in a Christian family and environment. I spent years seeing God as primarily focused on judgment: these are the rules, and how well you keep them or fail to keep them will determine how God judges you, in this life or when you die. I had a relationship with God; I prayed to him, trusted him, heard his voice, saw him work in my life. I read the Bible faithfully, memorizing hundreds of passages from it.

One day, decades after becoming a Christian, I heard a song that contains the line, "Mercy triumphs over judgment."[5] Singing it in church, and later, in a small group during worship time, that line overwhelmed me; I wept for what seemed like half an hour. But something in me said that I was just being overly emotional, and that the line about mercy triumphing over judgment wasn't really scriptural. I mentioned this to a close friend, and he directed me to James 2:13 in the New International Version, which translates that part of the verse, "Mercy triumphs over judgment." (Several other translations word this passage exactly the same way.) For most of my Christian life up to that point—over 20 years—I had been reading the old King James translation, which renders that part of James 2:13 as, "mercy rejoiceth against judgment"—whatever that's supposed to mean. No wonder I never connected with that passage.

This new understanding of God's mercy was a major turning point in my life. I began to see God as more merciful than judgmental. How could I have misunderstood the message given throughout the Bible about the greatness of God's mercy?[6] I could look for someone to blame, which would totally defeat what God was trying to do in me—to help me to become more merciful and to recognize his mercy as a backdrop to so many of the stories and episodes of the Bible, in history, and in my own life. Surrendering to that view of God has transformed me.

So we need to allow God to change our understanding of who He is, and that means we have to surrender to him even our mental image of who he is—on a regular basis. That's right, even our image of God can become an idol. The Pharisees prided themselves on not being idolatrous, yet they were among the worst idolaters in history. Their idols were not of wood and stone; their idols were their mental image of God—who they believed God to be; they bowed to this false image of God rather than allowing God to be who he was. As a result, they didn't recognize the Messiah they claimed to long for. He was in their midst, in their faces, yet they crucified him because he didn't fit the image, the idol, of God in their minds and in their doctrines.

One of the most important aspects of centering prayer is that it is an opportunity to daily surrender to God your concept of who he is and to invite him to change your mind. We don't have to be stuck in Pharisee mode. Like Paul, we can let God change us so that we can see him, not as our own minds interpret the Bible, but as God reveals himself to us in his Word and in the world.

Just Me and You, God

I remember hearing a preacher years ago mock the idea of people going off by themselves and just "doing their own thing with God—just me and you, God." Frustrated with churches, don't believe in organized religion, just want to find Jesus on your own, stay home and pray and read the Bible and worship and fellowship with God by yourself, that sort of thing. This pastor was talking about how that's wrong, self-focused, it's the body of Christ, we all need each other, and so forth. We've all heard messages like that, and they're right, we do need each other; there's no such thing as do-it-yourself Christianity. I Cor. 12:14-18 and other Bible passages make that clear: can one part of the body say to the rest, "I don't need you?" Of course not.

But at the same time, that longing just to be alone with God doesn't go away. That old hunger for "just me and you, God" is part of who we are; it's basic to how we're made. On the other hand, part of us is afraid to sit down alone with someone who knows all the details of our dark, dirty secrets, especially when that someone is all-powerful. But he is all-loving too; he's so crazy about us that we can't even comprehend that kind of love—we have to experience it, and it can take years to put enough of the pieces together to begin seeing the big picture of just how much God loves us. All of that is why it's important to have a "quiet time" with God every day. But for many, that tends to look like this: read several chapters of the Bible, mumble self-consciously for a minute or two about God blessing you and everyone you can think of, maybe confess some sin, maybe start singing a worship song as you go hit the shower and get ready for work. Those who have a more effective quiet time can sit and listen for God to speak, for a minute or two at least; taking more time than that gets pretty uncomfortable, and your mind wanders.

Think about when you were a child hanging out with your dad or mom, or going somewhere with one of them, just the two of you. There's something so special about such times for a child; family times around the dinner table or playing games are great, but each child needs a time just to be alone with Mommy or Daddy. Even if the parent and child don't talk much, or at all (fishing comes to mind, or hiking; watching TV, not so much), just being together with a parent builds something deep within a child that nothing can replace; no other activity fills that craving.

If it doesn't happen often, it's easy for the child to think he or she is getting the "silent treatment." What did I do wrong, they ask silently; why is my parent mad at me. But if it happens on a regular basis, the child—or the adult in centering prayer—learns the peace and freedom of just being together when love is all that's needed, when words would just clutter things up. For children under ten or so, and especially under five or six, a time to just sit on Daddy's knee and be held is so important, not only when the child has done something wrong, but "just because." So it is with us and our Heavenly Father. We still have that longing, no matter how old we get, to sit on Daddy's lap and just be with him.

Another favorite worship song of mine for many years says, "Father God, I am here to spend this time in drawing near. I have not come to ask of you; I just want to be with you."[7] To me, that's what centering prayer is all about. Just being with the Father in silence changes us into his image, ties our heart closer to his, bonds us with God, builds love and acceptance and freedom deep inside to be who he has made us to be. There's a time to talk about stuff with God, and as with our earthly fathers, there's a time to just be together in silence. Making centering prayer a part of your daily quiet time gives God a chance to work something in you that usually doesn't come any other way. You begin to see that God is totally attentive to you, everything about you, and you also begin to learn to be totally attentive to God in ways you never knew you could be. It's like seeing God building a fire in us. At first it's just a little campfire, a few sticks and a small branch or two, but gradually over a period of years, God builds it into a great bonfire of love that warms all those around us, one that will never go out.

God As He Is in Himself

Christian contemplatives down through history have spoken of their hunger to know God more and more, including knowing him "as he is in himself." Let's explore that phrase and its meaning a little more. What exactly does it mean? To understand what the mystics mean by knowing or receiving a revelation of God as he is in himself, it's important to first understand that God cannot be comprehended by the mind or the senses; he is completely beyond us. As God himself, speaking through one of his Old Testament prophets, put it, "…my thoughts are not your thoughts, neither are your ways my ways, declares the Lord. As the heavens are higher than the earth, so are my ways higher than your ways and my thoughts than your thoughts" (Isaiah 55:8-9).

God is so much greater than us that our minds can no more comprehend who he really is or what he's actually like than an amoeba can comprehend a biologist studying it through a microscope. Really, it's much more complicated than that: if the scientist could speak to the heart of the amoeba and love the amoeba with perfect tender love that would be totally fulfilling to it, and even become an amoeba himself to give his life to make it so all amoebas (amoebi?) could know him personally, this analogy would be something close to the way it is between God and us. In other words, God is so completely different from us and so far above us that we can't even come up with perfect analogies for our relationship with him.

God knows this, but he gives us symbolic language to help us comprehend something about who he is, what he's like, and what our relationship with him is all about. Jesus called God Father, and helped us see God as a loving, kind, caring Father who provides for all our needs, is attentive to the smallest details of our lives, and disciplines us with love, all to make us more like he is. King David represented God as the gentle shepherd who cares for his flocks, and Jesus was at least a partial fulfillment of that promise. But the reality is, we aren't sheep, and God doesn't herd us around with a literal rod and staff. We aren't actual children of God in the sense that he would have to literally change our diapers, feed us baby food, lullaby us to sleep or spank us. There are spiritual things that happen in our relationship to God that are similar to all these things, but they aren't literally the same. Claiming we are actual, literal children of a God who is an actual, literal human father in heaven leads to big problems; that's one of the issues that led the Mormons astray.

The point is, everything we can say or think about God is symbolic, not literal. Jesus called himself the Light of the World, the Door and the Way (or road). But he isn't a literal light or a literal door or a literal road. These things are symbols given to help us trust and come ever closer to God, but what God really is—that's completely beyond our comprehension. Quoting Isaiah again, Paul in I Cor. 2:9-10 says "No eye has seen, no ear has heard, no mind has conceived what God has prepared for those who love him—but God has revealed it to us by his Spirit. The Spirit searches all things, even the deep things of God." (You can say that's about heaven, and that's partly true, but what God has prepared for those who love him, more than anything else, is God himself.) Another way to say all this is that whatever we think God is, he is infinitely more, infinitely beyond our comprehension, infinitely greater than anything we can relate to. The miracle of it all is that, in spite of the great gap between God and the finite, sinful, extremely limited realm of what it means to be human, God still loves us and we can somehow still know him. We can be friends with God. The amoeba and the Ph.D. biologist can have a relationship.

But the mystics say that God, who can't be known by our minds or our senses, can be loved by our hearts, and that he responds to our weak, imperfect love with his perfect love; he empties us of ourselves and fills us with his own love, his own being. The God who can't be comprehended or represented by any concept our minds can understand thus makes himself known in ways we have no words for. The closest the mystics can come to a description of the God they know beyond concepts, beyond the mind and the senses, is to refer to him as "God as he is in himself."

So how does this knowledge of God-as-he-is-in-himself come about? We empty ourselves completely, including our concepts of God, so that he will fill us completely, revealing to us himself as he is in himself, not as our limited human minds can conceive of him, and without any input from our own minds. It's a whole new process, this emptying and filling, a paradox that goes beyond what the mind can discover, as paradoxes do. They are clues to the true nature of God-as-he-is-in-himself, which is at least part of the reason Jesus spoke in paradoxes: they reflect the reality of God beyond human reasoning. I have a saying by Eastern Orthodox priest Hieromonk Damascene on the wall of my office: "Pleasure of the senses is emptiness ever filling itself, yet remaining ever empty. Pleasure of the soul is fullness ever emptying itself, yet remaining ever full." That saying, I believe, reflects the nature of God-as-he-is-in-himself. What it depicts, you can't exactly picture in your mind, because it's something that doesn't exist in our world except in the form of God's presence, but we can at least get the drift. If you meditate on that saying awhile, you may begin to receive from God a sense, a glimpse, of what it means to know God-as-he-is-in-himself, for real.

Worship and the Tabernacle

Worship (not just the musical variety, but true worship from the heart) follows the pattern of the Tabernacle and Temple in the Hebrew Bible, the Old Covenant. What we're still learning is, we don't have to stop at the Holy Place; as Christ's body was torn, the veil is torn so that we can enter the Holy of Holies and stay there in silence with God.

But because we've been taught against anything that might seem "new-agey" or "mystical," and because the Church has been under the influence of the Enlightenment for four hundred years, we haven't even tried to go there. We sing praise and worship songs, and then we stop and meet and greet and take the offering, or go eat donuts and drink coffee. We read our Bibles, but so often we don't allow God to take us beyond, from "the Word was with God" to "the Word was God," into the place of rest beyond where the natural mind can go. We pray, and then we brush our teeth and go to work. By God's grace he takes us into the Holy of Holies at times anyway, but it's a special occasion kind of thing; we haven't fully recognized that it's okay, it's good, it's God's will, to enter behind the Veil, even to live there.

Following the tabernacle/temple pattern, worship begins with sacrifice (the brazen altar)—identifying with Christ on the cross, the Lamb of God, where we lay down our life to God with him. Next is our cleansing from sin by Christ (the bronze laver). It continues with recognizing Christ the Word of God as the Bread of Life (the table of showbread), the Light of the World (the golden lampstand), and the Great Intercessor (the altar of incense), and joining our prayers with his (incense is symbolic of prayer).

But all that—as vitally important, as utterly essential to our spiritual life as it all is—is not what worship is all about. It's not the heart of worship. It is preparation for the Holy of Holies, the true heart of worship where we meet alone with God, set aside from the world, dead to the world and the world to us, dead to self, to the past, to the future, alone with God in the present. So often our worship and Bible study and prayer stop short of the Holy of Holies; we don't see the torn body of Christ as a torn Veil inviting us into God's rest, God's perfect peace, participating in the life of God, the love of Father, Son and Spirit for each other and for us. But that's what contemplative prayer is: going beyond words, beyond asking, beyond ourselves and our weak human understanding, beyond the things of God, beyond theology, into God's goodness, into God himself. It is pouring the self out and being filled with God, being made full and complete in God.

Within this paradigm, contemplative prayer is the equivalent of being in the Holy of Holies. Entering in through the Veil is where it all changes. Up to that point, we're in the light—daylight from outside, or candlelight from the golden lampstand—but once we enter behind the Veil, it's dark, lit only by the shekinah glory of God himself, which the natural eyes can't see. That's where we must stop relying on our sensory input and our natural reasoning, and trust only in God.

Yes, there's some hardware in there too—the Ark of the Covenant, Aaron's rod that budded, and the pot of manna; the Mercy Seat is atop the Ark, where the Lord's presence dwells between the outstretched wings of the cherubim. But unlike in the Outer Court and Holy Place where human activity is required, what's in the Holy of Holies is all miracle stuff—God doing something to interact with his creation, without our help or involvement in any way except that he's invited us in, allowing us to be bathed in his light as Peter, James and John were in it at the Transfiguration.

In coming to know "God as he is in himself"—beyond symbolism, beyond anything the rational mind can relate to—our senses are of no help at all. We can't touch or see or hear or taste or smell God, and the intellectual abilities of even an Einstein can't begin to figure him out.[8] We're completely out of our element—all the elements of everyday life—and completely lost in God, in his territory, a wilderness to us that's a wonderland of God in which our human nature is as ill-equipped to cope as an infant alone on a sailboat in a hurricane.

That's the Holy of Holies—the place of absolute trust in God's miracle-working authority (Aaron's rod that budded), because there's nothing else there to lean on, nothing of human knowledge to trust in. It's there that we learn to rely wholly on God's miraculous provision (the pot of manna), because we are unable to do anything to sustain our life there; it's God or nothing.

And it's there in the silence, where the rational mind and the senses are completely in the dark, that we learn to dwell in the secret place of the Most High, to rest under the shadow of the Almighty, El Shaddai (Psalm 91:1), between the outstretched wings of the cherubim, where God sits enthroned on the Mercy Seat. It's there that we learn to see with the heart, through the eyes of mercy and grace. It's there that we begin to see as God sees, to feel as God feels, to love as God loves, and thus to know God as he is in himself.

In the womb of God

What was it like for us in the womb? A time we've forgotten, a time without time. A dark awareness of our mother, and perhaps at some point, a very dim awareness of our own existence as separate from hers. Silence, until our ears are formed; then, the constant sound of our mother's heartbeat, her breathing, occasionally her voice, her laughter, her crying, her singing; a faint recognition of the difference between sound and silence (though we know not complete silence except what existed before our ears began to function). And more distantly, other voices, other sounds. Darkness, until our eyes are formed; then, sometimes a light from outside, sometimes glowing, usually faint and dim; other times, still darkness; a simple, emergent sense of the difference between light and darkness.

Also, a gradual awareness, at some point, of sensation, of being able to feel with our hands and feet and head and back, a vague realization of our own movement, a slight realization of the difference between motion and stillness. We become aware of our own heartbeat, and probably a hazy recognition that it is like our mother's, but smaller and faster. We live surrounded by a warm sense of comfort, protection, security—and yet, since we have never known anything else, we have no concept of warmth, comfort, protection, or security, since they are the sum total of our experience; they have no opposites, therefore no meaning to us. But while still in the womb, I believe we are able to experience a rudimentary sense of our mother's love for us, and the beginnings of a love response for her in return.

In response to Christ's words about being born again, Nicodemus asked him, "Can a man go back into his mother's womb and be born a second time?" Jesus let Nicodemus know that he was speaking of being born of the Spirit (see John 3:1-8). So, can we enter into the womb of God, as it were? Once we begin to talk of spiritual realities, we can only speak in the language of symbol and metaphor, as Christ and all the prophets and apostles did. Reality is different in the spiritual realm than in the physical world we live in; for instance, Jesus said there is no marriage in heaven, and thus, apparently no sexuality. Bearing this in mind, is there an analogy for entering into God's womb once we have been born again, once we have come to know God? Contemplation could be such an analogy. In centering prayer, we go to a place of silence, of stillness, of closeness to God, a place of being only dimly aware of the outside world yet deeply aware of God's lovingkindness and faithfulness.

In centering prayer, we may be aware of our own heartbeat and be able to sense a connection between our mother's when we were in the womb, and the "heartbeat" of God for us—God's passionate love for us, conveyed through our awareness of his Spirit. In Hebrew, Greek, and many other languages, the word for "spirit" is also the word for "breath" and "wind." Our very breath is therefore a reflection of God's presence and of his Spirit that gives life to us (Genesis 2:7, John 3:6-8). We often sense his great love for us, and we begin to develop a level of affection, passion, and love for God that we never knew. We eventually come to the place where there is nothing but warmth, comfort, protection, security surrounding us. Timeless resting in God, beyond time. We even reach the point where there is nothing but us and God, and eventually nothing but God. Nothing but pure love into which we have been completely absorbed. God and God alone. That's the transformation in love that God passionately desires for all of us.

The Genesis 22 Sacrifice

"Take your son, your only son, Isaac, whom you love, and go to the region of Moriah. Sacrifice him there..." Genesis 22: 2

Talk about being between a rock and a hard place! Put yourself in Abraham's sandals. The one person you care about most in life, you must give up—the promised one you spent decades praying and hoping and longing for, and whose arrival in life was the high point of your own. You must surrender that child to God, never to see him again in this life—not because some disaster takes him away, like Job, whose children all died in a whirlwind. No, in this case, it's because of a command from God. An incomprehensible paradox: the One who loves you most forever, demands that you give up the one you love most in this life. The one given to you by God, God now commands you to kill. It seems to contradict everything you know about God, everything you've experienced with him in years of walking with him. And it seems to contradict common sense.

It's the most bizarre turn of events imaginable—a worst-case scenario far worse than you ever imagined.

And, strangely, we see nothing of Abraham begging God to change his mind. The one who negotiated successfully with allies, princes, and God himself, doesn't seem to say a word; he's completely silent on this matter—which means he knows that he knows that he knows he has heard from God on this matter. He gets up early the next morning, gathers Isaac and his servants and some animals for them to ride, and takes off with them, as if they were headed for Disney World. It takes them three days to get to the mountain where the sacrifice will take place, afterward known as Mount Moriah, which means "the manifestation of the Lord" or "the vision of Yahweh"—in other words, the mountain where you see the God whom no one can ever see. It's symbolic of the place in each of our lives where God reveals himself as the one who sees us, loves us and will take care of us. And it's also the place of our total surrender to him—surrender of everything, especially of the one thing it's hardest for us to let go of. For Abraham, this was the place where he had to recognize with brutal honesty that Isaac was God's, not his. We all have to realize that whatever God gives to us, he really just lends to us. It's still his. All of it. This is also the exact same place God chose through David, many generations later, for the Temple to be built. And it's also the same area where Christ was crucified (Golgotha was probably a mile or so away from the Temple). One commentator[9] notes that this is the first place in the Bible that the word "love" is used.[10]

After Abraham had bound Isaac and almost killed him, and after God provided the ram caught in the thicket for a sacrifice instead of Isaac, Abraham named the place where it happened (as translated into King James English) Jehovah-Jireh, literally, The Lord Sees, which some scholars say can be taken to mean The Lord Sees To It or The Lord Provides. So if you look at the whole story from the point of view of the main verbs, the number one verb in the story is "to see." Moriah: the place where the Lord is seen. The sacrifice: the Lord will see (to it). Jehovah-Jireh: the Lord sees. And, it's all about how a child of God can come to the place of fully seeing, with the eye of the heart, who God really is, in a way he or she can never forget or deny.

So sacrifice, dying to self, is the place where we see God the unseen, where we realize that God sees us and every detail of our entire lives, and where we know beyond all doubt that God will always see to it that we are taken care of. It's the place where we surrender everything to the God who sees everything, whose seeing and loving is vast beyond words. That's what centering prayer is all about. Abraham's sacrifice of Isaac is symbolic of God the Father's sacrifice of his only Son on the cross. But it's also symbolic of the kind of absolute surrender practiced by untold numbers of Christ-followers who bow in silence before the Cross daily and yield up to God all that's most precious to them, who let even their thoughts and feelings die daily before God who sees all and who loves and restores us in ways our thoughts can't begin to comprehend.

Centerpiece: A Meditation on Isaiah 40:6b-8

All people are like grass,
and all their faithfulness
is like the flowers of the field.
The grass withers
and the flowers fade,
because the breath of the Lord
blows upon them.
Surely the people are grass.
The grass withers
and the flowers fade,
but the word of our God
endures forever.

Sitting in silence, waiting on God
with the heart of a true servant,
we become passively open
to all things life may bring.
At the same time, we are actively aware
of God's gracious lovingkindness,
of God as the Logos,
the eternal Word of truth,
in all that we think and feel
and in all that we are.
In this place of waiting,
we watch our breaths come and go,
arise and pass away.
We watch our thoughts arise,
flourish in our minds
for a few moments or long minutes,
then gradually fade away.
We behold sensations, memories, emotions,
all come to birth in our conscious awareness,

run their course, and melt into oblivion
like chunks of ice at the edge of a river,
each in its turn.
Each idea, each fantasy,
each moment from our past
longing to be relived
or refashioned into something better—
each creature that arises in our minds
lives its brief but unique and self-important life,
then thins like the waning moon
and finally disappears, never to be seen again.
Thus pass our hours, our meals, our days,
our projects, our desires, our plans,
our years and our lives.
Over the course of history,
philosophies surface, evolve,
gather adherents convinced of the purity
and rightness of their beliefs.

Books are written about them,
political adherents cluster together around them,
legislation that affects the lives of millions
is built upon them,
nations go to war over them,
blood is shed for them,
lives are laid down for them.
Then, one day, those philosophies
once thought to be impregnable fortresses
show signs of aging.
The fortress walls begin to wear out, to weaken,
and eventually to waste away
to crumbled nothing,
to be all but forgotten,
as new philosophies show their faces,
gain strength and become preeminent
for the brief centuries given them,
only to be in turn relegated to

archaic words on faded pages
in forgotten history books
on dusty shelves in lonely libraries.
So go the ways and works of humanity.
So pass the nations and empires
and ages of the world.
So are the generations of man.

Plant species appear, flower,
spread to regions and cover continents,
then a few thousand-year days later,
they have given way to newer, hardier species
pushing them to extinction.
Dinosaur families have burgeoned and thrived,
only to surrender the sound of their thundering gaits
to silence
as their world changes
and they are gone.

Mountain ranges host assemblies of creatures
both rooted to the ground
in tall and glorious green floral grandeur,
and passing over it
with their lives of lordly animal eloquence,
yet they vanish forever
once their time has passed.
Seas full of crustaceans and nameless ferns
dry up, their sediments and fossils left
to be fashioned into mythological gods by one race,
then studied by scientists
and placed in museums by another.
The earth itself, like fabled Atlas,
carries continents on its shoulders,
moving them about
like a mighty slave rolling boulders,
forming Stonehenges on its own curved surface
to make its contribution
to the art galleries of the galaxy.

Epochs and eons lift their voices,
sing their sonatas, falter and fade away,
as if the earth that hosts them had become
the Mayan god who carries time
in a sack on his back.

And in the midst of all this change
is the Unchanging One
who alone can change our hearts to be like his.
Lord of the Harvest, I've heard him called;
Jehovah, Yahweh,
I Am That I Am,
the All-in-All,
King of Kings and Lord of Lords,
the Lion and the Lamb,
Alpha and Omega.
His word creates all things;
his breath gives life to all things;
his will establishes or allows or ends all things;

his love covers all things.
All men, all creatures, all lands, the earth,
even the universe itself,
are the grass that withers, the flowers that fade;
but the word of our God will stand forever.
May we rest in him,
and may our breath flow as one with his breath,
our thoughts surrender to his mind,
our hearts beat with his heart,
our spirits reflect his beauty,
our lives be signposts to point to his glory.

God sits motionless,
watching the centuries, the millenia,
pass like clouds on a summer day.
From his throne in heaven
he sees the kingdoms of the world come and go
like pieces of driftwood floating on a river.

Resting in his love,
he sees the minutes, the seconds of our lives;
he observes our thoughts, our emotions,
our dreams, our aspirations,
and he longs to rejoice over us with singing;
he longs for us to rest in his love
and receive his fullness of joy.
As we sit in contemplative prayer,
we too learn to see the passing of breaths,
the parade of thoughts,
the ticking of the clock, the songs of birds,
as God-breathed,
as gems of his generosity,
as flowers of his love.
And we learn to rest in his love with him,
to open to the incomprehensible wonder
of his presence in all he has created,
from the blink of an eye

to the flash of lightning on a nearby hill,
from the wag of a dog's tail
to the turning of the earth.
We learn to see the life cycles
of mountain ranges, rivers and deserts
like the rising and falling
of our own shoulders
as we breathe.
We begin to recognize
the eons of earth's history
as mere breaths
rushing in, out, and away,
flowing out of and back into eternity.

And we begin to sense,
in the moments of our days and nights,
the infinite goodness and love of God
who is beyond all our thoughts,

beyond all our concepts,
beyond time,
beyond the beyond.
And all we can say,
with every heartbeat, is:
God is love.
God is love.
God is love.

Chapter 6

For Those who have Ears to Hear and Eyes to See

...nothing's small!
No lily-muffled hum of a summer-bee,
But finds some coupling with the spinning stars;
No pebble at your foot, but proves a sphere;
No chaffinch, but implies the cherubim...
Earth's crammed with heaven,
And every common bush afire with God;
But only he who sees takes off his shoes,
The rest sit round it and pluck blackberries,
And daub their natural faces unaware...

-from "Aurora Leigh"
Elizabeth Barrett Browning

What is heaven like? We all try to imagine if it's like earth, or completely different. Jesus said, "Blessed are the poor in spirit, for theirs is the kingdom of Heaven...Blessed are the pure in heart, for they will see God...Blessed are those who are persecuted for the sake of righteousness, for theirs is the Kingdom of Heaven (see Matt. 5:3-10)." Why is it that in churches where the leaders are legalistic, prideful, and selfish (and yes, sadly, there are churches like that), some people still grow strong in God? Because to the pure, all things are pure (Titus 1:15). For the innocent, whatever they look at, they see God because they are pure in heart.

The same passage tells us that the opposite is true as well: to those who are defiled and unbelieving, nothing is pure, which is why even in the best of churches, there are those who become bitter, prideful, or selfish. Some people—especially children and the childlike—see God in all things; from the quote at the head of this chapter, Elizabeth Barrett Browning was perhaps one of these. Others see God in nothing; "in all (their) thoughts there is no room for God" (Psalm 10:4).

I think that Heaven will be way different from earth, yet much of the beauty and spellbound wonder we will experience there will have to do with the fact that our eyes will be opened to see God in all things. At that point, we will also recognize that in our earthly lives, God could be seen in everything as well, but that most of us, most of the time, were unable to see God that way because our eyes were focused on ourselves. Blessed are those who, in this life, in this world, can see God in all things.

"notw" – Not Of This World: the Cross in the middle of Now

There's a logo I've been seeing on T-shirts and in the back windows of cars for a few years now. It says "notw" which stands for "Not Of This World," and it's a rather catchy Christian logo, a brand name actually, for a company which also sells jewelry and other things some refer to as "Jesus junk." It's marketed as a way for Christian young people to let their friends know about their faith without walking up to them and throwing out clichés like, "Are you washed in the blood of the Lamb?" It's also called a lifestyle (by the company that makes the T-shirts and stuff). So in other words, it's a Christian cultural phenomenon.

But what I notice about the "notw" logo is that it looks like the word "now" with a cross stuck in the middle of it. And from that perspective, I really like that. Because that's really where we find the cross in our lives, Jesus in our lives, God in our lives, the Holy Spirit in our lives, most poignantly: in the now. In the Bible, yes, and prayer—but the bottom line is, what is God doing in your life *right now*? Hint: if you think the answer is "nothing," you're wrong. It wouldn't be too hard to compile a long list of all the things the Bible says God does for us on an ongoing basis, but that's not the point. The real question is, is the cross in the middle of your "now," and what does that mean? Am I standing in God at this moment? Am I in his will? Do I have to be doing anything special in order to be in his presence? Am I aware of his beauty? Do I sense his love for me? Do I see and hear him in the world around me? He's there, so if I don't recognize him, why not?

That "notw" logo contains a paradox: there's more to being "not of this world" than just going around wearing a certain kind of T-shirt or saying you're a Christian, going to church or youth group or Bible study. It's more than going through the motions of being a Christian, more than doing all the stuff Christians are "supposed" to do. To truly be "not of this world," you have to be present to the present moment, and present to God in it—surrendered to God, attentive to God, fully invested in God in the now. Really, being "of this world" means being into everything external to the now. It means taking seriously all the stuff the world around you says is important—the latest fashions, the coolest TV shows, what certain celebrities are doing, etc.—which really means whatever feeds your ego. And that means not being into the now, because when you really get into the now, it tends to crucify the ego. So at least part of what being truly "notw" means is being dead to self enough to fully participate in whatever God is doing in the now, not just reading in your Bible about what God did a couple thousand years ago, but living it out in the eternal now. The paradox comes down to this: I strongly suspect that some of the most "notw" people there are, have never heard of the "notw" cultural thing.

Those who are truly "notw" are often the kind of people about whom others might disparagingly say, "he's so heavenly minded he's no earthly good." Not that loving God and others is an excuse for absent-mindedness. But in my experience, those who are absent-minded are those who are caught up in their own little world, not God's. (Been there, done that, a lot. Got the space-case T-shirt to prove it.) Those who are really into the "now" are the people who are aware of all that's going on around them, to the point that they can be self-forgetful.

So to be really "notw" means to be aware of the world around you, the people around you, and God in the midst of all of it, and what he is saying about all of it. It means recognizing who is hurting, who is confused, who is angry, and praying for them or with them. Or, it can also mean feeling God's love, sharing his pleasure in what he has created. Or feeling his crackling, bubbling energy in everything that exists. Or sensing his sadness over what we've done and are doing with his beautiful creation. Or just being deeply aware of our own brokenness, our own weakness, our deep need for Christ and for dying with him to be risen with him. That's some of what it means to be "not of this world." You don't need to buy a T-shirt or car window decal for that.

Stealing from the Future, vs. Being with God in the Present Moment

A young man on a crotch-rocket style motorcycle zips in and out of traffic on the freeway. It's outside the city, the speed limit is 65, traffic is averaging around 70, and he's going nearly 90 miles an hour...till he makes a mistake, loses control, crashes and is severely injured, crippled for life...or dead. He was just trying to push ahead into the future as fast and hard as possible. He ended up stealing from his own future...and getting caught.

A woman of 34 takes crystal meth for the first time. She has used many types of drugs, and this one brings her a satisfaction she can't describe. She realizes some of the drugs she has used in the past weakened her; she's had flashes of becoming an old lady, having abused herself with drugs until, by her early forties, she will have the mind, organs and body of a woman of eighty. But she doesn't care. She knows she may not live to see old age anyway. She's killing off brain cells and healthy tissue in her body at an astounding rate, but in her own twisted way, she's enjoying life now. She's stealing from her future, and she's starting to learn the hard way that there are consequences.

A couple with three children takes out a second mortgage on their house to pay down the credit cards they've maxed out. The wife takes a second job and the husband works a third; they both dread the realization that they'll have to work well into old age to pay for the toys they just had to buy but have no time to enjoy. Their older son spends much of his time raising his younger brother and sister, and resenting having to miss his childhood. His parents are stealing from their future—and from his as well.

A government lets its deficit spiral higher and higher, knowing the nation's children and grandchildren will be left with the bill. They're stealing from their nation's future. From mine and yours.

Contrast these scenes with the Church, when it's functioning as God intended. A young single mother can't pay her bills on her minimum-wage part time job. She's thin, missing meals, trying to feed her little boy and keep him healthy with food from the bargain shelves at the supermarket. She asks the local church for assistance. A year later, she has a better apartment, a better job, and both mother and son are healthier and happier. They have become valued members of the church. The mother is dating a godly man who leads an intercessory prayer group there, and her son has more friends than he could ever have imagined a year earlier. People at the church have given of their time, energy and resources to better the life of the woman and her son. They took freely of the gifts Jesus gives from the future Kingdom of Heaven to make the Kingdom of God a reality today.

A child of nine is paralyzed from the waist down in a tragic automobile accident. The doctors say he's facing life in a wheelchair. Then a family friend from the local church brings some friends over to pray for him, and the unbelievable happens. He rises up, walks across the room, dances around, jumps on top of the coffee table and over to the couch to hug his formerly grief-stricken parents, who have gone from dumbfounded to overwhelmed with joy at the grace and love of God, who takes from the future gifts of heaven and gives one of those gifts to their son so he can live a normal life now.

God can take from the future, since he lives outside of time. But we cannot; one of Satan's greatest lies, one that reappears in every generation in countless forms, is that we can steal from the future with no negative consequences. But what we can do, any time we want, is take our entire future as well as the past, and put it all in God's hands. Then we can delight in God in the now, where his presence is also our presence, in the present, a gift greater and more beautiful than anything we think we can steal from the future.

We can start with giving all our thoughts, feelings, memories and desires to God and resting with him in silence, in the present, forgetting the past and the future. We can love God with all our heart, soul, mind and strength in the now, and only in the now. It's hard to love God when we're hanging onto our past or our dreams of the future, because they can become idols. Only in the now are we completely surrendered to God; only when we've let go of all else—past, present, future, and all thoughts including who and what we think we are—only when we've let go of everything but God—only then can we truly love him as he loves us, in the pure freedom of now.

The Sacrament of the Present Moment and the Least of These

God hides, and is found, precisely in the depths of everything."
- Richard Rohr[1]

Living in the present moment is referred to by more than one of the Christian mystics as a sacrament—something holy that God uses to draw us to himself and strengthen us in the work of his Spirit. Richard Rohr, a contemplative Catholic priest, says, "One great idea of the biblical revelation is that God is manifest in the ordinary, in the actual, in the daily, in the now, in the concrete incarnations of life, and not through purity codes and moral achievement contests."[2]

There are good reasons for calling the Now, the present moment, a sacrament.[3] First, here and now is where we deal with that "Thy will be done" thing from the Lord's Prayer. We can go to church, we can pray and read our Bibles, we can listen to worship music—but it's in the commonplace here-and-now of everyday life, living moment to moment, that we really choose obedience to the will of God. Secondly, and similarly, in the present moment is where we find God. If our minds are somewhere other than in the Now, how can we connect with God? Yes, he's outside of time, but we aren't. It's been well said that the memory is about the past and the imagination is about the future, but the true self is all about the Now. It's also been said, trite but true, that Now is a gift from God—that's why it's called the present.

How can something so ordinary as right now be holy? My fingers are on the keyboard of my computer, creating this document, something that didn't exist until a few minutes ago. I write this word, then this one, words that didn't exist here as part of this document till just now. That fascinates me, like cracking open a nut; I see its insides, and nobody but

God and I have ever seen the inside of this particular nut. Just now, my dog is scratching at the front door, wanting inside; I walk out to let her in, delighted by the smell of rain in the air and feeling a bit of moisture on her fur. Returning, I see my glasses lying on the desk upside down, staring upside down at a pile of new guitar picks I just remembered to take out of my pocket a few minutes ago. There they lie, randomly artistic, three red ones and two gray ones, waiting for me to pick one of them up and go play a song. The computer hums, the evening grows dark, the moon is rising out the window between the clouds; the arrangement of moon and clouds has never, ever looked exactly the same before this moment, and they will never look exactly the same again. And even if they did, that was then and this is Now...and God is here, now.

What could be more mundane than this moment? The dust on the shelves, the carpet on the hardwood floor, the moonlight on the tree outside, the breeze ruffling the curtains. All just ordinary stuff. And yet, God is here. He cares about it all. No other moment in all my life, or in all history, has ever been the same as this one. I draw a deep breath, "Breathe Deep the Breath of God," as the band Lost Dogs sang two decades ago; I don't need to listen to the CD to hear, in my mind, their grainy masculine voices ringing out, singing out the notes of their powerful exhortation to love all people as freely as breathing. I can remember where I was the first time I heard it, and how beautifully ordinary that cheap old third-story walk-up apartment was. Hearing the song that first time, and discovering that an old friend was one of the backup musicians, was a holy time for me; the forty-seventh time I heard it, it was just as holy. I can say the same about hundreds of other songs, and not just Christian songs. Every time I think of this one, it's still another holy time for me—including right now. And as they seemed to be saying in the song, every deep breath is a holy connection to God and to all other people and to the holy Now, holy in ways I can't really put into words.

And yet...Now is so ordinary, so plain. And that's why we tend to ignore the present moment. It's sort of "the least of these" among things to do (not to lessen the importance of the human "least of these" in our lives; more on that below). We can watch TV or a movie, or read a book or magazine, or play a game on a smart phone, all of which take us out of

Now into the world of fantasy or entertainment. We can dream about the future; we can remember the past; we can do any number of things that take us away from the Now. But when we choose to just "be here now," as the title of a popular book from the early '70's put it,[4] we find God in the present moment.

The great artists, musicians and poets of the world know about the sacrament of the present moment. They fully realize that it's in the Now that their greatest inspirations come. As a musician, I've realized for many years that music performance is a fantastic way to be in the moment, to worship and encounter God in the Now; even playing from sheet music, it's always a new experience. And improvisational music is truly amazing: often, it's as if the song is playing itself through you. And poetry is, to me, the art of putting the Now into words. I'm not a painter or sculptor, but I've watched some of them work, and what they do is very much a matter of transferring the gifts of the present moment onto a canvas or into a sculpture. For that matter, just watching them is a fascinating way of joining with and learning from the Now.

An acquaintance of mine, Dave Blakeslee, is a former pastor and also a potter. Now "retired," he's found a great way to combine his gifts. Dave travels to churches and sets up his potter's wheel on the altar, where he proceeds to give "potter-and-the-clay" teachings in a mesmerizing display of the craft of ceramics. No two pieces he makes are exactly alike. And watching him create vases, bowls, cups, or whatever he chooses to make, as he explains the spiritual implications of his craft, is a most wonderfully spellbinding in-the-moment experience indeed.

But there's something about turning away from the enticements of the world to be with God in the least-of-these Now moments, that tends to open a person's eyes to seeing Jesus in the "least of these" people in our midst. God can also bring you to see that there are times when he wants to gift you with *being* "the least of these," and what a great gift it is— yet, not one most people seek after; it usually involves feeling ignored or shunned, or even hated. "With the lowly is wisdom," the Bible says,[5] but it's the least of these—and those who seek and find the treasure of God's presence in the least-of-these Now moments—who learn to walk in that kind of wisdom. This, more than anything else, is what makes the present moment worthy of being called a sacrament.

The Four Beasts of Revelation

The four strange beasts John saw around the throne of God in Revelation Chapter 4 sound about as bizarre as anything you can imagine. The weirdest thing about them is that they were covered with eyes all over their bodies and even within their bodies. Talk about peripheral vision! And, since they were so holy and so close to God, my guess is that every eye had perfect 20/20 vision, or perhaps more like 20/2,000 vision. They were capable of seeing every tiny detail of everything going on around them, above them, below them, behind them. They were also capable of seeing with perfect clarity their every thought, every motive, every emotion, every memory, in the pure light of holiness and absolute truth, because they were always very close to God.

And yet, their focus wasn't on the things going on around and within them; they were fully focused on God. They never took their eyes—all of them—off God. They were heavenly worship leaders, messengers for God who waited to do his will in any task he gave them. In Chapter 6, they saw and called forth the four horsemen of the Apocalypse, and called John's attention to them when they rode out. But even with all those eyes, with all those things to distract them, their total attention was on God, always.

To me as a contemplative, the four living creatures with their eyes all around and within are symbolic[6] of total awareness. The more we focus on God through centering prayer, the more we become aware of all that's going on around us and within us; the more we are able to live in the present moment, and to see God in the present moment—to practice the Sacrament of the Present Moment. Turning our thoughts away from everything but God in contemplation causes us to see his face, hear his voice, feel his touch, sense his artistry and grace and love in the little things we experience outside the prayer room.

The four living creatures John saw were created that way; God gave them all those eyes. But for us, we only have two—and one nose, two ears, one tongue, lots of skin, but not even a hundredth of the perceptive ability of the four strange creatures gathered around God's throne. So for us, total awareness isn't something we're born with. We are pretty perceptive as children; it's amazing what children notice and how much of the world they perceive, but then gradually lose sight of as they grow up, and forget all about once they become adults. So contemplation is, among other things, a restoration of that childlike perception—one in which we can experience, not just the beauty and wonder of creation as children do, but the hand and heart and face of God in creation as well.

Does our gazing on God in contemplation bring greater awareness, or does greater awareness increase our attention to God? Both, I would say. It's part of the beautiful upward spiral of mystical spirituality, like slowly climbing a spiral staircase in a great tall castle tower with windows. As you keep climbing higher, most of the time you are aware only of stairs and walls and railings. But each window reveals more and more—not just the acres of land where the castle stands; not just the forests and meadows nearby; not just the hills and ridges a few thousand feet away—but the rivers, lakes, mountains, deserts, beaches, islands, and oceans beyond the horizon, and the hands and feet and face of God who created them, the wind that carries his voice, the gentle brush of his hand on your face as a soft breeze blows through the open window.

Seeing with New Eyes

"Therefore I tell you, do not worry about your life, what you will eat or drink; or about your body, what you will wear. Is not life more important than food, and the body more important than clothes? Look at the birds of the air; they do not sow or reap or store away in barns, and yet your heavenly Father feeds them. Are you not much more valuable than they? Who of you by worrying can add a single hour to his life? And why do you worry about clothes? See how the lilies of the field grow. They do not labor or spin. Yet I tell you that not even Solomon in all his splendor was dressed like one of these. If that is how God clothes the grass of the field, which is here today and tomorrow is thrown into the fire, will he not much more clothe you, O you of little faith? So do not worry, saying, "what shall we eat?" or "what shall we drink?" or "what shall we wear?" For the pagans run after all these things, and your heavenly Father knows that you need them. But seek first his kingdom and his righteousness, and all these things will be given to you as well. Therefore do not worry about tomorrow, for tomorrow will worry about itself. Each day has enough trouble of its own." (Matt. 6:25-34)

The Sermon on the Mount has often been called the greatest sermon ever preached. But contemplatives also see it as one of the greatest mystical teachings of all time. Taking a look at one well-known section, we find everything that's part of contemplation: letting go of worries and thoughts to focus solely on God, and the new way of seeing that comes to us when this happens; finding God in the present moment as he speaks to us through such simple, everyday things as birds and wildflowers; non-attachment to the things of the world such as food and clothing; the great love of God for us and for all things—the King for his kingdom— which we become more and more aware of as we crucify our false self with its thoughts and attachments; living out of the true self, which is what his righteousness is—the righteousness of God which we are to seek above all by seeking God alone, the key to the kingdom.

Righteousness is usually seen in Christian circles in the following terms: we are righteous because of what Jesus did on the Cross. That's true, but in this passage, he was speaking to people about three years before he went to the Cross. When they thought about God's righteousness, they didn't think in terms of the Cross. What Jesus's audience—those who had ears to hear—would have heard in the overall message of the Sermon on the Mount, and in his sayings and parables throughout his ministry, was this mystical message: From God's view, the world is upside down. Make God your everything, all that you live for, and God will turn you right-side up, so you can see the world as he sees it.

That's exactly what God's righteousness is: letting go of our own righteousness—our self-sufficiency, our dependence on *self* to meet our needs, which builds a false kingdom in our hearts and puts self on the throne—and instead using our minds and hearts to look to God as our all-in-all. The example of Jesus in his humanity was to look to the Father this same way in times of silence and solitude. There is a time to pray with words, and there is a time to just *be* with God, alone in his presence, without words—letting him work in us his freedom and grace, without our help—a time to just let God be God in us. That's what "seeking first his kingdom and his righteousness" is all about. That's how the house of a person's life gets built on the rock—the true self, "Christ in you, the hope of glory"—rather than on the sand of the false self.

And when we do this, we come to *see*—not just know by faith, but really see with new eyes, new spiritual vision—that the whole world, the whole universe, is in God's hands. This is non-dual thinking: in God we are one with all things. We can love our neighbors as ourselves, and we can also love our enemies, because God loves them, because we are one with God and one with all other people through God. We are part of all God is doing in the world: feeding the birds, clothing the wildflowers, loving those who hate him and hate us, and changing the world one person, one transformed mind and heart, at a time. That's God's kingdom and God's righteousness that Jesus was telling us to seek first—above all else. And it all starts with the dismantling of our own kingdom by seeking God in silence and solitude, as Jesus did.

An Undivided Heart for God

"The light of the body is the eye: if therefore thine eye be single, thy whole body shall be full of light" (Matthew 6:22, KJV).

I don't usually use the King James translation; the KJV was the only Bible I read for many years, until I realized some of the recent translations were better for me personally. But not many Bible versions translate the above verse literally in regard to the word "single." And to me, that's the key to the whole verse and a major clue in understanding the Sermon on the Mount.

Taken in context, Jesus is speaking in the Sermon on the Mount about loving God wholeheartedly. He says, don't pray or fast or live in such a way as to be honored by people. He says in effect, keep your focus on God, not on self, and keep it simple (the word "*haplous*," translated "single," can also mean "simple"). He offers a prayer we've come to know as the Lord's Prayer, which focuses on love for God and on simplicity. Then, in verses 6:19-24 of Matthew, he gives three examples of how we can view and evaluate our relationship with God. Jesus says three things in this passage:

1. 1. Store up treasures in heaven, not on earth, for where your treasure is, that's where your heart is.
2. 2. Let your vision be single for God so that your life will be full of light, so that you won't walk in darkness.
3. 3. Serve only one master—God, not money—because you really can't serve two masters. It just doesn't work.

I have a name for Matthew 6:19-24: One Treasure, One Vision, One Master.

It's all about serving God with an undivided heart. And that term, *undivided heart*, is what that whole section (and, really, the entire Sermon on the Mount) is all about. Another way to think of what having an undivided heart means is union with God. A very similar verse to Matthew 6:22 is Psalm 86:11, which says, "Give me an undivided heart, that I may fear your name." My paraphrase of this is: "Lord, bring all the broken pieces of my heart together into a single focus on you and in you—in union with you—so that I can worship you wholeheartedly, with true abandon, in the now, in humble awe and silent wonder at the way you unite all of creation under your glorious name."

Now, back to the "single eye" part of Matthew 6:22. This is generally considered one of the hardest verses in Scripture to understand. I struggled with it for years, partly due to the translation issues. In attempts to make it easier to understand, various translations render the Greek word "*haplous*" as "sound," or "whole," or "good," or "clear," or even "pure." There may be occasions where this word is used to signify one of these other meanings. A similar situation in English is the word "bright." When we say someone is "bright," we mean they're smart; we don't mean they light up like a light bulb. But in the original Greek, the primary meaning of the word used here—*haplous*—is "single." So this verse doesn't say "if your eye is "sound," or "whole," or "good," or "clear," or "pure." It says "if your eye is *single.*" And that's hard for us Americans to understand, and apparently for those in many other cultures to understand as well. I believe the reason it's so hard to understand is because unitive or non-dualistic thinking—which is thinking from the heart, not the head—isn't taught in most churches today.

Jesus is talking about our spiritual vision, about how we see God and how we see the world. He is saying, if you see according to what the Jews call the Shema (Deuteronomy 6:4)—"The Lord our God, the Lord is One, and you shall love the Lord your God with all your heart and soul and strength"—then God is number one in your life, and there is no number two. He is your everything, and he is the one that everything in the universe is surrendered to or will ultimately surrender to. And you are so surrendered to him that you have no other way of looking at the world except through the eyes of God. He is your vision, and whatever there is in you that wants to see things your way, to have things your way, is kept crucified. Your eye (not eyes, *eye,* singular, as in single vision) is single. Your vision is "clear, pure, sound, whole, good," because it's all about Jesus.

Oh dear, did I contradict myself? I said the word sometimes translated "clear, pure, sound, whole, or good," didn't mean those things in this passage. But, no contradiction here. *Haplous* (Strong's Greek 573), literally means single or simple. In the context of your vision being so focused on God that he is your everything, and only in that context, can it also mean vision that is clear, pure, sound, whole, or good. The word *haplous* comes from a combination of two words: *a,* the first letter in both Hebrew and Greek and which means *first,* and a derivative of a verb (*pleko*) which means *to braid together.* Picture a braid of hair, leather, or other material: it is something in which several things, or several strands of the same thing, are woven together to form a single unit, one thing. So in its essence and in its etymology, the word *haplous* means "*single*"! Compare what it says on our money: *e pluribus unum,* a Latin phrase which means "from many, one." When we are fully in God's will, we are in union with God: we are mind, emotions, conscience, will, memory, body, all woven into a single strand by God, for God, one single entity in love with God, and God's presence fills us. The Holy Spirit is braided together into us like strands of golden ribbon—made from pure gold— braided in with the human hair, or like the beauty and cleanness and radiance of that braid of hair. That is single vision, focused on God and forgetting self. That is unity with God. A church full of people caught up in worship is, to me, the most beautiful expression there is of unity: many people and God, all joined together, hearts beating as one, braided together into one glorious unity.

One Single Vision

When Jesus speaks of the eye being single, you may picture a Cyclops—a one-eyed mythical monster. I don't think that's what Jesus had in mind. Maybe that's the evil-eye he spoke of in verse 23! There, he said, "But if your eye is evil, your whole body will be full of darkness. Therefore, if the light within you has turned into darkness, how great is that darkness!" Seriously, what did he mean by this? It's interesting how the alternative to a "single eye" is an "evil eye." We can see these terms—single eye, evil eye—in terms of the true and false self: the false self keeps your vision focused on you; it's the ultimate idolatry because it takes God off the throne and puts the false self there. And we all do it, at least at times. The false self makes us compare ourselves with others and judge them to be less worthy. It gives us an us-versus-them mentality. It says we can do as we please, because we're better than others. And that's the opposite of love, the opposite of having a single eye. It fills us with darkness, and how great is that darkness!

If you lack that singleness of vision for God, it's easy to believe you and your church are the greatest in God's kingdom, as Jesus's disciples wanted to be. If he had let them follow that path, what would Christianity have ended up like? Sadly, there are many churches you can find today that have followed that false path. It's all about them, about their pastor, about the way they worship, about their building and the programs they have. And true servanthood is seldom seen in such places. Sometimes their version of servanthood is cleaning the pastor's house or mowing his lawn, not out of love, but out of a legalistic sense of duty, or because another church leader says to do so and you know you'll be made to feel condemned or ostracized if you don't. Truly, how great is that darkness.

The term "single eye" may bring to mind the "third eye" dot tattooed on the forehead of a Hindu. And what that dot means to the Hindus is the same: singleness of vision, seeing with the eye of God. And how does God see? He sees all things in love, with singleness of vision. Non-dualistic vision, unitive seeing. And what, exactly, is that? If you stand on the North Pole, there is no east or west or north; everything is south. That's how God sees us and all people, even the most sinful.

We see humanity, including ourselves, as sinful and in violation of God's standard of perfection. Is this what it means to see as God sees? That's what many churches teach. But this is true only to the extent that, with a heart of mercy and love incomprehensible to us, God sees us all as being in need of him. In the example of the woman caught in adultery in John 8, Jesus showed that with God, there is no us-and-them. He loved her, Zacchaeus, Barabbas, even Judas, as he loved himself. We can reject God, separate ourselves from him, refuse to believe he exists, but we can never make him stop loving us.

God also sees all things together as his creation, and therefore as a reflection of himself. And he sees all of humanity as created in his image. Like him, we are capable of both mercy and judgment, love and hate. But unlike him, we are capable of not just wisdom but also foolishness, not just of kindness but also cruelty.

And yet, as perhaps the greatest reflection of our Maker, we are also capable of going beyond these dichotomies—of being in the place where, like God and the way he sees all things in love, there is no us-versus-them, no weak-versus-strong, no good-versus-evil.[7] We are made by God to be capable of joining together with him to see the world and ourselves as one with him, created to be vessels of his glory, glorified as we glorify him. We are created to be co-workers with him to accomplish the fulfillment of his Kingdom through both giving and receiving, through both working with him and resting in him, and through prayer, both word-prayer and silent prayer.

And we are also able to come to a place where the dividing walls between all these things are broken, where there is neither Jew nor Gentile, slave nor free, male nor female (Galatians 3:28); even to a place where dark and light are the same (Psalm 139:12), where now and eternity are the same (Revelation 21:5) —where we "behold I Am, making all things new." And when we can rest in the Now, in the place where all things are new every moment, made so by I Am, where there is no self to divide between us-and-them, where there is nothing that is not held in the loving hands of God—the place where God is all in all—we then can truly see as God sees. There, we have one Treasure—God—one Master, and one single vision with God at the center of our lives and at the center of all things. There, in the place of ultimate healing and wholeness, our eye—our vision—is clear, pure, sound, whole, good. There, our eye is single.

Judging our own judgmentalism

We're not to judge others. "Judge not, lest you be judged," Jesus said, and in another place, "With the same measure you measure to others, it will be measured to you." And yet, after nearly 40 years of being a Christian, I've heard very few sermons on this subject, and I have to admit that this thing of not being judgmental is something I'm not good at. When someone cuts me off in traffic or wrongs me, even in some minor way, my first impulse is to decide they deserve

We are called to love as Jesus loved. Through the self-denial of centering prayer, I learn to deny the judgmental attitude that suspects the worst of others. I learn that even among the "lost" there are people in whom God has planted good-heartedness, truthfulness, purity of heart, compassion. I learn to allow God to teach me through others—including non-Christians. I learn that all people are created in God's image, and that I must look for God in every person, whether that person is a Christ-follower or not.

severe punishment – a few nights in jail, at least. Of course, when I wrong someone, I can always find a way to justify it.

I know I'm not alone. Judging (oops!) from the amount of judgmentalism I encounter among Christians in general, I doubt that this subject is preached on much in most churches. Learning right from wrong is part of growing up, but maturity includes loving others and treating them—and viewing them—as we would want others to treat or view us. Unfortunately, judgmentalism among Christians shows how few of us really grow up. We judge ourselves to be high on the scale of Christian virtue and maturity, and often we judge others to be lower than us on that same scale. But the words of Jesus lead me to believe that part of what constitutes true spiritual maturity is throwing the scale out altogether, at least in regard to injuries done to us by others. Paul tells us, "If we will judge ourselves we will not need to be judged" (I Cor. 11:31).

I once saw a guy strutting down the street with dreads, tattoos, lots of jewelry, and goth clothes. Rapping aloud, dancing as he walked, moving his hands in funny ways, he presented quite an image. I thought, "how many layers of phoniness are there to you?" and I heard God say to me, "And how about you? How many are there to you?" I then heard him reminding me that almost all people wear many masks. I've found that one long-range effect of centering prayer, if done right, is that it helps us remove those layers. But it takes a long, long time. What mask should we wear? A Christian one? Really, the true self is what's left after all the masks are stripped away. That's when people can look at us or talk to us and see "Christ in you, the hope of glory." And that goes way beyond the outward appearance. Another time, my wife was watching TV and I stopped for a minute to check out what she was so captivated by. It was a Barbara Walters special in which she was interviewing Oprah Winfrey. I was turning to walk away from something I thought unworthy of me, when I felt a sort of tap on the shoulder. God was asking me to examine my attitude toward these two women.

Early in my Christian walk, I remember how people in the church I attended would speak disparagingly of someone famous, or just come right out and lambaste them. "They aren't really the righteous, good-hearted person they claim to be," someone might say. "They're not setting such a great example for the world like they want you to think," another might intone. A third would perhaps chime in with, "These people aren't speaking truth—they're just leading people astray." The person or people these Christians would be speaking about could be TV news or sports personalities, actors, comedians, politicians, or whatever; they would always be someone in the limelight, and it would be assumed that they were far from God and deserved to be taken with several grains of salt. (I'm also quite sure there were and are other believers around who have heard me say such things as well. In my own defense, and in defense of those who have made similar comments as those above in my hearing, it was part of the "Christian" culture of the time—the '70's and '80's. And it didn't stop at the end of that period; the same attitude is alive and well today in many churches and in the hearts of millions of people who consider themselves Christian, including—sometimes—yours truly.)

At the time in my life that I'm speaking of, I assumed—I was taught to assume—that if someone was famous, they got to that position not by talent or intelligence, but by some kind of devious means. If it was a woman, she had probably slept with the producer of whatever TV show or movie she was in, or she had connections—maybe her uncle was a network mucky-muck. If it was a man, he had probably bribed his way into his envied position or done other unscrupulous things to make his way to the top. Of course, in sports and most other forms of entertainment, a person has to have a certain amount of talent to get into an important position, but that didn't mean they hadn't used cash or favors of some kind or stepped on others—any ungodly means available—to raise themselves to a position of power, wealth and acclaim. That's how the thinking went.

I won't deny that a certain amount of underhandedness accompanies the careers of many in Hollywood, Washington, and other places of influence. It happens quite a bit in the Church as well. But when that tap came on my shoulder, God was not pointing out the flaws and failings of others; he was asking me to look into my own heart and to recognize that there is value in every person.

What is it that makes us so susceptible to suspicion? What is it about Christians, specifically, that causes us to think that most unbelievers are contemptible? Why can't we accept others—especially the famous—as honest, hard-working, humble, kind and sincere? I recall, early in my Christian life, putting a question like that to someone who had been around the "Christian" (Churchianity) track for a few years, and this person pointed me to some scripture verses that said the whole world lies under the influence of Satan. I accepted that and soon became one of the Christian cynics, the bitter-pill believers, like those I was surrounded with. But there's something about the contemplative pursuit that changes a person's outlook.

What God was leading me to in those shoulder-tap experiences was the recognition that regardless of what Satan does or how powerful he is, God is still on the throne. And that means I am called to love as Jesus loved. In the self-denial of centering prayer, one part of me that I deny is the judgmental attitude that suspects the worst of others, especially unbelievers. I learn to recognize that even among the "lost" there are people whom God has influenced, in whom God has planted good-heartedness, truthfulness, purity of heart, compassion and other Godly traits. I learn to look for the good in others, expect the best of others, allow God to teach me through others—including non-Christians. I learn that all people are created in God's image, and that I must look for God in every person, whether that person is a Christ-follower or not.

And what of that rancid, poisoned attitude that sees only the negative in others? Often it is something in myself that I am subconsciously reacting to when I think I see something sick or evil in another person. If I can tune my heart to God when such thoughts arise, often I can recognize the Holy Spirit pointing out something I need to deal with. At other times, it is Satan putting his dark thoughts into me. When I have unloving thoughts toward others, where else would they come from but Satan? And why would I ever think such thoughts came from God? His heart, his desire, is for me to pray for those I believe are caught in Satan's evil grip—and also to see them as people God loves with great passion. God's heart is for me to love like Jesus did and does.

Chapter 7

The Mystical Christ

> And his name will be called Wonderful, Counselor, Mighty God, Everlasting Father, Prince of Peace. Of the increase of his government and peace there will be no end...
>
> Isaiah 9:6-7

> When I turned to see who was speaking to me, I saw seven golden lampstands. And standing in the middle of the lampstands was the Son of Man. He was wearing a long robe with a golden sash across his chest. His head and his hair were white like wool, as white as snow. And his eyes were bright like flames of fire. His feet were as bright as bronze refined in a furnace, and his voice thundered like mighty ocean waves. He held seven stars in his right hand, and a sharp two-edged sword came from his mouth. And his face was as bright as the sun in all its brilliance.
>
> John the Apostle, Revelation 1:12-15, NLT

For many in the Church, calling Jesus "mystical" conjures up in their minds the "cosmic Christ" of the New Age Movement—an "exalted Master" of strange worlds and bizarre experiences that have little if anything to do with the Jesus of the Bible. This is not the mystical Christ. The Jesus I'm talking about appears in many guises in the Bible, from the Angel of the Lord who appeared to Abraham and Melchizedek whom he honored, to the whirlwind that took Elijah up to heaven, to the Holy One seen by Isaiah, high and lifted up, his train filling the temple, to the white-haired, fire-eyed Ancient of Days revealed to John in the Book of Revelation. The mystical Christ appeared to two believers on Resurrection Day on the road to Emmaus, and to Paul on the road to Damascus. He appeared to the Promised Land-bound Israelites as the Pillar of Cloud and Fire, and to Peter, James and John as the transfigured Christ, speaking with Moses and Elijah. He is the burning bush that spoke to Moses, the fourth Man in the fire in the book of Daniel, the slain Lamb and Lion of Judah on the heavenly throne of Revelation. He is the Carpenter who alone can build a house for the Lord, and the Son of Man who can walk on water, who can change water to wine. The mystical Christ himself is the Mystery of mysteries, the true pearl of great price.

This is not the Christ of those who are content to merely accept, by faith, that there is a promised land they will someday see, a Savior they will someday know. This is not a pie-in-the-sky-by-and-by Christ. This is the Christ of those who say, don't tell me about the giants in that promised land—God himself is my Zion, my promised land flowing with milk and honey (though it may seem a barren wilderness to others), and I won't stop until, with his help, I've slain all the giants of the false self that stand in the way. This is the Christ of those who are willing to lay down their lives for the One who laid down his life for them, the Christ of those who live in the reality that walking in Christlike love *is* the true promised land. This is the Christ who reveals himself to those who just won't settle for anything less than God, who will crawl across deserts and swim away from shipwrecks to follow the Savior who loves them. This is the Christ of passion, the revealed Christ who is the same now as in the New Testament, the same yesterday and today and forever. This is the resurrected Christ. The mystical Christ.

I'm not presenting a different Jesus than the Jesus presented by Paul and the Apostles. If it seems like I am, that's because, for foolish reasons, our Christian culture has at times presented a distorted view of Christ that excludes the mystical aspects of his I-Am-ness, or simply refuses to call him mystical. Contemplative practice tends to open one's eyes to the mystical aspects of Jesus that have always been there. But, like Peter, we have denied this Jesus, which is the real in-your-face Jesus, not the nice mama's boy mamby-pamby Jesus taught in so many churches today. Like Aslan in C. S. Lewis's Chronicles of Narnia, the mystical Christ is not a tame lion. If all you've heard about is gentle-Jesus-meek-and-mild, I can tell you about a few encounters I've personally had with him where he revealed himself as the Lion of Judah, and he had me by the leg! (More on that at the end of this chapter.) There are many in the Church who don't want to hear about that Jesus. But all down through Christian history, the mystical Christ has continued to reveal himself to believers in ways that are often every bit as strange—and strangely beautiful—as the above examples from the Bible. Some of these, we will explore in this chapter.

Two Trees in Eden

For years, I never understood that thing about the two trees in the Garden of Eden, the tree of the knowledge of good and evil and the tree of life. Something about that whole thing just never made sense to me; it was a blind spot in my spiritual understanding. When I finally got enlightened about it, it was such a rich experience, I was on a cloud for a week. What it boils down to is this: the Tree of Life is relationship with God, God's hand reaching out to man, the living experience of the presence of God. And the Tree of the Knowledge of Good and Evil is human religion—man's efforts to reach God or heaven on his own terms, like the Tower of Babel and all the idolatry described and proscribed in the Bible. Author Frank Viola, in his book *From Eternity to Here,* explains the whole thing in a simple yet powerful way: "The Tree of Life… represents reliance upon God for our life and service. The Tree of the Knowledge of Good and Evil represents reliance upon *our* ability to do good, serve God, and avoid evil. The Tree of Life represents dependence on Christ. The Tree of the Knowledge of Good and Evil represents independence from Him."[1]

All this is in the context of partaking of Christ, which is a matter, Viola says, of eating from the Tree of Life. He is our sustenance; Jesus is presented to us as food and drink: the Bread of Life (John 6:35), the living water (John 4:10), the Lamb of God eaten at Passover (John 1:29), the bread and wine of communion/Eucharist (Matthew 26:26-28). We are to constantly partake of Jesus; he is our life, more than physical food. Job said, "I have treasured God's words more than my natural food" (Job 23:12). When we eat from the tree of life, we are eating Christ, and as they say, you are what you eat. What we consume, we become. Every time we put a bite of good, healthy food in our mouths, chew it and swallow it and begin to digest it, that's a simple picture of transformation into the mystical Christ.

When we eat from the tree of the knowledge of good and evil, what happens? Exactly what Paul spoke of in Romans 7: "When I want to do good, evil is right there with me." Both good and evil come from the same tree. The message of religion, morality and ethics is: do good. Figure out what's good and do it; figure out what's evil and avoid it. But it's never that simple, because that duality of good and evil come together; they're a package deal. "When I want to do good, evil is right there with me." Paul concludes about this situation, "Oh what a wretch I am! Who will rescue me from this dead religious body I live in? Jesus has and will—thank God for Jesus, the Tree of Life, the true God-food instead of religious food!" (My paraphrase.)

What was it like for Adam and Eve in Eden before their encounter with the serpent, before they ate the fruit of the tree of the knowledge of good and evil? There were no dualities: no good/evil, no clothed/naked, no love/hate, no right/wrong, no true/false. In other words, they saw from a non-dualistic viewpoint. And they saw God—they hung out with him— so they must have been pure in heart (Matt. 5:8). So the unitive soul— the person whose mind and heart is free of dualities—is pure in heart.

That's what loving your enemies means: they're still your enemies, at first anyway, but you love them and that breaks down the friend/enemy duality until they are enemies no more in your mind and heart—even if they continue to hate and persecute you. Blessed are those who are persecuted for the sake of righteousness—those who have reached the highest levels of spiritual development, who can love their persecutors— for theirs is the kingdom of heaven, which brings the beatitudes full circle, back to the same reward as for the poor in spirit, the first beatitude. They are the ones who have become most Christlike. That's how Christ was on earth, and that's how he is throughout eternity.

But the big question here is, how do we partake of Christ? Reading the Bible? Well, that's part of it, as long as it's getting into the heart and not just into the head. Praying? That's part of it too, as long as we can learn not to pray out of our ego but to die to self, to pray out of the true self, the resurrected self. What happens when you get done with your Bible reading, praying, or worshipping? As soon as the buzzer goes off, the usual response of many Christians is to head for the coffee pot and cookie jar, to feed the flesh. But at that point, if we can learn to wait on God, to sit silently in his presence, that's where much of the real work is accomplished; that's the real meal, not cookies and coffee. That's where we see whether our prayer and worship and Bible reading is being done by us or by God through us—whether it's for transformation or just religious exercise—whether we're feeding on God or just feeding our own ego.

Sitting in the stillness with God, even beyond the point of pondering his Word in our minds, to the place of green pastures and still waters, the place of just *being* with God, where we've surrendered all doing— that's the place where we most deeply partake of God. Every breath is a taste of God's life; every mental gaze of love for God is a drink of God. The thoughts that come are forsaken for the true food, being in the depths of God, where the Spirit searches all things. That's true spiritual sustenance. That's where we meet the mystical Christ. That's where true transformation takes place.

Becoming like Children

Jesus said we must become like children in order to enter the kingdom of Heaven, or even to see it. What did he mean? The standard take on this passage in many churches is that it refers to morality, to having a pure heart like a child, to innocence; some make a point of saying that Jesus was *not* referring to having a childlike outlook. But contemplatives say, and I agree, that along with purity of heart, Jesus was referring to living in the moment and seeing all things as new, as if for the first time—the way a child sees: from the heart.

If that's true, how does that differentiate Christianity from the mystical schools of other religious traditions? Most talk about becoming like a child again; for example, the Tao te Ching, the Taoist sacred book of ancient China, says the mind of a sage—a wise man—is the mind of a child. So how would Christianity be different from Taoism, the Raja yoga

Contemplation is not about an "experience" with God, but about absolute surrender to the Lion of Judah who was found on heaven's throne as a slain lamb. The world is not conquered by force and strength, but by sacrificial love, the laying down of life. We daily lay our lives down in silence before the Crucified One and enter into the mystical encounter with him. Through his death, his life becomes our life. And our lives become his to live through as the risen, glorious, victorious least-of-these Lamb/Lion King who rules through love.

of Hinduism, Zen Buddhism, Islamic Sufism, and so forth? Or, a better question might be, how might they be connected (other than examples like the one just mentioned), what do these connections mean, and—the crucial question—do they ultimately worship the same God as Christians? Could Christ be "the unknown God" (Acts 17:23) not just to the ancient Greeks, but to people of all religious traditions?

One answer to all this would be mythologist Joseph Campbell's ideas about what he called the Animal Master. I'll speak more about that later in this chapter. For now, suffice it to say I think there are things in every religious tradition that point to Jesus; I think he's the fulfillment of the longing for a savior that's expressed in all religions. Most cultures have had stories and myths[2] about someone who is able to heal the sick, raise the dead, perform miracles, provide for the poor, weak and elderly, and be the greatest and wisest of leaders. There are also many myths from around the world about a hero who bears the sins of the people, who dies for the world, who rises from the dead. I think Jesus is the fulfillment of all those things as well as Isaiah 53, Psalm 22, and all the other Hebrew Messianic prophecies.

The point of view so often seen in Christianity is that we have to say we're better than all the other religions, and that to say otherwise is demeaning to God and takes glory away from him. But I say the exact opposite: it glorifies God more for Jesus to be the fulfillment of not just the Hebrew traditions, but the fulfillment of many traditions all throughout history, all around the world. This is the key that makes this lock open: is there any connection between other religions and Christianity? The answer is, God reveals himself to all peoples of the world, not just to the Christians. Christ is the fullest revelation of God there is, but that doesn't mean there is no truth revealed to those in other religions. As with the Jews, it's hidden, but it's still there—hidden in plain sight, you might say.

The Bible itself makes it clear that the whole us-versus-them thing is man's idea, not God's. A few examples: John 11:49-52 - Caiaphas's inadvertent prophecy: " "...it is better for you that one man die for the people than that the whole nation perish." He did not say this on his own, but as high priest that year he prophesied that Jesus would die for the Jewish nation, and *not only for that nation but also for the scattered children of God,* to bring them together and make them one." I Peter 1:12 says in reference to the prophets of Israel, "it was revealed to them that they were not serving themselves but you..." (I Peter was written primarily to Gentile believers, according to the greeting in 1:1; the prophets were "serving" the Gentiles long before the Gentiles ever heard of Christ.) Hebrews 11:4-10 lists, among the "heroes of faith," Abel, Enoch, and Noah, who were Gentiles; Abraham, up until his covenant with God and the promises God made to him, was a Gentile. There must have been untold thousands among the nations throughout history with hearts that longed for God and were in total obedience to him to the extent that they were able, i.e. they walked in the light that they had and thus pleased God. Jesus died for them too, even if his name and story were completely unknown to them.

The Cross of Christ

As the subtitle of this book suggests, the real bottom line of Christ-followership is the Cross. Christ died and rose again; this is the basis of our faith. If he didn't die, he couldn't have been resurrected, and the same is true for us. And it's just as hard to understand today as it has been since the day Jesus walked out of the tomb. ""God is not removed from the world...[He] enters the world and gets nailed to a cross. And unless we accept Christ crucified, which is a scandal to those who want God to be some kind of power figure, and total foolishness to those who want it all to fall into place intellectually in our terms, there's no Gospel." ...[The crucified Christ] is a reality reflecting the nature of reality itself."[3] The reality that Christ crucified reflects is that there's something in all of us that hates God. The creation rebels against the Creator. And by his love the Creator enters creation to heal it, to make it completely whole, just as he himself is. That's not something humanity could have ever thought up, and yet, the idea of redemptive sacrifice appears again and again through all the religions of the world. But recognizing the part of us that hates God, and choosing to unite with God to crucify everything in us that will not submit to his rule and reign—this is part and parcel of contemplative prayer. It is not about an "experience" with God, but about absolute surrender to the Lion of Judah who was found on heaven's throne as a slain lamb. The world is not conquered by force and strength, but by sacrificial love, the laying down of life. We daily lay our lives down in silence before the Crucified One and enter into the mystical encounter with him. Through his death, his life becomes our life. And our lives become his to live through as the risen, glorious, victorious least-of-these Lamb/Lion King who rules through love.

The Bride of Christ

Some of the old hymns we used to sing when I was a young Christian spoke of the Church as the Bride of Christ. That always seemed a little weird to me, and I didn't really understand it. I wasn't at all sure what I should do with that information. (I suppose they teach this in seminary, but I haven't been there.) Eventually, with the help of a good Bible study, I came to the realization that if Christ is the second Adam, we are the second Eve. God took a piece of Adam's side and "fashioned a woman" after God put him into a deep sleep; Christ's side was pierced just after he went into the sleep of death before the Resurrection, and you could say the Church was taken from his side and fashioned to be his helpmate, his beloved, made in his image, bone of his bone and flesh of his flesh.

This fascinates me; it's mystical. The Christ who is the second Adam is the mystical Christ. That's amazing enough, but the next step is even more amazing, because it's about us: We are the people of God, and John says that "what we will be has not yet been made known. But we know that when he appears, we shall be like him, for we shall see him as he is" (I John 3: 2). We shall be like him—just as Eve was like Adam. This goes beyond the bounds of life on earth, beyond the standard go-to-church-and-try-to-live-a-good-life kind of Christianity. This is mystical theology. It's by faith, by daily walking and living on the path of faith. But not just out in the back yard on that path—it's way out on the side of a mountain in the wilderness of faith. It's beauty and wonder we can't see, hear, feel or smell or taste. It's totally beyond our five senses. It's God preparing us for something in the future that we have barely caught a glimpse of—being the Bride of Christ forever. That's the kind of mystical relationship we are called to have with Christ. And it's real! It's not just in the future, not just Book of Revelation stuff that will happen when Christ returns. It's here and now!

Psalm 45 speaks of this relationship. It first talks about the glory and majesty of Christ the triumphant King (Hebrews 1:8-9 quotes Psalm 45 as referring directly to Christ); then it presents the Church at his side: "At your right hand is the royal bride in gold of Ophir." Ophir was a mysterious place in the ancient world, location unknown today, where the purest gold was found in abundance; the meaning of the word Ophir is also unknown, but Ophir was a son of Joktan whose name means "he will be made little"—in other words, humility. So the Bride clothed in the finest of gold jewelry and gold-embroidered dress and robe speaks of mystery and of great beauty in deep humility.

Peter admonishes us to clothe ourselves in humility, like the Bride of Psalm 45. More than her rich clothing, it was her inner beauty that made the King crazy for her: "(Wives,) let your beauty not be [merely] external—the braiding of hair and wearing of gold jewelry and fine clothes—but [let it be] the inner person of the heart, the lasting beauty of a gentle and tranquil spirit, which is precious in God's sight."[4] Psalm 45:10-11 instructs the Bride on how to act in the presence of the King, her husband. In the Message Bible, this reads like a direct word to us today: "Now listen, daughter, don't miss a word: forget your country, put your home behind you. Be *here*—the king is wild for you! Since he's your lord, adore him."

How can we adore the King, our betrothed, today? We can take the time to do absolutely nothing but love him with all our heart, soul, mind and strength. We can forget our self, put the world behind us, and be *here* for Christ our Lord. We can find out, in the new mercies he has for today, what it means to truly adore him. We can sit in the silence and stillness of contemplation and just simply love him. We can let every thought that's not about him be thrown away. And the thoughts about him? After pondering his love and grace, let these thoughts go too—our minds can't understand him, so go beyond thoughts and just rest in his love and grace, in what T.S. Eliot called "lucid stillness," adoring him in the mystery of the fullness of who he is. Let the Spirit strengthen you in your innermost being in love for the mystical Christ. He is our essence, our strength, our peace, our life, our love. Let the lover of your soul love you in silent mystery and awe. And love him back the same way.[5]

Christ in the Primitive World

Christ had a way, uniquely in history, of giving himself so completely as to make it all about others—healing, etc.—and yet making it ultimately all about himself. If he wasn't the Messiah he couldn't have done this; the resurrection is proof that he deserved to be called Lord, Master, Messiah and the Name Above All Names. Has he only been revealed to Israel, 2,000 years ago? Or has he also been revealed to other peoples, in other times and other places?

I have often considered the possibility that Jesus could have appeared to, say, an American Indian or Australian Aborigine tribe in the distant past. How would he have revealed himself to them? What would that have looked like? Would he show them a cross and explain it to them? If so, I doubt they would have understood what the cross was all about, because crucifixion wasn't a part of their culture. To them, a cross might have just looked like a crossing of paths, with an implied option to change directions. And that's exactly what it is. But could God have presented the reality of Christ to such a people in a way that would have revealed him to them within the context of their own culture? Again, what would that have been like?

Earlier in this chapter, I promised to talk about how ancient cultures can relate to Jesus as the ultimate fulfillment of what mythologist Joseph Campbell called the "animal master." Campbell, in his book *The Power of Myth* (from a series of interviews with Bill Moyers), says: "Early hunters usually had a kind of animal divinity—the technical name would be the animal master...[who] sends the flocks to be killed. You see, the basic hunting myth is of a kind of covenant between the animal world and the human world. The animal gives its life willingly, with the understanding that its life transcends its physical entity and will be returned...The hunters have to fulfill certain taboos of not doing this and not doing that in a kind of "participation mystique," a mystical participation in the death of the animal, whose meat has become their life, and whose death they have brought about...[There is] a recognition of your dependency on the voluntary giving of this food to you by the animal who has given its life...the religious attitude toward the principal animal is one of reverence and respect, and not only that—submission to the inspiration of that animal. The animal is the one that brings the gifts...that is why you have the rites...of thanks to the animal. For example, when the bear is killed, there is a ceremony of feeding the bear a piece of its own flesh. And then there will be a little ceremony with the bear's skin placed over a kind of rack, as though he were present—and he is present, he serves his own meat for dinner...That is the power of the animal master."[6]

Now, I don't know about you, but there's a lot in there that reminds me of Jesus—the real Jesus, the one I know, the one who gave his life for us so that we could live. To many Christians in the 21st century, the above quote sounds like a bunch of heathen rituals and beliefs we might tend to label as occultic, new-age or even satanic; many would call it a spiritual counterfeit of Christ. But put yourself in the place of someone a few thousand years ago in what is now Nebraska or Romania or Mongolia or

Nigeria or Argentina or Australia. Imagine yourself as one of your own ancient ancestors, part of a tribe that hunts and kills animals to survive.

Was God around then? Did he make himself known to those people then? Could Christ have been revealed to them, and if so, what would that have looked like to a nomadic hunter separated from the Judeo-Christian world by centuries and by thousands of miles? First, there's a covenant between the supernatural world and man. Second, there's someone who gives his life willingly so that others may live. Third, there's eating his flesh, drinking his blood—like our Communion/Eucharist. Fourth, there's sorrow over this death the tribe has caused, and joy because they can live due to the sacrifice. Fifth, there's the promise of resurrection, of new life. And so, for some there who can enter into the silence, the mystery, and find the God who is boundless love, perhaps there's Christ in their midst.

We tend to see ourselves as living in some kind of bubble that "the world" can't relate to, a hermetically sealed existence away from the rest of history. We speculate that Jesus may have been revealed to people in past ages and lands unknown to the Christian world, and made himself known to them as the Savior of the world. Again, what would that have looked like? We have a perfect description of exactly that from Joseph Campbell—and it's not Jesus entering their world for a one-time appearance, not a counterfeit of Christ by Satan, but a common mode of life for hundreds or even thousands of tribes lost in the mists of history, with Jesus revealed to them on a regular basis! Amazing! But if that isn't true, then how could it be that those who worship God at his throne throughout eternity will include those from every people, tribe, tongue and nation on earth? Yet that's what Revelation 5 tells us.

Of course, missionaries have usually been able to tap into the beliefs of whoever they're sent to minister to and come up with things that echo biblical principles, aspects of other religions and beliefs that point to Christ. So this is nothing new, really. We Christ-followers often don't get it, though; there's still a tendency to think us-and-them, when really, Jesus included them, all of the "thems" out there in the world who never heard of him, who practice idol worship or cannibalism or whatever. We're no better than them; the "us" is just as sinful, just as lost and just as desperately in need of Jesus every moment. Us lost folks need to know him, not just his written word (that's important) but the Word made alive in our hearts. We need the Word to go from an "it" to a "Him" and then to worship the living Word, and to pass beyond worship into wordless loving adoration and wonder, like a small band of buffalo hunters and their families a thousand years ago, grateful at some animal and the Animal Master behind it who gave his life and shed his blood so they could have life.

The Mystical Christ and Dreams

I find it interesting that two Josephs in the Bible—the one in Genesis, Jacob's son, and the earthly father of Jesus—were both dreamers. In both cases, their lives and the lives of millions of others were greatly affected by dreams given by God. I have a similar story. Whether my dreams affect millions, or just a few, is up to God. But they have certainly affected me and profoundly altered the course of my life. I spoke at the beginning of the book about having a series of dreams in which I saw and longed to explore some beautiful rock formations high in the mountains, and how these dreams seemed to precede and, later, to be fulfilled by God's invitation to me to become involved in contemplative prayer. I'd like to also share two other very powerful dreams that God used in my life.

While in college in the early 1970's, I was a dedicated believer in what some people called "hippie philosophy;" this meant, among other things, that drugs (mostly pot) had been a part of my life for a few years. During that time, a friend who had been influential in my introduction to the drug world had become a Christian, and she just kept telling me over and over about how she'd been "talking to Jesus." I could see that her life had changed for the better, in some ways at least. Eventually I made a choice to ask Jesus into my heart, not really knowing much about what that meant or what changes it entailed.

I soon began to find out, as God started revealing himself to me through the Bible and some dramatic personal encounters with him. Before long I recognized that following God's will was diametrically opposed to following the hippie lifestyle. Still, having been steeped in the pronouncements of the Beatles, Grace Slick, Timothy Leary and others like them since about age fifteen, as well as my own experiences, the drug culture had a strong pull for me. I kept finding myself in situations with friends who offered me pot and other drugs, much more often than with those who encouraged me to follow Christ. I needed to make a clean break, and I knew I needed God to help me do so. I asked, and he answered in a dramatic way.

One night in November 1973, I was at a friend's home, the pot and beer had come out, and we were all laughing, joking, and listening to music. At some point the words to a certain song with a humorous but obscene message hit us all at once, and we laughed hard and listened to it again and again. Walking home afterward, the song and laughter still ringing in my ears, I felt defiled, knowing I had displeased God once again. A sadness began to come over me and I started praying. After asking God's forgiveness, I let him know I felt bad about letting him down as I had so many times before. I began to despair of ever being able to leave that lifestyle, but I asked him once again for his help in this matter.

Sleeping a few hours later, I had a dream. I dreamed I was in a "head shop"—a store that sold pot pipes and other drug accessories—and there was a man who apparently worked there who fascinated me. He was sort of your average longhair like me and my friends, but he was wearing what appeared to be some very unusual glasses. They seemed to have stones for lenses—matching slices of beautiful rainbow agate or onyx. In the dream I thought, "That's the coolest thing I've ever seen," and I got closer to check them out. When I was a few feet away, I got a better look at the guy, and I realized the stones weren't glasses—they were his eyes. At the same time, I saw smoke pouring out of him. Just then God spoke very clearly to me. He said, "This man is a servant of Satan." (For some reason, I was aware that the man did not know this; he was totally deceived.) Somehow, in the smoke, I saw many forms of evil taking place. God spoke again regarding all the evil connected with this man: "Is this what you want to give your friends?"

I awoke, absolutely terrified and trembling. For a long time—it seemed like half an hour—I tried to pray but all I could say was, "God help me! God help me!" I felt like this was it, it was all over, I was going to hell and that was the end of it. After a while, I picked up my Bible which was lying near me, and opened it at random. It opened to Job, which I knew next to nothing about. Here's what I read:

"God is greater than man. Why do you contend against him, saying, 'He will answer none of my words?' For God speaks in one way, and in two, though man does not perceive it. *In a dream*, in a vision of the night, when deep sleep falls upon men, while they slumber on their beds, then *he opens the ears of men, and terrifies them with warnings*, that he may turn man aside from his deed, and cut off pride from man; he keeps back his soul from the Pit..." (Job 33:12b-18, RSV, italics mine.)

A wave of peace slowly began to wash over me as I realized that what I had just read about was exactly what had happened to me a few minutes earlier. Something very specific, written thousands of years ago, had been fulfilled in my life. All I could do was recognize that God wasn't finished with me, and that it was time for a total surrender of my life to him. This was the Christ I had invited into my life a year and a half earlier—not some imaginary Jesus to add to my collection of idols, not a hippie Jesus who would help me build my own cool kingdom of self, but the Master with fire in his eyes who had said, "Behold, I stand at the door and knock." I had chosen to open that door. Here he was again, not just knocking; this time, he was breaking it down. I said simply, "Okay, Lord, what do you want me to do?" He said I was to leave that little college town, leave my druggie friends behind, and get involved in a church. At the end of the semester I quit college, moved away, began following Jesus earnestly, and have continued to follow him to this day.

Many years later, a few years before I began practicing centering prayer, I had another dream. You'll need to know a little of my background in order to understand it. When I was about five years old, I would awaken early every morning and go out to the kitchen of our old clapboard house in Colorado, with its old-fashioned white cabinets and homemade white-and-blue curtains. There I would sit near the side door with the big window that faced east. The sunlight would be streaming in the window, and I would sit quietly in the warm sunshine for a long time on the blue linoleum floor that reminded me of the sky full of wispy clouds. I would remain there on the floor, just enjoying the warmth of the sun—much like I sit in centering prayer now.

Fast forward several decades. One night I dreamed that I was there in that kitchen again, but this time, the door was wide open. Once again, morning sunlight streamed in and filled the room, making it very bright. On the floor, there was a shadow in the light coming through the doorway, right over the place where I used to sit—the shadow of a man wearing something like a robe. His arms were spread out to the sides, hands open. In each hand, he appeared to be holding a star. But there was no one—no one I could see, anyway—standing in the doorway; only the shadow. I pondered this for a moment, and then it hit me: it was Jesus standing in the doorway, and the bright places in his hands were not stars. It was the sunlight coming through the holes in his hands.

It was the risen Christ—casting his long shadow over me, watching over me, protecting me, making me aware of his love, his power, his invisible yet ever-so-glorious presence—in my childhood long before I knew him, and throughout my life. This is the mystical Christ, the Lord who makes himself known to his people in dreams, in visions—and in the silence, where we can rest in him, rest in his love, rest in his beauty, as he rested in the silence before creation.

Chapter 8

Transformation

The good man suffers but to gain,
And every virtue springs from pain:
As aromatic plants bestow
No spicy fragrance while they grow;
But crush'd, or trodden to the ground,
Diffuse their balmy sweets around.
             Oliver Goldsmith, *The Captivity*

I have been crucified with Christ;
it is no longer I who live,
but Christ lives in me.
So the life I now live in the body,
I live because of the faithfulness of the Son of God,
Who loved me and gave himself for me.
             Galatians 2:20

Actually, the term "transformation" may be a bit misleading. It's about change, which is very much a Biblical value: God changes us. But the word also implies a shifting from one form to another, when in reality, one of the major things God does in us on the contemplative journey is to shift our focus away from form—the "outward appearance," the preoccupation of the false self—to substance. The substance of a person is the true self, which can only be seen by another true self, the "inner person of the heart," which is "Christ in you, the hope of glory." Man looks on the outward appearance, said the Lord to Samuel, but God sees the heart (1 Samuel 16:7). Peter tells Christian women—and the message is for men as well—that beauty isn't about clothing or hair styles or jewelry or tattoos, but about "the inner person of the heart, the lasting beauty of a gentle and tranquil spirit, which is precious in God's sight" (1 Peter 3:3-4; see the first part of verse 7 as well). But how does this kind of transformation come about? Is there a process God brings his people through to make us Christlike? How does contemplative prayer affect the process? And what do the great mystics of Christian history have to say about that? That's the subject of this chapter.

Freedom from Religion

> **Centering prayer is a face-to-face encounter with the One who knows all the games we play, all the masks we wear, all of our dirty little secrets. And he patiently, gently, lovingly insists that we take off the masks, throw down the toys, let down our defenses, give up all that's in our hands and our hearts, to cling to only him.**

Contemplative prayer is the simplest thing in the world. It's not a technique, not a method, not a religious exercise. It's just sitting silently in the presence of God. Nothing more than that. The false self wants to co-opt the whole thing, to make it all about how long we can remain in silence, how deep we can go with God, how many years we've been doing centering prayer, how much we've grown and changed. That doesn't work. If centering prayer is effective— and it almost can't help but be, if Christ-centered and practiced in a disciplined manner—the false self is being crucified, along with all its little schemes to make centering prayer a part of its kingdom, its rule. And it must be put to death. If allowed to have its way, the false self will take over and become the pope of its own little religion, reciting, *I am the master of my fate: I am the captain of my soul,*[1] as it bows to none but itself—not even God. This is the antithesis of what centering prayer is all about: bowing all we have, all we are, all we ever hope to be, in total submission to God. Emptying oneself, becoming nothing, as Christ did, with him as your guide. And the way to do that is just to sit in silence and humility, seemingly doing nothing, as you surrender every thought to Christ, until he is your all in all.

It's not religion. In fact, it's the end of religion as we know it. Religion allows us to create personas within us—masks we wear, games we play, rules and rituals we require. Centering prayer is nothing less than a face-to-face encounter with the One who knows all the games we play, all the masks we wear, all our dirty little secrets. And he patiently, gently, lovingly insists that we take off the masks, throw down the toys, let down all of our defenses, give up all that's in our hands and hearts, to cling to only him.

Once that process is underway, God's task is to teach us to live in the wild freedom of having nothing but God (and therefore having everything), of teaching us who we really are, introducing us to our true self which can only be found in him, utterly outside the false self's domain. That's what transformation is. It's so far beyond religion, there's not even a name for it. It's the glorious freedom of the children of God that Paul talked about (Rom. 8:21): freedom from religion and religiosity, freedom from religious law and legalism, freedom from pompous phariseeism and pseudo-religious anything-goes-ism. Freedom to love as Christ loved, give as Christ gave, speak as Christ spoke, care as Christ cared. It's the freedom to live in the moment at the Father's behest, at the beck and call of freedom itself, free in the knowledge that God is love and love is the ultimate freedom.

There's only one rule: no rules.[2] In other words, keep it simple. Once you begin imposing rules, conditions, etc., the freedom disappears and religion begins to rear its ugly head. And God will have no other gods before him. Never forget that religion itself can become a god, an idol, a puppet of the false self. And that false self which is so much a part of each of us—that is the greatest idol of all.

Deep Calls to Deep

King David, in Psalm 42, recounts in poetic language how he had seen a deer drinking from a brook and thought what so many of us think at some point in life: "I want to drink from the stream of you, God." The following is my paraphrase of David's great expression of spiritual thirst: "I want to drink deeply of you, to drink my fill of your very life, Lord. I have a great, deep, never-satisfied thirst for you; I want to drink you till I'm drunk with you, God. I want to drink you till I'm completely satisfied, till I'm complete in you. Will I ever arrive? Will I ever be at that place of constantly drinking in your presence, God? Will I ever learn how to satiate my great thirst with the absolute satisfaction and utter fulfillment of God himself? Not the things of God, not theology, not talking about God or reading about God or listening to sermons about God or singing about God, or even singing *to* God, but the actuality the reality of God—that's what I want; that's *all* I want! Baptize me in you, God! Drown me in that living stream, God—drown me in your presence, then resurrect me! Drown me till the 'I' is dead, till there's nothing left in me but you!"

Spending time alone with God, surrendering our emptiness to his fullness, our thirst to his satisfaction, our weakness to his strength, changes us. We have to be brought to a place of pouring out, of emptying ourselves as Christ emptied himself—a place beyond even worship, as we discussed in Chapter 1, though worship can lead us to that place of the pouring out of self.

> He is jealous for me
> Loves like a hurricane, I am a tree
> Bending beneath the weight
>   Of his wind and mercy...[3]

Psalm 40:3 says God puts a new song in our hearts—a song of praise to God—and that "many will see and fear and put their trust in the Lord." But the new song comes only after waiting patiently for God (v. 1)—a time of emptying out the self of its ideas and expectations, a time of making it all about Jesus and not about our agenda. Another way to look at it is, you don't get God's new song until you've made room for it by cleaning out your own stuff, getting rid of your own same-old-song.

The Message Bible translates the last part of Psalm 40:3 to say that people "enter the mystery, abandoning themselves to God." I picture that as being like getting in a rubber raft in a river at the mouth of a dark canyon, only to be carried to the wildest of rapids—and being overwhelmed, yet held safely in God's hands all the way to new life, though it may feel like a pretty rough ride at times. Downstream a few miles from where the deer drank his fill, the brook has become a raging torrent that answers the prayer of David: God's power drowns all that's not of God. "Deep calls to deep in the roar of your waterfalls; all your waves and breakers have swept over me" (Ps. 42:7)—or as the Message Bible puts it, "Chaos calls to chaos, to the tune of whitewater rapids. Your breaking surf, your thundering breakers crash and crush me."

And it doesn't end there: verse 8 goes on to say, "Then God promises to love me all day, sing songs all through the night! My life is God's prayer." He takes us where we can't go by ourselves, and he transforms us in the process until "my life is God's prayer." Peter, walking on the raging sea, was in God's will for him—and when he fell, he still was; he learned something that he couldn't have learned any other way. Peter, like Christ, learned obedience through the things he suffered. Through all those experiences, he was transformed, and his life became God's prayer.

So enter the mystery and abandon yourself to God. It won't always be smooth sailing, but he'll be with you, if you're obedient to the leading of the Spirit throughout the process. You can start from worship, from Bible reading, from praying, but don't stop there. Let God take you deeper into his life, into the Holy of Holies. Go beyond appearances, beyond the veil of this world, beyond the things of God, to God himself, and drink deeply of that living stream, of Christ the Living Water. That's the true heart of worship.

Loving You is Loving Me

One of the simplest and yet most profound spiritual realities—one found in some form in all religions—is the Law of Return. In Eastern religions this is known as the Law of Karma: what you do to others will come back to you. Jesus said, "Give, and it will be given to you—a full measure, pressed down, shaken together, and running over," and "Blessed are the merciful, for they shall receive mercy."[4] The opposite applies too: if you do something to harm another person, even if they don't know about it, you're harming yourself. Paul said, "A person will reap what he sows."[5]

I personally believe the Law of Return is at the heart of the Ten Commandments. In light of that, here's my paraphrase of the Big Ten:[6]

1. No other gods. God is One, and if you try to fragment God into a bunch of little gods, you fragment your own soul.

2. If you make gods for yourself out of wood or stone or metal or plastic or computer chips, you take away from yourself the reality of God's infiniteness and holiness; trivialize God and you trivialize your own soul.

3. If you misuse God's name by using it as a curse word, you curse yourself; or if you try to manipulate luck or God or nature by using his name in a way that's against his will, you bring bad luck on yourself.

4. If you forget the day of resting in God, you become a restless soul.

5. If you disrespect your parents, you disrespect yourself, your own roots, and you miss out on the promise of long life—you cut yourself off from the abundant life in the promised land—God's life in you.

6. If you kill others, something inside you dies too.

7. If you're unfaithful in your marriage, you're unfaithful to yourself too.

8. If you steal, you also steal your own innocence and grace.

9. If you lie to or about others, you lie to yourself.

10. If you covet something that belongs to someone else, you impoverish yourself by tricking yourself into thinking you need that thing, and you lose out on the promise that, in God, you already have everything you could need or want, and more.

There's also an underlying connection between the Law of Return and what has been called, in traditional Christianity, the Golden Rule: do for others what you would want them to do for you. Why? Not just because it's so nice to be nice. Not just to do the religious thing. Not just because your mother told you to. Do for others what you would want them to do for you, because in God's kingdom, God's reality—the only true, eternal reality there is—you *are* one with others; everyone you see is your brother or sister (whether they're Christian or not), and what you do to them, you do to yourself. Cain was wrong: I *am* my brother's keeper, and so are you. What we give to others is what we give to ourselves. How we care for others is how we care for ourselves. Love others as you love yourself— that's the paramount rule. Understanding that when I love another I *am* loving myself, frees me to love others in ways I never could before.

I think all this is exactly what James, the brother of Jesus, meant when he said, "Anyone who sets himself up as "religious" by talking a good game is self-deceived. This kind of religion is hot air and only hot air. Real religion, the kind that passes muster before God the Father, is this: Reach out to the homeless and loveless in their plight, and guard against corruption from the godless world" (James 1:26-27, The Message).

The godless world around us twists our thinking, and twists us, into believing we can do whatever we want, and it won't make any difference. Helping others won't help you, so why bother; hurting others won't hurt you, so go ahead. Do whatever you feel like. That's how life looks to us before we've experienced the setting-things-right of God that Eugene

Peterson talks about again and again in the Message Bible, because until God straightens us out, we're twisted around upside down and backwards, and we don't even know it.

That's why, in this world we inhabit, the simple truths of the Ten Commandments and the Golden Rule/Law of Return are so seldom recognized, so poorly understood, even among Christians. Like the Laodiceans, we think because we go to church on Sundays, glance at our Bibles now and then, and pray to God for parking spaces and for our favorite teams to win, we're rich and have need of nothing, when in truth, we're wretched, pitiful, poor, blind and naked.

James is saying in 1:26-27, prove you're really straightened out by God. Give to those who have nothing, recognizing that in doing so, you're giving to yourself. Care for those nobody else cares for. Encourage the discouraged. Help those whose souls are in the lost and found to find their true Owner. Love the unlovable, because when you do, you're loving and caring for and helping and encouraging yourself. You're binding yourself to God by doing the things Jesus did, being the kind of person Jesus was. You're becoming Christlike and learning to think with the mind of Christ when you act like Christ acted toward others and feel what Christ felt for others. It's then that you begin to see that you are one with God.

Union with God

As I said earlier in the book, when I first encountered the term "union with God,"[7] I said, no way. I even thought about throwing out the book I read it in. To the average non-liturgical Protestant mind, "union with God" sounds like becoming equal with God, or worse, becoming God—something that's anathema to my understanding of truth. A former pastor of mine used to say the main thing to always keep in mind is: He's God, I'm not. So, union with God, no thanks, don't want to get led astray into some strange kind of false doctrine, that's how I saw it. But what the writer said about it intrigued me, and everything else I'd read in the book up to that point seemed right on (or as much as possible given the fact that it was about the paradoxes of Meister Eckhart, who said things like "Every creature is a word of God.") So, I prayed about it, and guess what

God showed me? A lot, actually, including (eventually) strong scriptural basis for the idea. But first, he showed me an analogy.

In the 1980's, divers searching for old shipwrecks in Lake Superior found a different type of treasure: submerged logs—many thousands of them, including huge ancient birch, maple and oak trees—from logging operations going back to the 1800's or earlier. This tight-grained old-growth hardwood timber is mostly gone from our forests today, the result of less than environmentally sound lumbering practices. Lying in the pristine waters of the lake for centuries has made the wood in the logs—some of them up to 800 years old when cut down—even more special than when they were first harvested. Something about the temperature, low oxygen content and freshness of the water at the bottom of Lake Superior actually alters the wood at the cellular level, making it truly "superior;" some logs go for tens of thousands of dollars. In addition to being used for expensive custom furniture, the action of the water on the wood brings out colors not seen in normal wood, so it's great for intarsia and parquetry, highly intricate wood inlay art forms. And musical instrument makers find the wood has exceptional acoustic resonances, making it perfect for making great instruments. Ever since the discovery of the Lake Superior submerged logs, limited-edition violins, guitars, harps and other instruments—highly prized for their brilliant sound— have been made from these long lost logs.[8]

No, what you just read wasn't just a random paragraph about wood; it didn't get into this book by accident. Around the time I started practicing centering prayer, I read about the Lake Superior submerged woods and, as a musician and amateur woodcraft artist, I was fascinated. When I began asking God to help me understand what this divine-union thing was all about, he brought to my mind these hardwoods and the way the water had changed them. When the logs were in the water, completely waterlogged, there was a merging of wood and water, to the point that it would be hard to tell what was wood and what was water, and this changed the structure of every single cell in the entire log. In the embrace of God's love, we can be changed; something amazing can come from divine union, so that we can know and express levels of love we couldn't have been capable of prior to this experience.[9]

The analogy goes beyond the simple merging of water and wood. From the tree's point of view, God allowed it to have exactly the right soil nutrients, light and other factors to grow hundreds of years, so that he could create within it the finest of woods, such as top quality tiger maple, for instance. The tree was cut down—sacrificed, in keeping with God's will—and its limbs cut off, but before it could be milled, it became waterlogged, sank to the bottom of Lake Superior and rested there in stillness, silence and solitude for perhaps two hundred years.

During that time, God allowed the total saturation of its top-quality, fine-grain wood by low-oxygen water, at just the right temperature, to create an accordance of wood and water that changed its identity. The saturation in water raised the superiority of the wood to almost unheard-of levels, perhaps comparable to that used in a Stradivarius violin. When finally resurrected from the lake, God saw to it that the wood was cut into smaller pieces, slowly kiln-dried for nearly three months, then examined by some of the world's finest wood experts. Afterward, some of the tree's wood was carefully crafted by world-class violin makers into instruments of great beauty. In the hands of God and a master violinist, what was once just wood hidden inside a single mighty tree lost in a vast forest is now a magnificent, very expensive violin capable of producing music imbued with a truly magical sound for centuries to come.

In much the same way, say the mystics, being in stillness, silence and solitude, hidden in the depths of God for long periods of time, changes them. In miraculous ways, they experience transformation beyond man's ability to change himself through education, morality or any other human power. The Holy Spirit brings them through long periods of isolation, suffering, self-denial, and loving adoration of God—even during times when they can't sense his presence at all—to a place of union, of knowing God in the very depths of their being, in ways no words can ever convey. There, they are brought to a place where freedom in God becomes real as never before; just like the Lake Superior woods, they take on a new identity. Through long hours deep in God's presence they are changed into men and women who can see as Christ saw and love as Christ loved, who can be a ray of light from God to all, even—especially—with "the least of these." The work of God in them is transforming them into something precious to God that the world can't recognize. They become the Stradivarius violins lost in the attics of humanity, the Mother Teresas of the world—loving, compassionate, generous, kind, self-sacrificing, pure in heart, like pure gold refined in God's fire.

This "union with God" thing raises a lot of questions. For one, does this mean that we *become* God? Because, as I said before, I have a problem with that idea. Looking at what some of the theologians say, you can get pretty bogged down; their writings can be very confusing, though it's usually worth the time to try to understand what they are saying. So I did some research on the subject. There are many references to union with God in the writings of Christian leaders from the first five centuries of Church history. For example, Augustine, writing in the late fourth or early fifth century, said, in connection with taking Communion/ Eucharist, "Not only do we become Christians; we become Christ…If He is the head and we the members, then together he and we are the whole man." [10]

We can look at God this way: God's actions are the same as his essence. In other words, unlike us, God's actions always line up perfectly with who he is in his heart, his essence. That is a theological way of saying God is perfect, in sharp contrast to us humans, whose actions and essences—our core values—are never completely in sync and who are utterly incapable of being perfect, let alone being God. At the end of the day, we're still just clay and he's the potter. But in union with God, we are invited by God to *participate* in God.

Peter tells us in 2 Peter 1:4 that God "has given us his very great and precious promises, so that through them you may participate in the divine nature." This participatory relationship means that in the experience of union with God, we are brought into a place of identifying with him in a more profound way than ever before; our actions and essences become closer to perfect alignment, and closer to God's essence. Like the Lake Superior wood, we begin to take on a new identity as his children when we come into relationship with him; in union with God, we have fully accepted his invitation to participate in him, and he gives us an even deeper, closer identity with him.

Does this mean we reach sinless perfection? From what I see in the Bible, I have to doubt it. I sure don't know anyone like that. Again, he's God and we're not—and yet, in his perfect love for us, God invites his people—at the highest level of contemplative prayer—to experience full participatory union with him. Thomas Aquinas, one of Christianity's greatest theologians, commented in the 1200's regarding 2 Peter 1:4 that "full participation in divinity...is humankind's true beatitude [deepest blessing] and the destiny of human life."[11]

Following from 1:4, Peter goes on to describe a progression, a sort of pathway to sharing in the divine nature which is that "full participation in divinity." It's a path called "escaping the corruption caused by desire." The way stations on the path (and it's a very long path) are: faith (a basic belief in God), excellence (good character), knowledge (spiritual understanding), self-control (alert discipline), perseverance (passionate patience), godliness (reverent wonder), brotherly affection (warm, kind friendliness), and finally, love (unselfish, generous love). For each station, there's no shortcut; you have to go through all the previous ones to get to the next one. This path leads deeper and deeper into the forest of participation in the divine nature, or what some contemplatives call transforming union; the path ends in what the mystics refer to as full union with God: pure, full-hearted, unselfish divine love. Peter says continuing on this path will keep you from being ineffective and unproductive in your Christ-followership, which he describes as a path of moving toward knowing Christ more and more intimately. Conversely, those who camp at the entrance to the path but never really venture down it, Peter calls "blind" or "nearsighted."[12]

As I've said before (quoting some of the great theologians and mystics), although we can know God personally, God is so completely "other" to man that the things of God can only be expressed symbolically. Because contemplative prayer is all about a deep relationship of love with God, mystics since King Solomon, writer of the Song of Songs, have characterized this rapturous love between God and man as being best symbolized by the deepest kind of human-relationship love, the sexual union between a husband and wife totally in love. For some believers, this is a bridge too far; those who denounce and try to refute contemplative spirituality have sometimes accused the mystics of claiming to have sex with God, which, of course, is blasphemy. No Christian mystic I've ever heard of has ever said anything of the kind—only that, in trying to find a comparison people can understand, the sexual relationship of a man and woman fully in love is one of the best metaphors for what happens in divine union.

Paths of Transformation I – John of the Cross

Many of the great Christian mystics have written books on the stages of transformation. I don't consider myself qualified to do that, and that's not my purpose anyway. My purpose in writing this book has been to give those who are interested a glimpse of what it's like to move into the area of contemplative spirituality. Rather than give an overview of the various stages of progression that different Christian contemplatives have come up with, I'd rather just take a brief look at two of the most important—John of the Cross and Thomas Keating—and their views.

John was born into a poor family in Spain in the middle of the 16th century. As a young man full of zeal for God, he became a monk, striving to learn as much about God and the Bible as possible in order to live a godly life. After attempting to reform the Carmelite monastic order of which he was a monk, he was imprisoned in a tiny cell by others in his organization who opposed the reforms. He escaped after nine months, but while in prison, he sought God passionately through contemplative prayer and experienced a profound change in his heart and in his relationship with God. While still in prison, John wrote a long poem, the *Spiritual Canticle*, basically a shortened poetic version of the Biblical *Song of Songs*. The poem is an allegory of a bride (the Bride of Christ) searching many places for her beloved (Christ, the Bridegroom), finally finding him in a beautiful garden. The poem describes the mystical process the soul encounters in seeking union with God through meditation. The beauty of John's poetry has also brought great literary acclaim to him for the *Spiritual Canticle* and another poem, *Dark Night of the Soul,* which are considered to be among the great classics of Spanish literature.

After his escape, John's poem was circulated among others in the reformed wing of the Carmelites; some of them asked him to write a commentary on the poem to help them better understand how to live out the truths his poem taught. The result is *The Ascent of Mount Carmel* and its poetic counterpart, *Dark Night of the Soul*, which describe all the difficulties a person may have during a period referred to as the "dark night of the soul," a time of adversity and deprivation—both spiritually and physically—in a quest for union with God. Darkness symbolizes the hardships and struggles one meets in becoming detached from the world on the journey toward divine union. The term "dark night of the soul" has become a part of our language. It is generally used to refer to a crisis of faith; it is also used to mean a time of difficulty for anyone in any walk of life. But in the original context, it refers specifically to contemplative practice.

The book of the *Ascent* included John's hand-drawn diagram, explained in the text, that detailed in allegorical fashion the journey to the summit of Mt. Carmel, a symbol for union with God (the word Carmel in Hebrew means a garden). The poem is divided into two parts, each representing one of the two stages of the dark night. The first, the night of sense, is referred to as the purification of the senses. The second, the night of spirit, is the more difficult of the two and is referred to as the purification of the spirit. *Dark Night of the Soul* poetically elucidates the ten steps of the ladder of mystical love expounded a few centuries earlier by two of history's greatest Christian mystics, Thomas Aquinas and Bernard of Clairvaux.

The night of sense—which can last anywhere from a few weeks to several years—is often referred to as a purification of the senses. During this time, a sort of lackluster dreariness sets in, reminiscent of Solomon's declaration in Ecclesiastes: "There is nothing new under the sun." It's all been done before; the prayer life and relationship to God, in particular, become monotonous and tiresome. It's as if God is no longer there to inspire the mind and heart; the senses—sight, sound, taste—seem dull. Life itself seems lifeless; your prayer seems meaningless. It feels like you're on your own, set adrift from the presence of God, so that you just don't seem to be able to pray at all with words anymore. Without help from someone who understands this stage—a maturing similar to adolescence—it's hard not to just throw in the towel on God and any further hope of relationship with him. How sad it is that so many believers have reached this point and fallen away because there is so little teaching in the churches today on the process of purification God brings us through in the dark night of the soul. Why doesn't God just let us bypass this step? Because, more than anything else, the dark nights are a purification of our deepest motives.

What John of the Cross says is that those experiencing the night of sense need to learn to just *be* with God, in silence, at peace, not trying to offer word-prayers, not attaching to thoughts, but continually looking to God in silent love. Rather than try to run from this stage, John says a person in this position should welcome it, and that once the night of sense is accepted, God will feed your soul directly, at a subconscious level, with no help from you and unknown to you. Think of this as being like an adolescent who feels he has lost the close relationship with his father that he had when he was younger. The father is still there, protecting and providing—more than ever in some ways—but behind the scenes. John goes on to say that God will be doing a work of grace in your will to attract you to him more and more. Once you come out the other side of the dark nights, the result will be an ability to make decisions by relying purely on God—the house built on the rock—with no input from the false self, the house built on the sand, and the false motives it is built upon.

Again, without proper guidance, once you're in this state, your spiritual walk seems to have become a long uphill crawl. You want to pray with words but it seems you can't; you still like spending time with God although it's not really enjoyable any more. The tendency of many at this point, especially under the influence of the age of reason, is to conclude that their entire walk with God has been a huge illusion, and that they should just walk away from religion altogether. But if you allow yourself to rest in the night of sense, the love God is building deep inside your heart toward him will eventually grow into a fire—what John calls the "living flame of love."

The night of spirit is similar to the night of sense, but is even more intense. The purpose of the night of sense is to weaken the false self and its system inside you; the purpose of the night of spirit is to finish it off once and for all. In both, you come to recognize, more and more, that there is absolutely nothing in you that you can lean on—only God. And what Catholics call the "consolations"—the blessings, the sense of peace, joy, or just the presence of God—seem to dry up completely. Generally, between the two "nights," there is a period of time where things seem to be more or less back to normal between you and God (although God does things differently with each individual); come to find out, it's only coming up for a breath of air before being plunged back down into the darkness of feeling like God is gone from your life.

Some believers experience the dark night without ever touching on or knowing of contemplation, but it is most commonly associated with those who have spent many years in contemplative practice. Because of this, prior to the dark night experience there is the temptation to think you have reached a level of spiritual greatness far above the average mortal. So, following the humiliation of the night of sense, the night of spirit is what God uses to bring an even deeper level of humility, such that you recognize selfishness in even your most noble motivations. You come to realize that you are capable of even the vilest of sins and therefore utterly unworthy of even the crumbs from the Master's table. Through this process, because you can identify with all men, the line between "us" and "them" is erased, so that you are able to eventually see Christ in you and in the world around you more than ever before, even in the smallest of things and in people you may have formerly just written off as "sinners"—"the least of these."

At the onset of the night of spirit, you tend to feel like, "oh, no, here we go again." Again you feel cut off, orphaned, deprived of God's peace , lost, deserted, unable to understand what's going on. Your hunger for God is greater than ever before, but it seems he has stopped feeding you. Remember, it's a purification—sort of like fasting—this time going after the roots of the false self: pride and other spiritual issues. You are flooded with self-knowledge, and you see all kinds of weaknesses in yourself that you never recognized before. The beatitude, or stage of spiritual development, that corresponds to the dark night of the soul, is: Blessed are the pure in heart, for they shall see God. In the night of spirit especially, the Holy Spirit will burn out everything inside you, even your human ideas of who God is and what it means to be a follower of Christ. He does this in order to fill you with pure truth directly from the Throne and the glorious light of his splendor, once all that's still left over from the worldly culture and the false self system is completely gone. It's a difficult journey, but if you continue to wait on God in pure faith, even though you sense nothing of his presence, it more than pays off in the long run; as the Psalmist says, "they weep as they go to plant their seed, but they sing as they return with the harvest" (126:6).[13]

Paths of Transformation II–Thomas Keating

Father Thomas Keating is a monk and former abbot of the Cistercian (Trappist) St. Benedict's Monastery at Snowmass, Colorado. Now in his nineties, he has been an ardent practitioner of contemplation all his adult life. He is a prolific author, writing or co-writing over 35 books on contemplative prayer, and is credited with helping found the modern centering prayer movement, bringing contemplative spirituality from the dark ages to the twentieth and twenty-first centuries. Perhaps Keating's primary contribution to our understanding of contemplation has been his ability to express in modern psychological terms what happens in the human psyche between birth and adulthood that leads to the development of the false self system, and how centering prayer is able to help us get back on the path of living to please God instead of self.

In his many books and videos, Keating explains the development of the false self in the following way. After spending nine months as a fetus, with all our needs lovingly taken care of in the gentle warmth of our mother's womb, we are thrust into the cold, hard world, where we experience pain, hunger, sickness, and numerous other difficulties we are unprepared to deal with. In response to these issues, Keating says, we begin to develop patterns of activity based around three psychological need centers: the need for power and control, the need for safety and security, and the need for affection and esteem. As we grow up, we organize our lives around these areas, creating what Keating calls "emotional programs for happiness" based on these three sets of needs, which gradually become what he refers to as the "energy centers" around which the false self develops.

For example, as we are weaned from milk to more substantial food, something as simple as thumb-sucking may develop in us as a way of replacing the sense of security and affection that we felt at our mother's breast—a measure of control that can serve as a sort of protection (however illusive) against the unpredictable future we are beginning to face. As we grow older, we learn to rely more and more on self to meet the ever-increasing demands of the energy centers, which in turn tends to cause us to focus more and more on self as the center of our universe.

At this point, sin begins to rear its ugly head. When something happens that makes us feel insecure, for instance, such as leaving a neighborhood where we're comfortable and moving to a new town, we may learn that lying and deception appear to give a measure of power, security and esteem. Even a modest measure of distinction or achievement, rewarded by any level of recognition or appreciation, real or imagined, whether on the playground, in the classroom, in the kitchen, or wherever, teaches us that certain actions on our part lead to certain benefits which feed one or more of the energy centers. By the time we reach age eight or so, we are well on the way to building our own little world around our needs and desires, and already becoming the king or queen of our own little kingdom of self.

None of this is particularly new; these ideas are standard psychology theory. What Keating brings to the table is the idea that, since the energy centers which comprise the false self are built largely around self-talk (our "emotional programs for happiness"), the silence of contemplation tends to gradually erode and dismantle these programs. Being still in God's loving presence also, slowly but surely, reveals the true self hidden under the layers of the false self's beliefs and corresponding activities. "Silence," says Keating, "is God's first language; everything else is a poor translation." [14]

Keating also outlines what happens at the subconscious level during contemplation. Over a period of years (or, sometimes, shorter periods), the disciplined practice of centering prayer makes us more and more aware of God's omnipresence and helps us consent in deeper and deeper ways to his action in us; at these times, God becomes, in Keating's words, the "Divine Therapist." With the gentle stirring of our innermost depths by this Therapist, we may become vaguely aware that in the hidden abyss of our subconscious, we are still being affected by painful things that we experienced very early in life.

As we learn to come to a place of profound rest and interior silence in God's Spirit, our psychological defense mechanisms are able to relax and let go of these experiences and the crusts of raw emotion that have built up around them. At these times, occasionally our unconscious releases a barrage of thoughts or emotions, the result of these emotionally painful early-childhood experiences which we were unable to process at the time. Keating refers to this releasing as the "unloading of the unconscious." During these times of spiritual turbulence and emotional pain (which are sort of like ripping a large band-aid off of our emotional self), it's helpful to know that God in his love is allowing this to happen as part of the process of purification and healing. The result is that we are able to love and trust him in greater ways than before, and then we in turn find we have a greater capacity to love others with God's healing love.

Keating likens the divine therapy process of centering prayer to an archaeological dig. The early stages begin to reveal the most recent parts of our lives; the longer we are involved with contemplation, the deeper we are allowing God to dig into our unconscious—the rubble of our false self. Consequently, through this process of self-knowledge, we gradually come to understand more and more about our own life and about how various experiences have affected us. We learn more about the false self system we have built than we ever wanted to know—and we also learn that God has been there all along, in all that has happened to us, in every detail. All that we've buried and hidden is revealed to us, so it's a very humbling process. As with John of the Cross's dark nights, Keating sees this process as God's work of dismantling the false self.

Love is the Hard Part

Walking in love is the goal and the crowning achievement of the contemplative life and of the Christian life. If that's not there, as 1 Cor. 13 says, we're wasting our time. The biblical lists of the fruits of the Spirit and the fruits of the flesh (Galatians 5) give a pretty good indication of whether a person is walking in love or in self.

It's not easy; as singer-songwriter Michael Anderson said so well, "Love is patient, love is kind/Love is tender, love is blind/Love is clean and love is true/Love's the hardest thing to do/Love is the hard part/It's the one light in the dark/It's the arrow through your heart/Love is the hard part."[15] But more than anything else—more than hours of daily centering prayer, more than living in the present moment, more than reciting the Jesus Prayer all your waking hours, more than all the candles and incense and prayer bells in the world—walking in love helps us die to self. It helps us crucify the old nature. It makes us like Jesus to the world around us.

This has always been recognized by the great Christian mystics. William Johnston, in his book *Mystical Theology*, says this: "John of the Cross does not begin by advocating long hours of silent prayer nor does he tell the would-be contemplative to spend many years in solitude. More important is the imitation of Jesus in daily life—"behave in all events as he would." This point is made even more forcefully by [John's] saintly collaborator Teresa of Avila. For all her ecstasies and flights of the spirit, Teresa always insists imitation of Jesus and love of neighbor are more important than sublime experiences in prayer....And this commonsense teaching entered into subsequent mystical theology which held that Christian perfection consists in charity, listing among the adversaries those who held that perfection consists in sublime contemplation."[16]

Love is truly the crown jewel of contemplation. This point cannot be emphasized strongly enough. If our contemplative practice is not moving us closer to loving as Jesus loved, something is wrong. It cannot become a way of making us feel we are better than others. The Pharisees of Jesus's time were a perfect example of how pursuit of God can become mere human religion, all about rules, forgetting love and truth. And contemplative prayer does not exempt us from becoming Pharisees. Those who pursue God through contemplation, according to the Spirit's leading, learn to love; those who don't learn to love end up missing the whole point of who Jesus is and why he came.

If you read through the parable commonly known as The Prodigal Son from the point of view of the culture in which Jesus lived, it looks a lot different than it does to us through the filter of our own cultural context.[17] It's helpful to know the story's background: Jesus told this story, along with The Lost Sheep and The Lost Coin, really a three-in-one parable, in response to the Pharisees' attempt to shame him for eating with "sinners." The Pharisees saw themselves as defenders of God's honor, and Jesus didn't condemn them for that. But they extrapolated on the Ten Commandments and came up with 631, including the rules about not touching or eating with "sinners."

This went along with the Middle Eastern cultural view that eating with someone was the same as accepting them into your family. Since their whole culture was based on shame, this would bring shame on the person who ate with "sinners," their family, and their village as well. So, in keeping with the dictates of their culture, and contrary to the heart of God, the Pharisees drew the line at eating with certain categories of people, choosing instead to disassociate with them and call them "sinners."

But Jesus wasn't in the habit of calling people sinners;[18] that was the Pharisees' term for tax collectors, prostitutes, and other persons they considered to be of ill repute. Many of the people Jesus hung out with fit into that category. He told the three stories to let the Pharisees know that their view of the lost was exactly the opposite of God's, and that such people, contrary to being considered "sinners" by God, were incredibly precious to him. In the three stories, it's not the coin, the sheep, or the son who is the main character; it's the finder of what was lost – God. So the Prodigal Son story should really be called The Waiting Father or The Loving Father.

For the younger son (or any son) to say to his father, "give me my inheritance," was the same as saying "I wish you were dead." It was an unbelievably disrespectful thing, a demand from son to father (disrespectful in itself, and in that culture, a point of deep shame for the family) to give now what he would have received upon the father's death. Those hearing Jesus tell this story would have been deeply shocked at this statement—it was almost unthinkable in their culture for a son to speak this way to his father. Amazingly, instead of backhanding the kid, the father complies. That meant he gave him, not lots of money, but lots of stuff—cattle, sheep, clothing, jewelry, etc.—that the son would have then quickly sold off to the villagers to convert to cash.

Even in our culture today this would be considered a disgrace. But as with Jesus's act of eating with "sinners," the son's actions would have brought tremendous shame not only on him, not only on his family, but also on his whole village. Of course, he would have been selling things at bargain-basement prices, so most of them would have seen these things as an offer too good to refuse; a sheep or a set of pearl earrings at less than half of its value would have been snatched up, knowing that if they didn't take it, someone else would have.

As soon as he was finished with his transactions, the younger son took off for parts unknown—"a distant country"—to leave behind his father and the great shame he had caused. But the Father kept waiting for him to come back, watching the road for his son's return. Here's where we really begin to see the Father heart of God. And after partying it up for a while and spending all his money, after feeding pigs and having nothing to eat himself—a picture of the son's spiritual condition—when the son finally did return (hastened by famine and economic disaster in that distant land, engineered no doubt by God himself), it was the father's turn to do the unthinkable: he ran to his son. For the father to even leave his house was a show of humility; for him to run was shameful, because in order to run, he would have had to lift up his robe and show his legs—something a man of respect in that cultural setting would never do. He runs, embraces and kisses his son—who is still covered with dirt, sweat, the smell of pigs and their manure—and lavishes love on him, giving him full acceptance.

Part of the reason he ran to his son was to get there before anyone else, so that he could let the son and everyone else know that he had his full forgiveness and acceptance, and to shield the son from any criticism that might come from the other villagers. The son had his speech all prepared; he'd been practicing it: "Father, I've sinned against Heaven and against you; I'm not worthy to be called your son; let me be one of your servants." The father let him say the first two parts—confession and recognition of the consequences of his sin—but he stopped him before he could say the third part, because he wanted him to know he had full acceptance as a son and would never be on the same level with the servants.

Meanwhile, the older son is coming in from the fields and hears a party going on. Asking one of the servants what the excitement is all about, he learns that his wayward brother has returned, and that his father has killed the grain-fed heifer. To anyone in that culture, that would mean that this was the biggest celebration of the year, a wing-ding of major proportions. The older son is very offended and refuses to participate; normally he'd be expected to be the master of ceremonies at such an event, praising and complimenting his younger brother in whose honor the party was held. He speaks rudely to his father—again, unheard of in that culture—and says, what about me? I've worked hard for you.

That's the religious mindset: working for God. The younger brother was willing to come back on that basis. The father wouldn't hear of it, but the older brother had been living in that servant mindset for years, rather than living as the fully accepted son he really was. And he had something going on the side: he was thinking in terms of partying with the friends he hung out with, rather than being fully immersed in intimacy with the father who loved him. The father lets him know that "all that's mine is yours"—that he has full acceptance and is loved just as much as the younger son—but that the younger son's homecoming was like a resurrection: the only appropriate response would be the biggest celebration they could pull off.

Then, strangely enough, the story just ends there. Jesus doesn't tell us if the older son accepted his brother or not. He left it up to the Pharisees—and to each of us—to decide how the story ends, because each of us has a choice in the matter. That's because there's a younger brother and an older brother in each of us. The older brother wants rules, religion, everything by the book; the younger brother rebels, then returns and has a chance to experience God's invitation to full acceptance, intimacy, total grace.

Over the course of my life, I've read this story many times; I've read various commentaries on it; I've done Bible studies on it; every preacher whose church I've been a part of has preached on it. And after thirty or so years of being a Christian, I had come to realize that I was definitely the older brother. I had that religious mindset, that commitment to doing all the things a good boy should, not rocking the boat. I longed to have that fuller, deeper, closer walk with God that so many preachers and teachers and writers had promised I could have. Once in a blue moon I would receive God's wonderful outpourings of grace and find myself weeping before him, but most of the time, I just wasn't there. And my life was marked by that conservative, hold-'em-accountable, death-penalty, make-'em-work-for-every-dime, never-give-an-inch attitude that goes along with the older-son mindset. I really didn't understand grace; if you had asked me for a definition, I would have had a hard time giving one, and it wouldn't have been very accurate. In my understanding, mercy was good, but ultimately, God's judgment was more dominant than his mercy. So was mine.

Although I had begun to learn more about what the Bible says about the merciful side of God, my judgmental view didn't really start to change until I began practicing centering prayer. Though I couldn't have said this until a few years into the practice, I realize now that centering prayer fosters intimacy with God in ways that few other aspects of Christianity do. It opens us up to knowing God in ways we always wanted to but never could. It truly aids in the transformation process of becoming like Christ. So if you don't want to change, don't get into centering prayer. If you do, God will most certainly change you. And if you see too much of the religious older-brother heart in yourself—if you long to see the promise of Ezekiel 36:26 fulfilled in your life—"I will give you a new heart...I will take out your stony, stubborn heart and give you a tender, responsive heart"—ask God the Father about the gift of contemplation.

Epilogue

Contemplation and the River of Life

> There inside my dream
> I heard the river roar.
> I stumbled through the darkened mist
> But I couldn't find the shore.
> A voice within the mist said,
> "Tell me, what do you seek?"
> I said, "I have a mighty thirst,
> But I feel so tired and weak!"
> He said, "I am the river
> Full of power and truth.
> You've been looking outside yourself
> When it's there inside of you."
> And the river will flow
> The river will flow
> Through all of the times of your life
> The river will flow
> And the river is love
> The river is peace
> And the river will flow through the hearts
> Of those who believe...
>
> - Whiteheart, "The River Will Flow" (Gersmehl, Smiley)

The life cycle of a large river is a fascinating study. Many world-class rivers, such as the Colorado, the Yangtze, or the Nile, begin high in a mountainous region, fed by melting snowdrifts and tiny springs. A tiny but wild rivulet tumbling under and around boulders, joined by other tiny rivulets to become a small brook, it soon leaps down precipitous mountain faces and over small cliffs to form tiny waterfalls frequented only by marmots, mountain goats, and the occasional snow leopard or condor. The embryonic river, clear as crystal and cold as ice, gradually grows in size as other, smaller water sources feed into it. Before long, it has become an alpine creek, carving its way through mountaintop tundra and down a steep canyon into the high windswept timberline forests, demonstrating from its earliest stages a powerful ability to shape the earth. Joined by other, less significant streams which add their own variations to its unique mineral content, the creek leads past magnificent rock formations, the habitats of eagles' nests.

As the stream becomes wider and stronger, ravens, jays, martens and squirrels dwell in the forests near its bright waters dancing in the sunlight; trout race its rapids and hide in its shadows. The canyon traversed by the creek becomes less steep, more accessible to humans. Soon, hiking trails appear along its banks; hikers marvel at the beauty of the creek and the roar of its waters as their dogs splash among its boulders and drink from its bounty. Further downstream, children dangle their legs from bridges built across the creek's swift current; an occasional fisherman tries his luck in its pools. Dusty rutted roads begin to appear; above the quiet rush of the stream, the roar of all-terrain vehicles can be heard. Houses, colorful in their rustic solitude, can be seen near the creek's banks and waterfalls. Without the stream to bring life, little if anything of human habitation would be seen there.

Eventually, what was once a wild canyon becomes a high mountain valley with the stream, now a small willow-lined river, winding its way through. Herds of deer and elk graze its meadows, foxes chase rabbits on its wooded fringe. Kayakers and whitewater rafters ride its rapids. Ranches begin to appear; cattle graze on its banks and horses cavort near its cataracts. Within a few miles, fields of hay are cultivated, their bales lying like fallen game pieces in the pastures, waiting to be stacked or gathered into barns. As the valley broadens, dusty pickup trucks bump along washboard roads, greeted by the barking of dogs from nearby farms and cabins. Spring snowmelt and summer rain make the river overflow its banks occasionally, while droughts cause it to dwindle to a narrow, languorous trickle amid pools of dying fish.

As the small river becomes gradually larger and slower, a little wider and deeper by the mile, villages and small towns take advantage of its wealth. Railways follow its shores, carrying loads of coal and cattle. Gravel roads give way to two-lane asphalt thoroughfares which eventually become rivers of automobiles, and mountains give way to hills and hills to plains. Hikers give way to camera-wielding tourists bent on taking some nature back with them to the big cities. Their left-behind cigarette butts, cans and bottles begin to be seen on the river's ever-broadening banks and at the edges of the reservoirs its waters now fill. Orchards grow up on the rich soil the river's wanderings have produced over the millennia; bridges cross it, and canals and ditches carry its water into the fields.

The outpourings of contemplative spirituality at various seasons through the centuries are springs of pure water for the Church. Contemplation is a river in the desert, a placid current churning relentlessly through the prairie, the silent water in the depths of lakes fed by and feeding the river, the vast reservoirs of the purest water on earth in aquifers thousands of feet beneath the surface of the ground.

A few dozen miles farther on, larger towns and cities tap into the plentiful water of the river. Power plants make use of its cooling flow, and water purification plants transform the polluted liquid, making it clean and safe. Nevertheless, the level of pollution and trash in the river increases with every city it passes. The inflows from tributaries and springs help to cleanse it as it grows ever wider, but the river is no longer the pristine watercourse it once was. In the cities, the channel is straitjacketed by hydroengineering, so that it can no longer wind freely through the land. Still, dirt banks give way and houses are swallowed by the current every few decades, when heavy rains transform the river into a raging, churning torrent. Such deluges remind those who live nearby that nature is not subject to the will of man.

Growing and flowing through the heartland of a nation, passing factory farms, green fields and forested hills, the river is now a hundred yards wide and growing ever wider. Where Indian canoes once traversed the waters near its shores, speedboats now race across its surface; barges towing lumber begin to appear in its channels. Its twists and turns sometimes allow it to catch up with itself, creating oxbow lakes, proof of the river's ever-changing flow, like a living entity, a vast serpent writhing its way across the land, across the centuries. These lost remnants are sometimes re-crossed by the river long after it has left them to stagnate; the river can even cross itself at times. As it nears the ocean, its course becomes so tangled and confused, like an old graveyard of ancient river passages, that even experienced boat captains and barge pilots at times find it difficult to know which way to go.

And finally, the river reaches the sea, the vast fullness of life, the end for which it began as a surging rill so far away in the high mountains. Its journey completed, the river passes into the great beyond, the mysterious unknown for which it has longed every weary mile of the way, proof that everything in creation changes, that nothing lasts forever. Such is the life of a river.

And such is the life of the Church—from babblers full of joyful noise on the day of Pentecost to weary pilgrims trudging the stations of the Cross on Good Friday, to tiny storefront churches full of the newly born-again, to monks and nuns chanting psalms at midnight in candlelit monasteries, to smiling people serving food at homeless shelters. From its start, the early Church was like a tiny high-mountain brook, fresh and sparkling with the news that the Messiah has risen, leaping wildly over rocks like those newly healed and set free, rushing with vitality even through the rockslides of persecution. And today's Church still is at times like a swift mountain stream bounding over the boulders in its path and moving forward rapidly in the power of the Spirit.

We have also seen our share of slow, plodding faith as well—stalwarts in elderly congregations singing hymns in dusty, steepled buildings full of stained glass, church boards arguing over budgets and policies, murky as the Missouri at times, and just as determined that the work of the Kingdom trudge forward mile by weary mile. Disagreements sometimes cleave the river like large islands in midstream; congregations stuck on minor points of doctrine get cut off from the main stream, then stagnate and die like oxbow lakes under the prairie sun.

The river of Christianity loops and lurches from side to side, from fundamentalist dogmas to liberal precepts, sometimes crossing over itself; the thousands of denominations today make the Church much like a great river delta, with its numerous streams and channels crossing and intertwining with each other. Like the crowds who followed Jesus, there were so many they were stepping on each other (Luke 12:1). In such a situation, there is bound to be plenty of confusion, with many believers just going with the flow, not knowing or caring which part of the river they are in, trusting the Spirit to lead, eyes and hearts intent on reaching heaven as the river flows finally to the open sea.

And like a great river system, when you come down to it, it's all water. Some streams—and some churches—can get so polluted that the water is poison. Much of the water is polluted to some degree. But like pure springs flowing into a river, the Spirit of God quickens the water of the Church, bringing freshness and renovation to grimy, stale streams. Over the history of Christianity, names like Augustine and Martin Luther, as well as movements like the Desert Fathers and the Charismatic Renewal, are these freshets flowing from the springs of heaven to revive, heal and restore the Church.

Not only the Church, but the world around us is at a crossroads as never before—the great river delta of history. As Daniel prophesied many centuries ago, people run to and fro and knowledge has increased—yet our vast knowledge has not brought us closer to God or helped us to know him more fully. Life is stressful and confusing. What the people around us need to see is not more confusion and stress, but the peace that passes understanding. Historically, the Church has been a source of at least some of the confusion, when we should be, as Jesus was, the eye of the hurricane, the hope in the midst of the turmoil of our times. In order for that to happen, we must learn to rest in God, to wait on God, to let the river of God's pure love flow through us. Contemplation is one of the greatest gifts God has given the Church for helping us learn the kind of humility that is at the heart of true Christlike servanthood and selfless, sacrificial love.

The outpourings of contemplative spirituality at various seasons down through the centuries have been springs of pure water for the Church, reawakening multitudes of believers who learn to wait on God in silence. Contemplation is the fresh inflow of life from brooks streaming down amid the boulders in steep canyons above timberline. Contemplation is a river in the desert, a placid current churning relentlessly through the prairie, the silent water in the depths of lakes fed by and feeding the river, the vast reservoirs of the purest water on earth in aquifers thousands of feet beneath the surface of the ground. Contemplation is forsaking everything in life to drink deep of God. Contemplation is finding yourself in water ankle-deep, then knee-deep, waist-deep, chest-deep, chin-deep, and finally over your head (Ezekiel 47:1-5). It is pure water, purer than any on earth: the river of life, sparkling as clear as crystal, flowing out from the throne of the Lamb (Revelation 22).

Contemplation isn't just a way to personal peace, a method for relaxation or a way to get rid of stress. It's so much more, so far beyond anything this world can offer. Contemplation is a way for us as individuals to flow with God's plan for the world, to recognize it and work hand in hand. It's not just you sitting on your chair or cushion meditating. Contemplation is daily laying down your own yoke—your own vision for how your life should look, how it should play out, who you are and what you will be— and taking on Christ's yoke, and then you and Christ pulling together in the same yoke. His yoke is easy and his burden light; he's the one who gives us peace and rest in our souls as we labor with him.

If your Christian life or contemplative practice is all about you, you're doing it wrong, and it will just lead you in circles and end up stagnant and dead, like a bayou or an oxbow lake. But if you're in Christ's yoke, pulling with him, you're part of that great river that flows to the sea, to eternity. And the eternal waters of the Kingdom return to water you, again and again, forever.

Appendix 1

Frequently Asked Questions

Q. Aren't contemplative prayer and all types of meditation a new-age thing?
A. The new age movement began in the 1970's; Christian contemplative prayer began at least 1600 years earlier, in the fourth century Church, with roots going back clearly to the second century Church Fathers and to Christ himself. There is strong evidence that various types of meditation were practiced by the Jews long before Jesus. There's also a lot of reason (though no hard evidence) for thinking that Paul, John and other first-century Church leaders, as well as Christ himself, practiced extended "be-still-and know-that-I-am-God" sessions similar to what we know today as centering prayer. It's important to realize that the character and nature of centering prayer and contemplation, while seeming similar in some ways to new-age and occult practices, is actually the opposite in purpose and design: rather than trying to gain spiritual power or channel a spirit, the objective of contemplation is to lay down one's life to God— to yield to Christ in total surrender, to submit to the Holy Spirit— one day at a time, one thought at a time.

Q. I've heard that meditation of any type, including meditative prayer such as contemplation, subjects the practitioners to demonic influence by emptying their minds.
A. I know that idea has been passed around in churches for decades, but I find no biblical basis for it. Luke 11:24-26 has been cited as a source for the idea. Here Jesus had been accused of casting out demons by the prince of demons. He shows how irrational that idea is, then says that for someone who has had a demon cast out, it's important to be filled with God, so the demon can't re-enter. The teaching has nothing to do with emptying the mind of the thoughts one's false self feeds on to build its own kingdom. On the contrary, Isaiah 26:3 makes it clear that we need

to keep our minds on God, which entails getting rid of thoughts to be attentive to God's presence alone. The next FAQ deals with numerous places in the Bible that address the issue of contemplative prayer and spirituality.

Q. Is contemplation Biblical?

A. Countless millions of Christians from the fourth century (or earlier) to our time have certainly thought so. Let's just take a look at a few places in the Bible that we consider to be "contemplative" scriptures.

Gen. 24:63 – Isaac went out to the field to meditate, and God brought him Rebekah.

Psalm 46:10 – "Be still and know that I am God."

Psalm 62:1a – "My soul finds rest in God alone" (NIV); "For God alone my soul waits in silence" (NRSV)

Psalm 104:34 – let my meditation be pleasing to him.

Matt. 14:13, Mark 1:34, etc. – Jesus went off by himself to seek God in quiet and solitude. (I suspect that most of the great men and women of God in the Bible did the same, from Enoch and Noah to Paul and Timothy, and that this was a common enough practice that it usually wasn't mentioned or commented on in the Biblical accounts.)

I Corinthians 15: 31 – Paul's pronouncement, "I die daily."

II Corinthians 4:16, 18 – ..."Though outwardly we are wasting away, yet inwardly we are being renewed day by day...So we fix our eyes not on what is seen, but what is unseen. For what is seen is temporary, but what is unseen is eternal."

Philippians 2:5-8 – Paul's encouragement to believers to take on, as Christ did, the attitude of a servant and to die to self.

Ephesians 3:16-19 – Paul's prayer for all believers "to know this love that surpasses knowledge, that you may be filled with the very nature of God."

Hebrews 3:1 (with reference to Heb. 2:14-18) – we must fix our eyes on Jesus. That's a call to contemplative prayer.

Hebrews 4:9-11 – about God's rest and our labor to enter into it.

Hebrews 11: 27 – Moses "persevered because he saw him who is invisible."

And, consider this: II Corinthians 3:18 – "And we, who with unveiled faces all reflect the Lord's glory, are being transformed into his likeness with ever-increasing glory, which comes from the Lord..." (NIV); notably, an alternate translation for the word "reflect" is "contemplate" in

NIV. A historical study of the word "contemplation" will show it to mean more than just pondering; it refers to "a state of mystical awareness of God's being" (Webster's Ninth New Collegiate Dictionary).

Q. What's Christian about contemplative prayer?

A. Dying to self to be transformed into the image of Christ. This is the heart of contemplative prayer. It's a way of laying down your life, taking up your cross and following Jesus; it's a way of allowing the Holy Spirit to change you more into the life of Christlike love, service and surrender.

Q. What do you do when centering prayer is difficult?

A. When the thoughts just won't leave you alone and you can't seem to focus on God for more than a second or two, there are two methods that I've found to be helpful. One is to use a short "active prayer" such as the Jesus Prayer; the other is to focus on your breathing. Or you can combine the two. The Jesus Prayer has been used for many centuries in the Orthodox Church and was introduced to the rest of the world in the late 1800's by the book *The Way of a Pilgrim*, written by an anonymous Russian Orthodox Christian. This short prayer is as follows: "Lord Jesus Christ, Son of God, have mercy on me, a sinner." Abbreviated versions are also used; after years of trying various formulations of this and other active prayers, I found that what works best for me is "Lord Jesus, have mercy." I use this prayer while driving, along with deep breathing; the "Lord Jesus" part goes with the inhalation and the "have mercy" part goes with the exhalation. When focusing on the breath, bear in mind that in Hebrew and many other languages, the words for breath, wind, and spirit are the same word. So in focusing on your breathing, you are, in a sense, focusing on the Holy Spirit. (There's more about the breath in Appendix 7: The Spirituality of Breathing.)

Q. Do you have to sit in a chair to do centering prayer?

A. No, if you can sit cross-legged or in the lotus or half-lotus position, that works well too. You can also kneel; there is a small bench called a "kneeler" or "meditation bench" that some people find helpful. What you don't want to do is sit on a couch or easy chair. It's not that you don't want to be comfortable; you just need to sit up straight so you don't fall asleep. It's best to sit so that your knees are lower than your rear; this keeps your blood flowing at an optimal rate, which enhances alertness.

Q. How is Christian contemplation different from, say, Zen Buddhist meditation?

A. Hindu and Buddhist meditation aim for mental clarity through awareness by way of concentrated attention. Centering prayer and contemplation aim for purity of heart by a constant practice of letting go of our selfish desires, thoughts and feelings, to make our minds and hearts available only to God. Also, the objective of Eastern meditation is to come to the point of realizing that you are one with the universe. The aim of contemplation is to attain what 16th century writer Jean-Pierre Caussade referred to as "abandonment to divine providence," that is, complete surrender of self and its desires, plans and goals to the will and work of God. One of the most common fruits of that complete surrender is union with God, the realization that God is all in all and that you are one with him and one with all things through him, which is similar to the Eastern objective of meditation, but again, for Christians, it's all about knowing God through Christ and the Holy Spirit, not about attaining that sense of universal oneness.

Q. Why is contemplation necessary?

A. It's not that you can't have a great walk with God without being a contemplative. It's all about having a passionate relationship with God, so much that he becomes the lover of your soul. Contemplation is a gift that I believe God is restoring to the 21st century Church, just as the gifts of prophecy, tongues, etc. were restored to the Church in the twentieth century. If God gifts you with contemplation, you will have a deeper, richer, more meaningful walk with God than if you choose not to accept the gift.

Q. Why hasn't the Church taught contemplation, if it's in the Bible?

A. Contemplation was very much a part of standard Christian teaching until the "Enlightenment" or "Age of Reason" convinced most in the Church, contrary to the Bible and Christian history, that this was not how God should be worshiped or followed. Since at least the third century, there have always been believers who practiced and taught contemplative prayer in the Church. In this book, I try to show as clearly as I can that contemplation goes back to Jesus and the Apostles, and to the Jewish culture before them.

Q. Are there dangers involved in contemplation?
A. There are potential risks if it is not practiced properly. The first risk is that someone will just decide on their own to follow the contemplative path, without waiting on God to see if it is a gift he has chosen for that person. You can't just do it on your own; it's all about God, and it's by his grace and constant guidance, or not at all—his way or the highway, but in a way that's more loving and gracious than you can imagine. Trying to pursue the contemplative journey without God can open the door to extreme egocentrism, because rather than the false self being crucified, it takes over and becomes a god to itself. I also think trying to become a contemplative without God's leading could perhaps lead to mental illness or demonic activity.

Q. If meditation is part of what led the New Age Movement astray, why should anyone believe it won't lead Christians astray as well?
A. If you don't know the Lord, your meditation will probably tend to be focused on self and on your frame of reference in life, whatever that is. If it's anything but God, you're likely to veer off into things that aren't of God but are of the god of this world, the father of lies (John 8:44). On the other hand, just as you can't say Jesus is Lord except by the Holy Spirit, you can't seek to die and be resurrected with Jesus in centering prayer except by the Holy Spirit. God's guidance is everything, bearing in mind that staying rooted into the Word is a vital part of his guidance.

Q. How does using the sacred word help you keep your focus on God? It seems like a lot of work.
A. If it seems like a lot of work, you're doing it wrong. In centering prayer, the sacred word is not used like a weapon against thoughts. It's incredibly gentle, like a snowflake landing on a fawn's nose, or like a baby's sigh. It's whispered to God, not with the voice, but in the heart and mind, as if calling softly to one's father in a dream, calling for a simple touch of reassurance, calling to make sure he's still there. It's as silent and gentle as a wordless glance into the eyes of the one you love the most.

Q. Does centering prayer help in spiritual warfare?
A. Yes, if done properly and consistently, it can. Centering prayer helps train your heart and mind to constantly look to God with every thought,

feeling, memory or desire, laying each of those things at his feet in poverty of spirit. Then, you carry that attitude into everyday life. That's a big help in the fight against temptation; when the temptation comes, you do the same thing that you do in centering prayer: look to God as you mentally say your sacred word, fix your gaze on him, and keep returning your focus to him every time it comes. I also find that deep breathing does the same thing—like the use of a sacred word, it can be a symbol for God, something to help you call on him, focus on him, and trust in him all at once. When combined with the centering prayer attitude of constantly looking to God, it's simple but powerful. The same is true with using an "active prayer" such as the Jesus Prayer. Unlike traditional spiritual warfare, with this type of spiritual warfare, you're not trying to rebuke or defeat Satan; like David in the caves, you're hiding in God and letting him deal with the enemy. To me, the use of centering prayer and the sacred breath for spiritual warfare helps us daily to see the truth that God's strength is perfected in our weakness. Another way of looking at it is this: every time you use the sacred word, sacred breath, or the Jesus Prayer, you're saying yes to God and no to whatever the enemy wants to distract you with. And if the intentions of your heart are pure and humble, God honors that every time.

Q: What does God say to you during centering prayer?
A: You seldom if ever hear from God during centering prayer, but you are often aware of his presence and his love for you. Think of Ecclesiastes chapter 3: it's a time for silence, not speaking; it's a time for embracing God and being embraced by him. But it tends to make you more open and sensitive to hearing from God at other times when you're not practicing centering prayer.

Appendix 2

Paradoxes I Have Known and Loved

Paradox: a statement or situation that seems contrary to common sense. Paradoxes can be true or false; some are in the form of word-illusions. Biblical paradoxes are true and can be gateways to help us grow in Christ if we look for and meditate on them in our personal worship time. I'm convinced Jesus himself did this; otherwise his own life and teachings would not have been so full of paradox. In this section, I present some of my favorite paradoxes. Some people may argue that some "paradoxes" are really more irony than paradox, and they may be right, but as far as I can tell, the examples I present really are paradoxes.

> "…For the power of paradox opens your eyes
> and blinds those who say they can see."[1]

Paradoxes of Nature and Everyday Life

Here's an example of a catch-22, a term coined from a novel by that name, by Joseph Heller. A catch-22 is a dilemma created by contradictory situations. Here's an example from my life: I work as a shuttle driver early in the morning, and traffic can be stressful. Centering prayer when I first get up helps, but that means I have to get up at 5 a.m. or, better, 4:30. And I'm not a morning person! So trying to get up early enough is stressful; getting up earlier in order to have time for centering prayer is more stressful. But without it, as I said before, my job is stressful. So I do my best to get up at 5 a.m. or earlier.

Here are a few everyday paradoxes:

- Sometimes we can't see the forest for the trees.

- Sometimes things are hidden in plain sight.

- When you stir a cup of tea, the leaves gather in the center, although centrifugal force pushes them outward.

- Why is water, which is so much more useful than diamonds, so much cheaper?

- Hegel's paradox: We learn from history that we do not learn from history.

- Murphy's law: Anything that can go wrong will go wrong.

- The more things change, the more they stay the same.

- If God knows everything, then at the instant he created you, he knew all the decisions you'll make in your life. So if that's true, how can there be free will?

- And, one from Einstein: "Why can we explain things at all?" [We must recall] Einstein's emphatic assertion that "The eternal mystery of the world is its comprehensibility." For Einstein, explicability itself clearly requires explanation. The most incomprehensible thing about the universe is that it is comprehensible."[2]

There are also linguistic paradoxes (why do we park in driveways and drive on parkways?) One example of this is an idea I've seen on bumper stickers around military bases: freedom isn't free. In other words, the liberty we enjoy in America comes at a cost—the lives of those who fight for it. The spiritual side of this is that Jesus bought our freedom, but he paid for it with his life. I consider the "freedom isn't free" saying a linguistic paradox because it involves two different meanings of the word "free;" I suspect that it would not translate well into other languages.

Some paradoxes of language are called autoantonyms—words that have two meanings which are opposite; an example is the word "bolt"—to fasten something so it can't move, or to move very rapidly. My favorite example, however, is the word "cleave." The English word "cleave" is a study in paradox all by itself. It has two definitions—two more or less *opposite* definitions. The first is "to adhere firmly and closely or loyally and unwaveringly;" it is synonymous with "to stick extremely close to (someone or something)." The second definition is "to divide by or as if by a cutting blow" (think of a meat cleaver); it is synonymous with "to split apart." And believe it or not, in contemplative spirituality, both definitions of "cleave" are meaningful at the same time. Contemplation teaches us to cleave *away from* our attachments to the things of the world—that is, we become *detached* or live in a state of *detachment*. And at the same time, through contemplation we cleave *to* God; we become so close with God that we become one with him—"union with God."

Interestingly, the word "contemplation" is also an autoantonym: it means both thinking deeply about something, and surrendering all thoughts to God and silence, until there are no more thoughts, just God. As I said at the start of Chapter 1, both meanings are valid in today's world, but the second—silence beyond thought—is the original meaning.

And, there are natural paradoxes that reflect God's truth:

- Light is what makes things visible, yet light itself is invisible. The same is true with God—he opens our eyes to truth and his Kingdom, yet he can't be seen.

- A seed can't bring forth life unless it dies (John 12:24).

- Water seeks the lowest level, so it is the humblest of elements; yet it can wear down mountains over time and, when flooding, can bring great destruction, so it is the most powerful of the natural elements.

- It is the empty space inside things that makes them useful and valuable. Consider a house: the walls and roof are important, but it's in the empty space that living takes place. [3]

Popular culture brings out many paradoxes. There are many songs whose lyrics contain paradoxes; here are a few of my favorites:

- Freedom's just another word for nothing left to lose
  ("Bobbie McGee," Kris Kristofferson)

- He who knows he knows, knows nothin'
  But he who knows he knows nothin' really knows
  ("Hangman Hang My Shell On A Tree," 60's-70's band Spooky Tooth; the idea goes back to Socrates).

And two from the 60's-70's band It's A Beautiful Day:
- Hot summer day carries me along to its end, where I begin
  ("Hot Summer Day")

And this amazing jigsaw puzzle of a paradox:
- Time is too slow for those who wait
- And time is too swift for those who fear
- And time is too long for those who grieve
- And time is too short for those that laugh
- And love is too slow for those who wait
- And love is too swift for those who fear
- And love is too long for those who grieve
- And love is too short for those that laugh
- But for those who love...Time is eternity
  ("Time Is")

Paradox: Beyond Logic to Spiritual Understanding

People try to avoid paradoxes; they seem like speedbumps in the road of understanding. But they aren't; truly, they're gateways to spiritual knowledge, which is a deeper kind of understanding that goes beyond logic. Without paradoxes we can't see into the deeper things of God. That's why Jesus spoke in paradoxes so often, and why is life is so full of them (more on that below). It's important to take paradoxes on their own terms and work through them, rather than try to steer around them. This is one of the places where the rubber meets the road in the Christian walk. Unfortunately, most churches do little if anything to foster the kind of spiritual seeing that comes from paradox meditation.

Here's an excellent view of paradox from the Jewish perspective, written by Rabbi Aryeh Kaplan:

> "The Shema[4] ends with "Adonoy is One" (*Adonoy Echad*). Here we are saying that no matter how many different ways we experience the Divine, they are all One and all have one source. We recognize that there is a basic Oneness in the universe and beyond, and in our search for the transcendental, it is precisely this Oneness that we are seeking. We see in God the most absolute Unity imaginable, the Oneness that unifies all creation.
>
> The more we realize this, the more we begin to see that on an ultimate level there is no plurality. If there is no plurality, then we are also one with God. When saying the word "One" (*Echad*) in the Shema, one can realize this in a deep sense.
>
> An objection might be raised here. If a person is one with God, how can he continue to exist? If he is one with God, then there is no room left for him to have an independent personality. How is it possible for a person to ever experience this oneness with God? The answer is that this situation is a paradox. To say that I exist and that God exists, and that I am one with God, is like saying 1 + 1 = 1, which is, of course, logically impossible.
>
> Nevertheless, we cannot say that logic is higher than God. Quite the contrary. Just as God created everything else, He also created logic. Logic is a tool of God's, but He is

never bound by it. Therefore, if He wants one plus one to be one, it is no problem for Him. And if he wants a person to be one with Him, and still be able to experience it, it is also possible for Him.

This principle allows us to understand all theological paradoxes. To a large degree, in creating the world, God bound himself by logic. Since he created man in "His image," man uses the same logic that went into creation and can therefore understand God's creation. However, when it suits God's purpose in creation to transcend logic, He can also do so, and this is what we perceive as a paradox. If God is the Creator of *all things*, then He must be the creator of the very concept of will. But how could God create will without this in itself being an act of will? In a sense, the creation of will is by its very nature paradoxical, like trying to pull yourself up by your own bootstraps."[5]

Biblical Paradoxes

The paradoxical sayings of Jesus have a way of overthrowing the mind to get to the heart:

- The last will be first and the first will be last. (Many of Christ's teachings revolve around this idea.)
- He who would save his life must lose it; he who loses his life for me will save it.
- You must be born again.
- Beatitudes:
  o Blessed are the poor in spirit, for theirs is the kingdom of heaven.
  o Blessed are the meek, for they shall inherit the earth.
  o Blessed are those who are persecuted for the sake of righteousness, for theirs is the kingdom of heaven.

Other Biblical paradoxes:

- We are in the world but not of the world (John 17:11-16).
- We must labor to enter God's rest (Heb. 4:11)
- There are many paradoxes in the Book of Proverbs; for example, 11:24-25: one person is stingy, yet never has enough for himself; another is generous yet always has more than enough.

Paul's paradox:

- 2 Cor. 12:9-10—God's strength is perfected in weakness, so Paul learned to rejoice in his weaknesses.

Paradoxes of the Christian life:

- Only the crucified can live the abundant life
- Only God, who never changes, can truly change us
- The four great paradoxes of the Christian life:
  - o the paradox of spiritual growth: The more you grow spiritually, the further from spiritual perfection you realize you are.
  - o the paradox of spiritual enlightenment: The more enlightened you become as an adult, the more childlike will be your wisdom.
  - o the paradox of knowing and mystery: If you are to know the Living God, you must be comfortable with mystery.
  - o the paradox of love: The more love you want to experience, the more love you must give away.[6]

And here are three different but related ideas from three different Bible passages. Each contains the words "all things" (or similar wording, depending on the translation). Taken together, these form a paradox which addresses the issue of nonattachment:

- Colossians 1:16-17, 20: "...all things were created by him...and in him all things hold together...and through him to reconcile to himself all things..."

- Romans 8:32: "He who did not spare his own Son, but gave him up for us all—how will he not also, along with him, freely give us <u>all things</u>?"
- Luke 14:33: "Anyone who does not give up <u>all things</u> he has cannot be my disciple."

Here's a similar view of nonattachment, seen from a different angle: By practicing nonattachment to things, we become aware that we are one with all things. We can't know that oneness as long as we are attached to things, but once we let go of everything, we discover that we have everything. The letting go is just losing what the ego thinks it has, which is all just illusion; once the soul is freed from that illusion, it discovers the real possessing of all things in the oneness of all things that we have in God, in love. I think that's at least part of what Jesus meant when He said, "If anyone wishes to come after me, he must deny himself, and take up his cross and follow me. For whoever wishes to save his life will lose it, but whoever loses his life for my sake and the gospel's will save it [or, find it, Mt. 10: 39]. For what does it profit a man to gain the whole world, and forfeit his soul?" (Mark 8: 34-36). From the contemplative point of view, it's all about letting go of things in the mind, all but God.

Paradoxes in the Life of Christ

The life of Jesus Christ is full of paradoxes; here are a few for you to consider:

- At his birth, the Creator of all became a helpless creature.
- The high and holy became meek and lowly.
- He began his ministry by being hungry from fasting, yet he is the Bread of Life.
- He wept, yet in the end he is the one who will wipe away all tears.
- He was sold for thirty pieces of silver, yet he redeemed the world.
- He ended his ministry by being thirsty on the Cross, yet he is the Living Water.
- He who knew no sin became sin for all sinful humanity.

- By his death he defeated death, so his death is the source of our eternal life.
- His defeat at the Cross was His ultimate triumph.

The Paradoxes of Jesus and the Centurion of Golgotha

Matthew 27:54—When the centurion and those with him who were guarding Jesus saw the earthquake and all that had happened, they were terrified and exclaimed, "Surely he was the Son of God!"

Mark 15:39—And when the centurion, who stood there in front of Jesus, heard his cry [at the moment of death] and saw how he died, he said, "Surely this man was the Son of God!"

Luke 23:47—The centurion, seeing what had happened [darkness over the land for several hours while Christ was on the Cross, followed by an earthquake and a violent windstorm just after his death], praised God and said, "Surely this was a righteous man."

We have no reason to believe this was the same centurion whose servant Jesus healed in Luke 7. There were many centurions in Israel at that time; the other was in the Galilee area, and this one was in the Jerusalem area nearly a hundred miles away. (He was apparently not Cornelius the centurion of Acts 10 either; that was in Caesarea, about 60 miles away.) Therefore, we can assume that until the Crucifixion this centurion had no awareness of Jesus being the Son of God or anything other than a convicted criminal, though perhaps he had heard rumors that Jesus claimed to be the Son of God. As Jesus was dying on the Cross, many who were present taunted him and hurled insults such as, "Jesus, come down from the Cross if you're really the Son of God!" So the centurion had probably heard the idea by the time Jesus died.

When Jesus breathed his last breath and surrendered to death, the centurion, seeing how he died and the darkness, the earthquake and the violent windstorm that took place at that time, cried out, "Surely this was the Son of God!" He may have just been fearful—or he may have experienced a genuine revelation of who Christ was, not through Christ's life or words, but through His death.

If the centurion indeed believed in Christ at this point, consider these paradoxical facts:

- Christ's life ended, saying "it is finished!" But for the centurion, those words and his own words—"Surely this was the Son of God!"—signaled that his new life was just beginning.

- Christ, a man of peace known as the Prince of Peace, suffered a violent, bloody death. The centurion, a man of war, found life and peace.

- The centurion, who was in charge of carrying out Jesus' crucifixion, was also the first post-crucifixion recipient of God's grace and the first post-crucifixion Gentile convert.

- Having probably heard Jesus say "Forgive them, Father, for they know not what they do," he became the first fruits of that forgiveness—the first proof that God the Father had answered Jesus' prayer.

If God had such grace and mercy as to make a glorious example of the person who was in charge of putting his own Son to death, we can be sure his grace is more than sufficient for us too. That's cause for celebration! That's why, as Paul said, we glory in the Cross—a gruesome ancient Roman instrument of torture and death—because Christ's death means life for us. And we learn to die with Christ, because only the crucified are truly alive.

Appendix 3

Lectio Divina

Lectio Divina is an ancient scripture meditation practice; in Latin, Lectio Divina means "sacred reading." Its purpose is to help cultivate a deeper, closer friendship with God; think of it as conversing with God about a specific short passage of Scripture, allowing God to direct the questions and to enlighten you regarding the meaning and application of the passage. Lectio works very well as a lead-in for centering prayer; the two practices are separate and distinct, yet they can feed and greatly complement each other. The lectio process typically takes anywhere from five to fifteen minutes. The most common format is the 4-R method: Read, Reflect, Respond, Rest. Take a short passage of scripture (a verse or two, or a parable of Jesus—not a whole chapter); generally, the shorter the passage the better. Many people read two or more chapters of the Bible daily. If you do this, ask God to show you what is the single most important thing in your reading for that day. Or just use one of the many daily-bible-verse resources available online; many Christian organizations have their own list. (If there's more than one basic idea, you're taking on too much. Simplify.)

Once you've chosen a passage, *read* it four times very slowly, following the pattern outlined below, asking God to speak to you in each part of the process. With the first reading of the chosen passage, focus on each word, each phrase, and the basic idea that ties it all together. Look for a word or phrase in the passage that seems to carry the most weight—the part you are most attracted to. Then, repeat that part over and over, till you feel it's planted in your mind and heart. Afterward, follow each of the three additional readings with one of the other three R's: Reflect, Respond, Rest.

After reading the passage again slowly the second time, *reflect* on what you have read. Turn it over in your mind and keep asking God to show you what he wants you to learn and understand about it. Throughout your reflection, be open and receptive to God. Some suggestions for reflection: What did the passage mean to the original writer or hearer(s)? Can you picture in your mind how the passage would have played out in the lives of the original hearers? How would it play out in your own life? Is there a play on words or a paradox involved? If so, how does that affect the meaning? You may also think of other Bible passages that relate to the one you're meditating on; if so, briefly think about one or two and how they connect to your main passage, then return to reflecting on that main passage. Again, be open to God's leading, more than to your own exploration of the passage.

When you feel you've gone as far in this direction as God is taking you, then read the passage again slowly and begin to *respond*. In other words, pray about the verse in terms of how it applies to people, and specifically, how God would have you apply it in your life or how he is applying it. Without getting off on rabbit trails, be open to memories the passage may trigger. Keep prayerfully returning to the passage and to God's presence in the silence around you, with a view toward living out the verse, and to giving thanks or praise to God. When you've gone as far as God is taking you, you will usually feel your focus turning more to God and away from the passage, although it will still form a background in your mind.

At that point, read the passage once more slowly, then let it go and let your focus return to God; without getting too cerebral, be passively aware of how the verse may have changed your view of God. Then, let go of everything but God—every thought, concept, memory, or emotion—and cling to nothing but God, as a feather floating in the air clings to nothing and yet is directed by the air itself, as if becoming one with the air. This is the *rest* stage, which quite naturally leads into centering prayer and contemplation.

Note: Don't be locked into the above order of the read-reflect-respond-rest pattern. God may lead you in a different order: sometimes God directs you to begin responding partway through the first reading. Or he may draw you back to further reflection after the response step. And sometimes he takes you straight from the first reading into the resting step. Let the Spirit lead; be sensitive to how he is leading. The more you practice lectio divina, the better you get at being sensitive to the Spirit. If things seem to stall out and you don't sense God's leading at all, or if at any point you notice that it's no longer God but you who is guiding things, go back to the passage and move on to the next step.

The Hidden Things of God

There are things in the will and purposes of God that are open, exposed to the world. "Do not kill," "Do not steal," "honor your parents"— pretty much everywhere, these things are understood; murder, theft and dishonoring one's parents are wrong in every society (though there are cultural tweaks to even these in some places, including America, and there can be much more depth to them than meets the eye; see Appendix 7, The Ten Commandments: Four perspectives). And then there are those parts of the Bible that are hard even for many Christians to understand: the finer points of Leviticus, the head-covering stuff in 2 Corinthians, much of the book of Revelation, etc.

Speaking of which, the scroll in Revelation that was sealed with seven seals, that no one in heaven or earth could open except the Lamb (Jesus), had writing on both the outside and the inside. Most of it was on the inside. (How John knew this, by the way, is one of the many mysteries of Revelation.) I think what that means is, what's written on the outside are the things easily understood; what's written on the inside consists of the "deep things of God" that the Spirit searches (1 Cor. 2:10). Most of the will of God revealed in the scroll involved God's wrath and judgment on humanity for ignoring and choosing to disobey him in regard to things they knew they should do or avoid.

But you don't get into the deep things that the Spirit searches just by a cursory reading of the Bible. Even most Bible studies won't reveal much more than surface stuff. We have to sit with the Word, open up to it, allow it to speak to our hearts. Like God himself, we must take his Word on its own terms, or not at all. You can't know God or have relationship with him based on your own agenda. It's the same with the Word.

"For the world to change, our thinking must become different, selfless, endlessly responsive, ethical. We must learn not to consume a text, but to allow it to call us. We must learn to listen, to receive and respond. Meaning becomes a gift that we allow to live within us and return to the giver with our whole being."[1]

Properly done, this is what Lectio Divina is all about. You don't dig into the Word like a backhoe digging up gravel. You wait on it, like a servant; you carefully, lovingly search the verses, the sentences, the phrases, the words, like a master gardener searching his rows for just the right tomatoes, cucumbers, spinach leaves, to make a salad for a king. You don't demand answers or understanding; you let it come to you. The Word, after all, is alive. Those who wait on it, walk with it, learn to feel it, to rest in it, to sense the smiles, the pain, to recognize the sly winks and the patient yearnings—they are the ones who eventually see the subtle nuances of the personality of God in his Word.

Again, the standard formula for Lectio Divina, if you can saddle something so wild and free as the living Word of God with such a human thing as a formula, is: read, reflect, respond, rest. But even that, you don't control. It comes in any order the Holy Spirit pleases. There are times when, as soon as you glance at the first word, God takes you straight into resting in that Word, resting in Him with just a single word. At other times, after reflecting on a passage—turning it over and over like a gemstone, trying to comprehend the incomprehensible—you can find yourself responding in prayer with words that surprise you, even shock you, because they don't come from you. At such times, you are no longer reading the Word—it is reading you, praying you, changing you.

Not that you never see things like this apart from Lectio Divina. Most people who read the Bible have experienced seeing a phrase "jump off the page" at them, or encountering a verse that appears to have been written for them alone, as if directly from God for the situation they're in at that moment. God is liberal with his gifts. He rewards those who diligently seek him. He feeds the ones who hunger for him with the bread of life even when they were only expecting natural food; he heals the dogs with the crumbs that fall from their master's table. All the more reason to forsake the mere reading of God's holy Word as if there will be a test to make sure our eyes are scanning every word.

Man looks on the outward appearance, but God sees the heart. That applies not just to our perceptions and treatment of others, but to our treatment of his Word as well. There are those who claim to love God and his Word, yet they treat the Word as its master. A true pastor, a person who truly loves God, is one who is the servant of the Word. Some people go to seminary to encounter God, only to learn to dissect his Word like a dead frog in a biology class. That's not the way to learn, to discover, to honor the living Word of the living God. The way to learn it is to sit at the feet of the Master, to wait on him as a servant, as a child hungry to learn. To hide under the shadow of his wings, to hide in God until the hidden things of his Word are revealed to you. To be transformed as the hidden things become real in you.

Appendix 4

Contemplation and Early Christian History

Origen, a believer in North Africa born near the end of the second century AD, is considered by many Christian scholars to be the greatest theologian of early Christianity. Origen was the first to canonize a list of books which eventually became our New Testament; he also wrote extensive commentaries on most of the books which became our Bible. Yet most American Christians today have never heard of Origen (pronounced like "origin"); some of those who know of him consider him a heretic, partly because he was one of the first Christian leaders to write about contemplation. Though some of Origen's writings were later condemned as heretical by the Catholic Church, his great influence on Christian theology is unmistakable. Given the extent of his positive impact on the Church, Origen's condemnation by believers who came after him appears to be somewhat like the following situation: a person climbs a hill to get a better view, stumbles over a stone, then condemns the hill for the stone and does not appreciate what he has seen from the hill's vantage point. It's not just the believers who condemned Origen in the past who are guilty of this; many Christians in our time condemn contemplative spirituality. By doing so, such people are also condemning the millions of contemplatives throughout Church history who have been faithful to the God of the Bible, whom they walked with closely, loved deeply and served obediently, and who passed on that love to us today.

But how did contemplative prayer get its start in Christianity? That's the subject of this appendix. As discussed previously in this book, centering prayer as a modern form of Christian contemplative spirituality was formulated in the 1970's by three Catholic monks in response to the droves of young people who were leaving the Christian faith to seek God by way of Eastern religions that emphasized forms of meditation. The three monks—Thomas Keating, William Meninger, and Basil

Pennington—had all been practitioners of contemplative prayer for years. They well knew of Christianity's own rich heritage of meditation and silent meditational prayer for the purpose of total surrender to God. They also knew contemplation had been almost completely forgotten, to the point that even many Catholics were unfamiliar with it, and that those within most Protestant churches knew nothing of contemplative spirituality at all. The writings of Thomas Merton, a 20th century Trappist monk as were Keating, Meninger and Pennington, were influential in the development of centering prayer. But centering prayer was primarily based, not on models of the meditation of Eastern religions, but mainly on *The Cloud of Unknowing,* a book written in 14th century England by an unknown monk, which in turn was a condensation of the contemplative teachings of the Bible and of many Christian contemplative writers since the second century.

But where did the earliest contemplative Christian writers get their ideas from? Did Christian leaders at that time make a change away from what Jesus and the Apostles originally taught? The short, simple and honest answer is, no. Christ was known to often seek God in solitude, a practice commensurate with ancient Jewish forms of meditation. Various Old Testament writings—especially the Psalms, Song of Solomon, Isaiah, and Moses' experience on Mt Sinai—have long been considered to be of a contemplative or mystical nature.[1] If this sounds strange and not much like what you were taught in Sunday school, that's because the book of Christian history we've been given in America has a lot of pages missing. The rest of this appendix will help you begin to fill in the blanks.

The roots of Christian contemplative prayer were, first of all, Jewish, and secondly, Greek. Jewish contemplative history is not well known outside various Hasidic and Kabbalist communities. Orthodox Rabbi Aryeh Kaplan wrote extensively on the subject prior to his death in 1983. Kaplan states, "There is ample evidence that meditative practices were widespread among Jews throughout Jewish history. References to meditation are found in major Jewish texts in every period from the biblical to the premodern era."..."There is also evidence that during the period when the [Jewish] Bible was written...meditation was practiced by a large proportion of the Israelite people...regular schools of meditation existed, led by master prophets."..."Virtually every method found in general meditation can be found in ancient Jewish texts, as well as a number of methods that are found nowhere else."…"In sum, during the entire First Commonwealth [the First Temple period] meditation and mysticism played a central role in Judaism" in which the schools of the prophets took the lead in teaching various forms of meditation as part of helping the Israelites to know, hear from, and fully obey God's Law.[2]

On the Day of Pentecost, those who heard the disciples speaking in their own languages included people from what is today Iraq, Iran, Afghanistan and the areas to the north. The message of Jesus spread far into Asia as well as Europe and Africa; tradition teaches that churches were planted in Persia (Iran) and as far east as India within the first century[3]–lands where contemplative practices had long been a part of the common culture. So the contemplative aspects of Judaism, reflected in Christ's life, were nurtured by Christians in lands that had a more mystical bent. The Apostles carried the message of Jesus in all directions. Paul helped make it clear that the Gospel was for all people, not just the Jews, but Paul himself spread the Gospel around the northern Mediterranean. We think of him as the most influential of the Apostles. Greek culture had been and continued to be dominant in the areas he traveled to, influencing European thought even to our time. Because European culture has dominated the world well into the 21st century, the Greek/Western version of what Christianity was all about is the only one most Christians in America are familiar with.

But much of the efforts of the other Apostles reached eastward with a record of success at least as great as Paul's; because of their efforts and those of their followers, many centuries later during the Age of Discovery, there were several instances where explorers in areas of Asia or Africa far distant from Europe found thriving Christian communities they had not known existed. But the churches in Jerusalem, Syria, Egypt, Iraq, Iran, and other parts of western Asia had cultural roots pointing east, not west, and their version of who Christ was and what the Church should look like had a distinctly Asian perspective.[4]

Bear in mind, too, that Judaism is itself an Asian religion, stemming originally not from a European/Western philosophical basis, but from the Middle East—an area whose cultures are, even to this day, tied more to China and India than to Europe. Abraham himself came from Ur, in what is now southeastern Iraq, near its border with Iran. In such areas, the mystical pursuit of God was sewn into the fabric of the culture. Historian Philip Jenkins says of the Eastern Christians in the early centuries after Christ, that they "continued to pursue mystical quests in ways that were familiar in the early church."[5] He also speaks of "the near-obsessive nature of the Eastern Christian mystical quest" in the faith's first 1000 years; he goes on to say that "the Eastern churches had lost virtually nothing of the ancient mysticism...Ideas of solitude, inner contemplation, and even the quest for divinity [union with God] pervade the stories and teachings" of Eastern Christianity.[6]

This cultural kinship with contemplative spirituality is one of many reasons for contemplatives' assertions that mysticism is not a later, outside addition to the edifice of Christianity, but a part of the original building blocks of the faith. It also, no doubt, has a lot to do with the fact that Christianity in Asia was much more widespread than is commonly recognized today; a map in Jenkins' book *The Lost History of Christianity* shows Nestorian Christian metropolitans (overseers of large populations, similar to archbishops) around 500 A.D. throughout the Middle East and in what is today Iran, Afghanistan, Turkmenistan, Uzbekistan, Tibet, northeast India, the Uighur area of western China, east-central China, and even near today's Beijing. In other words, in its first 500 years, Christianity had extended eastward through Asia pretty much all the way to the Pacific Ocean. The Western churches had very little knowledge of Asian Christianity; for example, in 1275, a Nestorian monk from China made quite an impact in the courts of the Christian kings of Europe. His Christian doctrine was quite surprising and also considered fully acceptable to the Western theologians of the time, who had no idea that their faith had traveled so far.[7]

There can be no doubt that Jewish culture and religion at the time of Christ were still thoroughly Asian. The stories Jesus told have a distinctly Eastern flavor, much more in keeping with the cultures of China and India than with Greece or Rome. Israel was at the western end of the Silk Road, on which caravans of traders traveled from Egypt, Israel, Arabia, Mesopotamia (today's Iraq), and Persia, to central Asia where they met with traders from China, India, Korea, and Southeast Asia to exchange goods, as well as news and cultural influences. Israel's connection with Silk Road traders reinforced their Asian worldview. And Nazareth, the town Jesus lived most of his life in, is near where the western terminus of the main Silk Road splits into northwestern and southwestern routes. Jesus himself spoke Aramaic, the common language of the area in his day. Aramaic is linked to a more earthy, mystical view of life than in the West,[8] with a rich tradition of wisdom teachers and contemplative practices. The Asian mystical aspects of early Christianity are closely related to Jewish mysticism[9] and, later, the Sufi mysticism of Islam[10], which was strongly influenced by the Nestorian Christian churches that preceded Islam in many areas of the Middle East. For centuries after Islam began taking hold, these Asian forms of Christianity continued to thrive and greatly impacted Islamic culture. Christian communities have continued to exist in various parts of central and western Asia to the present day.

Why, then, don't we read in the Bible about contemplative practices of the early Church? The short answer is, the Bible does mention mystical views and practices, but today's Christian culture (especially in the West) has not equipped us to recognize such things. More on that below. This discussion of Bible texts and historical context brings up another important point of history to bear in mind: the oral tradition. It's generally accepted among historians the world over that most ancient literature, including the Bible, was memorized, and that the main way it was passed on from one generation to the next was orally. The transition from oral to written literature began about four thousand years ago; stories, poetry, law codes, etc. that had always been transmitted orally from one generation to the next gradually began to be written down. The oral tradition has continued up to our own time in more primitive areas of the world. Most of the Hebrew Bible is believed to have made this transition somewhere between the time of Moses and the Babylonian exile, a span of about eight hundred years.

The upshot of the oral tradition is that for hundreds of years, many if not most of the books of the Bible were transmitted by the only means available prior to the development of writing—orally. Even after they were written down, the primary means of passing them along would still have been by word of mouth, since only a few people knew how to write and because the oral forms, thousands of years old at that point, carried the weight of tradition. So the books of Moses, the Psalms, etc. continued to be passed down to succeeding generations orally. Much of what we call the Old Testament may not have been written down prior to the 5th century BC. This means that many of the books of the Jewish Bible were not written down by the original prophets, poets and patriarchs who composed them and whose lives are recounted in them; they were memorized and passed around among the followers of the prophets.

So what Christians know as the Old Testament originally consisted of lengthy passages memorized and passed orally from father to son, from teacher to student, and from rabbi to synagogue congregation, for hundreds of years; some parts remained only in oral form for well over a thousand years before being written down in the four or five centuries before Christ's appearing. (For those among us who find it difficult to memorize even a single Bible verse, all this is hard to believe. However, bear in mind that even today when writing is so commonplace, many of us know the Lord's Prayer, not from taking the time to memorize it, but from hearing it repeated every Sunday as a child in church or every night by our parents. Before writing was common, memorization was the only way to learn a text.)

What does all this have to do with contemplative practices? What was true for literature was also true for methods of prayer and meditation. Contemplative spirituality had no handbooks we can point to as evidence for its existence prior to the Desert Fathers in the third and fourth centuries. But as Aryeh Kaplan points out, the language of mysticism was something that would have meant one thing to the average person, and another to a student chosen by a rabbi to study meditation and mystical practices. That's why some of the terms used in the Psalms and the Prophets that refer to types of meditation aren't recognized today by most Christians as pertaining to contemplative spirituality. Even most Jews by the time of Christ were not able to recognize the hidden references to meditation contained in certain Hebrew words. For example, the term *Maschil* used in the title of over a dozen Psalms can mean a teaching or instruction; it can also mean a meditation or contemplation. (See note in title, Psalm 42 and 89, in the New King James Version.)

Because Christianity was centered mainly within the Roman Empire and eventually became its official religion, and because Europeans conquered America, American Christianity ended up with a Western worldview. Much is being made of the importance of having a Christian or Biblical worldview today, but it would be hard to argue that the churches in the first century would have had that same worldview. In the first place, the Bible as we know it didn't exist at that time, and much of this "Christian" or "Biblical" worldview is based on the modern European/American cultural perspective, which also didn't exist then. The "Christian worldview" of a believer in, say, Arabia or Persia in 100 A.D., though no doubt still Christ-centered, would have been considerably different.

An example of the non-Western and mystical worldview is the idea reflected in Paul's assertion that in Christ there is neither circumcised or uncircumcised, barbarian or Scythian, Jew nor Greek, (nor any other ethnic differences), male nor female, slave nor free, "for you are all one in Christ Jesus" (Gal. 3:28); "but Christ is all, and in all" (Col. 3:11). Given the contemplative nature of these statements—that, in effect, all differences and dichotomies are resolved in God, in whom all things are one—why would it be strange for contemplative spirituality to be a part of Christianity? The same can be said of many other New Testament statements: Christ's observations about the lilies of the field and the birds of the air in the Sermon on the Mount; Paul's declaration that we can die and be resurrected with Christ through baptism and "dying daily;" and other ideas intrinsic to Christianity but reflective of Asian cultural and religious viewpoints.

Again, the Bible we have today was unknown to the early Church. Their Bible was the Old Testament (the Septuagint, a Greek translation of the Hebrew Bible), with additional input from numerous writings circulating during the First Century. These included but were certainly not limited to the writings of Paul, Peter, John, James, Matthew, Luke and other early Christian leaders. Through the Dead Sea Scrolls, the Nag Hammadi codex, and other groups of ancient manuscripts that have come to light in the past century and a half, we know today that early Christianity, like its ethnic makeup, was a hodgepodge of ideas reflecting numerous cultural views. Some of these came from the Greek and Roman cultures, but a considerable number of writings came from Jewish, Syrian, Assyrian and other Middle Eastern believers whose cultures were rooted in the Asian mindset. Remnants of Asian Christianity survive today in Coptic, Syriac, Eastern Orthodox and Russian Orthodox Christianity, all of which include strongly contemplative elements within their worship and liturgical practices.[11]

Our Bible—39 Old Testament books and 27 New Testament books— wasn't finalized until near the end of the fourth century. The Synod of Hippo, in 393—almost 400 years after the birth of Christ—established the Old and New Testaments as they stand today. So the Church in its early centuries was not, as it is often portrayed, a clear-cut group of people with the same ideas about everything, basing everything on the Bible. Again, what we know as the Bible was unknown to the early Church. Most if not all of the New Testament books were in circulation among the churches within one hundred years of Jesus's ministry, but so were various other writings such as the Didache, the Shepherd of Hermas, the Epistle of Barnabas, the Gospel of Peter, the Secret Book of James, and numerous others. All of these writings had their adherents for word-of-God candidacy among Christian leaders in the early centuries.

The Church for its first three or four centuries was a welter of different groups all claiming their version of Christianity was the true one. Actually, this is much like what we have today: Catholics, Orthodox, Lutherans, Episcopalians, Methodists, Presbyterians, Baptists, Congregationalists, Quakers, Mennonites, Reformed, Church of Christ, Brethren, Charismatic, Pentecostal, and a partridge in a pear tree! And each of the groups above is split into various sub-groups (American Baptist, Southern Baptist, etc.) and combinations (African Methodist Episcopal, for example)—and then of course there are the various evangelical denominations (Calvary Chapel, Evangelical Free, Foursquare, Vineyard, and so forth). And of course, today there are also millions of believers in non-denominational churches of various stripes. And that's not even counting all the pseudo-Christian religious groups like the Mormons and Jehovah's Witnesses. But, believe it or not, early Christianity was even more fragmented than it is today! For each of the above-mentioned groups, there were at least two or three in the centuries leading up to the First Council of Nicaea in 325.

Christians since the 2nd century have looked to the Apostolic Church born on the Day of Pentecost as the true model for what Christianity should look like, and that's how it should be. But in terms of culture, those first churches were Asian in culture and thought. We read in the Book of Acts about the beginnings of Greek influence in the Church. For Christians in the Roman Empire—especially the western half of it— Greek culture and ideas came more and more to dominate Christianity. But the Asian churches that existed in the first ten centuries—especially those outside the boundaries of the Roman Empire—carried the same ethnic, linguistic, and historical lineage as the Church that went from 120 to 3,000 in one day. The Western churches, with their roots in Hellenistic and Eurocentric traditions and customs, could not make that claim—and neither can the churches of Europe and America today, or those in other parts of the world which are planted out of and tied to European and American forms of Christianity.[12]

Dr. Samuel Moffett, historian and missionary to Korea, tells us that

> "The church began in Asia. Its earliest history, its first centers, were Asian. Asia produced the first known church building, the first New Testament translation, perhaps the first Christian king, the first Christian poets, and even arguably the first Christian [nation] state. Asian Christians endured the greatest persecutions. They mounted global ventures in missionary expansion the West could not match until after the thirteenth century."[13]

However, many of the existing writings of the first century which Christian scholars are familiar with today are in Greek and were written for Greeks. Primarily interested in the spread of the Christian faith to Europe, these writers were less concerned with chronicling the extensive expansion of Christianity to the east; to this day, the numerous writings focusing on Eastern Christianity have been largely ignored by modern and postmodern Christianity. Also, some of the Greek Christians of the early centuries may have been hostile to the Jewish and Syrian Christians, as evidenced perhaps by the growth of anti-Semitism in the western Church during that time.

The Book of Acts shows the transition from an all-Jewish church to one which opened its doors to the Gentiles as well. The Jewish culture was strongest in the area at the time, but a strong and growing second cultural influence was that of Greece. By the time of Christ, the Greek culture had had such a powerful impact on western Asia, where the Church was born, that it was bound to affect Christian history; the clashing and blending of the two cultures is a major theme of the New Testament and other writings of the first century in Israel and the surrounding areas. And the Greeks had their own forms of mysticism, tied both to the philosophers of Greece's Golden Age, and also to the mystery religions that flourished around the Mediterranean before, during and after the time of Christ. Greek mysticism included *theoria*, a form of meditation believed by the Greeks to please their gods and to make men more godlike. The Greek philosopher Aristotle believed *theoria* to be the greatest activity humans could engage in. Christian writers of the second and third centuries began to refer to *theoria*, which was translated into Latin as "contemplatio," as a form of prayer valued highly for leading a Christian to the place of full surrender to God.

Contemplative Christianity owes much of its early growth to some of the early Christian leaders known as the Church Fathers. To the Fathers who lived from the late second century on, the contemplative life was considered necessary for bringing a person to the height of Christian perfection.[14] Clement of Alexandria was the first of the Church Fathers to mention contemplation, presenting it as the "meat" of the mature believer. Clement successfully preached and taught Christ and Christian doctrine using the language of the Greek philosophers and the mystery religions, winning souls for Christ from both. He is believed to have been the teacher and mentor of Origen, mentioned at the beginning of this appendix. Among Origen's many commentaries on books of the Bible is one on the Song of Songs (Song of Solomon), considered "the first great work of Christian mysticism."[15] Origen thought of the Song of Songs as an allegory of the love between the Church (the Bride of Christ) and the Divine Lover, Christ himself—a mystical theme many others throughout Church history have pursued. "While the mystical element was present in Christianity from the start, it is with the Alexandrian teacher [Origen] that a formal biblically based mystical theory first emerges."[16] As mentioned earlier, Origen also gave us a list of books nearly identical to what later came to be called the New Testament.[17]

A stumbling-block for many twenty-first century evangelicals is the fact that much of Church history, both Eastern and Western, is inextricably tied to monasticism. Many non-Catholic believers today cringe when thinking of monks chanting in cathedrals. But the monasteries were centers of learning, somewhat akin to today's colleges and universities; most people were illiterate, so the average Christian would hear a sermon preached at a church presided over by monks. For much of Christian history, becoming a monk was the equivalent for us of attending Bible college or seminary, going on a long mission trip, or just becoming a full-time missionary.

So, contrary to the commonly accepted idea in American evangelical and fundamentalist churches that mysticism has no history in early Christianity, contemplative practices were a common part of the early Church, inherited from the Jewish culture out of which it grew. (In fact, Christianity was still viewed by many throughout the first century as a Jewish sect, not as a separate religion in its own right.) By the time the monastic movement was beginning in the Egyptian desert during the late Third and early Fourth Centuries, Greek culture—including Greek contemplative ideas and practices—had come to have as strong an influence on Christian thought as did the Jewish culture from which the Church sprang. But in its first few decades, the Early Church—yes, the one millions of American Christians today claim to emulate—was quite familiar with mystical ways of worshiping God.

The Desert Fathers, however, made contemplative prayer more a foundational part of their faith practices, which were modeled after Christ's 40 days in the desert and the lives of John the Baptist, Moses, Elijah and other prophets from Israel's history, as well as the Nazirites, all of whom were known for separating themselves from society to seek God. The Essenes and other groups were forerunners of the monastics who followed Anthony of Egypt and others to live solitary lives in the desert, choosing at some point to live in community so as to help each other with daily tasks in order to provide each person more time for seeking God in prayer and contemplation.

Much more could be said about the history of contemplation in Christianity; indeed, many volumes have been written on that subject. I wanted to use this appendix to simply draw a clear connection between Jesus, the early Church, and the great burgeoning growth of contemplative spirituality that developed in the fourth century and has played such a significant role in Christian history. Christian mysticism is not a modern product of occultic influence or a bleeding-in of the practices of East Asian religions; it has been very much a part of real, authentic Christianity since Jesus walked the earth. And it is my sincere conviction that the Holy Spirit is restoring the gift of contemplation to the Church in the 21st century.

Appendix 5

The Spirituality of Breathing

> This is the air I breathe
> This is the air I breathe
> Your holy presence
> Living in me
>
> This is my daily bread
> This is my daily bread
> Your very word
> Spoken to me
>
> And I,
> I'm desperate for you
> And I,
> I'm lost without you[1]

From day one in my centering prayer practice, I felt led by God to make deep breathing a part of it. For me, even more than using a "sacred word",[2] my breath is what keeps me focused on God. Every exhalation is a little dying, followed by a time of waiting in silence and peace... followed by...an inhalation. And every inhalation is a little resurrection.

If there was nothing more to be learned from the breath than that, it would be more than enough to tell us this: What God did in Jesus on Golgotha, and in the grave of Joseph of Arimathea and also outside it, after the stone was rolled away, is what God does in every one of us, thousands of times every day. We are in the process of dying all the time, in and of ourselves dead in sins and trespasses, and raised to newness of life in Christ, over and over again. It's pretty much the same whether you're a Jesus-follower or not: without that next breath we're all dead. With it, we're restored, revived, resurrected.

The world, and everything in the world, is always encroaching on us, trying to define us, to sculpt us, to make us in its image. But when I breathe using the breath as a symbol of God, in every inhalation I take in the whole world, and with every exhalation I let the whole world go, giving it all up in exchange for God, who is all I need…who is the breath of life, who is everything to me, in every breath.

Each in-breath is like the tide coming in on the beach of my life, cleansing me, revealing the new treasure of Now, each moment a gift of God. Each out-breath is like the tide sweeping away everything old, every old piece of driftwood, every dead starfish, every thought and memory and desire of my own. Each out-breath reminds me my life is nothing but sand, that I have nothing, I am nothing, and yet in that nothing I have everything because I have God, I know God, God's richness dwells in me. And though I am nothing, God brings me new treasures every moment, every Now, with every new breath. I can sit back and rest in God and silently watch each thought, each emotion come, then let it be swept away with the next incoming tide-breath before it sticks to me. And the part of me that is just sand, the part that watches the thoughts come and go and then forgets them, staying focused on the tide, the water of life that brings constant renewal, constant resurrection—that part of me is my spirit, my true self that isn't swayed by every thought, every emotion, every wind of doctrine, but gazes steadfastly at God who is unseen.

The rhythm of our days is reflected in the breath: each inhalation is like the sunrise and morning; each exhalation is like the afternoon and evening; afterward, waiting in silence a few seconds, not breathing out or in, just listening, is like the darkest night—and it often glows like the mountains under the full moon.

Taking in that breath, that fresh new moment of nourishment, of life, is like being an infant all over again, nursing at the mother's breast, receiving the milk that will sustain its life, and with not a care in the world but to receive the next mouthful of milk, the next breath God will send. Nothing matters but lying in the arms of God (who is neither male nor female, by the way, and whom David also compares to a mother in Psalm 130). There we can rest and forget everything, let everything else go, and just be in the arms of our Lord, and receive his nurturing care and love in ways that are as far beyond our understanding as the chemical composition and molecular structure of mother's milk is to an infant.

Paul the Apostle spoke about feeding the Corinthians with milk, but complained that they weren't ready for meat when they should be (1 Cor. 3:1-3). The writer of Hebrews says pretty much the same thing (Heb. 5:12-14). Yes, we need solid food to grow; you can't become a mature Christ-follower without knowing and practicing what the Word says. Peter, on the other hand, admonished his hearers to "crave pure spiritual milk" (1 Pt. 2:2-3), and it doesn't appear that he was speaking only to brand-new Christians. What's my point? We need the meat of what the Bible says, but too many believers get so much into the meat of the Word that they forget God's love which is the foundation of everything. No mercy, no kindness, no grace, just plenty of scripture floating around in their heads to throw at people, along with a colossal ego, a Christian mask which they mistake for true spirituality.

Without love toward others in our hearts, we're built on sand, even if we have the entire Bible memorized. Christians who pride themselves on how much scripture they know, and use it to beat others up, more than for self-correction, are Christians in name only; they aren't really following the path of Christ. They're like children who have been orphaned just as they were being weaned; they start eating meat, but the lost love of the mother is like a hole in their heart that they try to fill with scripture and doctrine. There has to be more to it than that; there has to be God's love, experienced daily. If the love isn't there, such believers become twisted; it's as if they become addicted to the action of chewing, and then start chewing up and devouring other believers they don't consider as spiritual as themselves.

So in deep-breathing meditation, it's not just the breath that feeds us, but the loving presence of God. It's the mother's love that feeds her infant's soul, and that's at least as important as the milk. Same with us and God and the breath. Yes, we need meat, not just milk; it's good to learn as much about the Bible as possible (and even more important to live it out!), to memorize Scripture and study doctrine. But here, we're talking about a different kind of milk, a paradoxical kind: milk that's better for you than the best banquet you could ever go to—the sweetness of the Lord, and your adoration.

I have included two poems below, both of which I wrote a few years ago about deep-breathing meditation (though it seems so mundane to label it that way!) What's even better than writing poetry about it, though, is to just rest in that silent wordless place, beyond thought and reason, lying peacefully in the hammock that's strung between one outgoing breath and the next incoming one, just staring up at the spaces between the stars. Okay, there, I just wrote another one. Anyway, hope you like it.

Slow Motion Breathing

adrift in the space between breaths,
i hang in silent eternity,
devoid of yesterday or tomorrow.
then like a hand reaching
out of a dream,
the inhalation pulls me
out of the now
into the new.
i pause for a brief moment,
like shot-off fireworks
arching on the sky
in the instant before they become
brilliant flowers of flame.
the exhalation pushes me
into the future,
like the prow of a boat
piercing the icy waters of night
until, far from the current
in the still backwaters,
i rest motionless,

pondering the reflection of the stars,
lost upon the luminescent sea of silence,
adrift once again
in the new,
in the now.

Sonnet for the Breath

Our breathing is an endless living prayer.
With each out-breath we die a little death,
With every inhalation rise again,
And by this constant miracle learn of Christ,
Identifying with him in his time
Of making this world new in those dark hours
Of leading us forever past the grave
Into uncharted liberation life
As, Spirit-led, we trust the voice of love
And dance upon all darkness and despair.
With every breath I learn a little more,
Grow freer as I learn to free the past.
I take the whole wide world inside myself,
And throw it all away again for You.

Appendix 6

The Ten Commandments: Four Perspectives

I. The Ten Commandments	II. The Ten Commandments Simplified[1]
1. You shall have no other gods before me.	1. Love God more than you love anything else.
2. You shall not make or worship idols.	2. Don't make anything in your life more important than God
3. You shall not misuse the name of the Lord your God.	3. Always say God's name with love and respect
4. Remember the Sabbath day by keeping it holy.	4. Honour the Lord by resting on the seventh day of the week.

III. The Ten Commandments (Nonattachment Perspective)

1. Love God more than you love everything else there is, all put together. Be attached fully to God and not attached in any way to anything else.

2. No idols. God punishes those who hate him but lavishes love on those who love him. Idols, including self, symbolize attachments to things and false-heartedness toward God.

3. Never misuse God's name in any way; always speak of God as the one you are attached to in love, your all-in-all, your everything, the lover of your soul.

4. One day a week, rest with God and rest from everything else; that one day, renew and strengthen your attachment to God and weaken your attachments to everything else.

IV. The Ten Commandments (Karma/Sowing-Reaping Perspective)

1. Love God as your All in All. God is One, and if you try to fragment God into a bunch of little gods, you fragment your own soul.

2. No other gods. If you make gods for yourself out of wood, stone, computer chips, etc., you take away from yourself the reality of God's infiniteness and holiness; trivialize God and you trivialize your own soul.

3. If you misuse God's name by using it as a curse word, you curse yourself; or if you try to manipulate luck or God or nature by using his name in a way that's against his will, you bring bad luck on yourself.

4. If you forget the day of resting in God, you become a restless soul.

I. The Ten Commandments	II. The Ten Commandments Simplified[1]
5. Honor your father and your mother.	5. Love and respect your parents.
6. You shall not murder.	6. Never hurt anyone.
7. You shall not commit adultery.	7. Always be faithful to your husband or wife.
8. You shall not steal.	8. Don't take anything that isn't yours.
9. You shall not give false testimony against your neighbor.	9. Always tell the truth.
10. You shall not covet.	10. Be happy with what you have. Don't wish for other people's things.

III. The Ten Commandments (Nonattachment Perspective)

5. Honoring your parents honors God; recognize them as the two greatest symbols of God to us in this life. In being attached to God, be appreciative of all he gives, beginning with those whom God used to give life to you.

6. Don't murder. Honor God by honoring life. Murder is the worst fruit of self-attachment; it is the epitome of selfishness.

7. Honor God by honoring the mate he gave you. Love that person as an extension of your love for God, but selflessly, for who they are and how they reflect God, not just for what they can do for you.

8. Honor God by honoring others and by not being attached to things that belong to others.

9. Honor God and others by honoring truth. All deception is self-honoring, self-attachment activity.

10. Honor God your provider by your contentment, by being attached to the Giver rather than the gifts, and especially by not being attached to what God has not given you.

IV. The Ten Commandments (Karma/Sowing-Reaping Perspective)

5. If you disrespect your parents, you disrespect yourself, your own roots, and you miss out on the promise of long life - you cut yourself off from the abundant life in the promised land – God's life in you.

6. If you kill others, something inside you dies too.

7. If you're unfaithful in your marriage, you're unfaithful to yourself too.

8. If you steal, you also steal your own innocence and grace.

9. If you lie to or about others, you lie to yourself.

10. If you covet something that belongs to someone else, you impoverish yourself by tricking yourself into thinking you need that thing, and you lose out on the promise that, in God, you already have everything you could need or want, and more.

Endnotes

Preface

1. For many Christians, the words "mystic," "mystical" and "mysticism" can be off-putting, to say the least; some would take my use of this word as proof that I'm teaching something false, something that's not connected with God and Christ and the Bible. Please be aware that this is a modern American cultural bias and that these terms have been used by Christians since at least the second century A.D. in reference to waiting on God and to the mysterious aspects of God. I have much more to say on this subject in Chapter 2, in the section on "Christianity and Mysticism."

2. For the purposes of simplification, throughout this book the term "contemplation" refers to all aspects of contemplative spirituality, although I will occasionally use other terms: contemplative prayer, centering prayer, meditation, mystical Christianity, etc. These terms are all more or less synonymous.

3. Don't let this description scare you. It's all Spirit-led. Just becoming a Christian and learning to walk with Christ could be described the same way, as perhaps you yourself can attest.

4. Colson heard theologian R. C. Sproul's assertion that "the Roman Catholic church is neither a Christian body nor a Christian church." Colson's brilliantly inspired sarcastic response: "Where does this lead us?...There are 900 million confessing Catholics out of the worldwide Christian body of 1.7 billion. So if Rome is not a church, more than 50 percent of what the world believes as the Christian church is gone. And to be logically consistent, of course, we would have to write off the Orthodox Church. There goes another 300 million. While we are at it, I don't know how we would hang on to Episcopalians or the mainline Presbyterians ..." (Charles W. Colson—A Life Redeemed, by Jonathan

Aitken. Doubleday, © 2005, page 385.) If you carry this kind of thinking to its logical conclusion, you end up with just you and your family, and you're not so sure about some of them, either. That's not the way of Christ. His disciples were quite the diverse bunch, with plenty of opportunities for divisiveness—and he handed the Kingdom over to them. We need to love and accept our fellow Christians on the common ground of Calvary rather than find reasons to disagree.

5. This doesn't mean that new believers are just naturally contemplatives, or that they should pursue contemplative spirituality. The fact that new believers often experience the wonder of the Kingdom more than their older counterparts can generally be taken to mean that they don't need to pursue contemplation at that point in their journey. In my experience, contemplative prayer tends to usually (though not always) be for older believers. It tends to go with the gradual surrender of youth, material things, and eventually everything else, right up to a person's very life itself; this stage of life generally begins around age 50. Not that you can't be a contemplative if you are in your 20's or 30's, but if you've been following the Lord less than 5 years, I would say the first order of business is to focus on learning the Bible as well as possible, and more importantly, learning to live it. Later on, when you start to sense a weariness in everything including your Christian walk, and a "there-must-be-more-than-this" kind of hunger (and you will), then pray about pursuing contemplative prayer. Of course, God occasionally chooses to gift a fairly new believer with contemplation. For each person, it has to be up to God whether or not one becomes a contemplative, and when. It's vitally important to know for sure that you're hearing from him before you jump into contemplation.

Introduction

1. "I Still Haven't Found What I'm Looking For," music by U2, lyrics by Bono, © 1987 Universal-Polygram International.

2. "Consuming Fire," written by Tim Hughes, copyright 2002 Thankyou Music. There are also quite a few other worship songs that express a similar sentiment.

Chapter 1: Beyond Worship

1. I like Thomas Merton's answer to the question, "what is contemplation?" He said, "Contemplation is the highest expression of man's intellectual and spiritual life. It is that life itself, fully awake, fully active, fully aware that it is alive. It is spiritual wonder. It is spontaneous awe at the sacredness of life, of being. It is gratitude for life, for awareness and for being. It is a vivid realization of the fact that life and being in us proceed from an invisible, transcendent and infinitely abundant Source. It knows the Source, obscurely, inexplicably, but with a certitude that goes both beyond reason and beyond simple faith. For contemplation is a kind of spiritual vision to which both reason and faith aspire, by their very nature, because without it they must always remain incomplete. Yet contemplation is not vision because it sees "without seeing" and knows "without knowing." It is a more profound depth of faith, a knowledge too deep to be grasped in images, in words or even in clear concepts. It can be suggested by words, by symbols, but in the very moment of trying to indicate what it knows the contemplative mind takes back what it has said, and denies what it has affirmed. For in contemplation we know by "unknowing." Or, better, we know beyond all knowing or "unknowing."" (from Thomas Merton, "What Is Contemplation?" in New Seeds of Contemplation, p. 1, copyright 1961 by The Abbey of Gethsemani, Inc., quoted in The Essential Writings of Christian Mysticism by Bernard McGinn, The Modern Library, New York, 2006.

Some contemplatives distinguish between two types of meditation or meditative prayer: apophatic and kataphatic. Basically, kataphatic meditation or prayer refers to focusing on something tangible, such as a specific prayer, a verse of Scripture, or an icon (picture) of Jesus. Apophatic prayer or meditation, on the other hand, focuses on nothing tangible or conceptual at all, including one's own thoughts—nothing but God who is beyond all that is tangible or conceptual. Lectio Divina—a form of meditation on Scripture—is a form of kataphatic meditation. Contemplation is apophatic meditational prayer. I will also add that in many of the great Christian mystics—Teresa of Avila, for example— there is a distinction between what they refer to as "mental prayer" and contemplation. Thus, contemplation is prayer that goes beyond words, beyond concepts, beyond all that the mind is capable of, into the realm of just sitting in stillness and silence at Jesus's feet, in silent adoration. It is allowing God to take us in our time of prayer beyond where we can go, to where there is no path we can follow; all we can do is cling to his hand. Perhaps contemplation is the deepest fulfillment of what is often referred to as "blind faith."

2. Centering prayer was developed in the 1970's by three Catholic Trappist monks to bring contemplative prayer as practiced by Christians for many centuries to twentieth century Christians in a form that is simple, practical and effective. The three monks—Thomas Keating, Basil Pennington and William Meninger—and many others have spent years teaching people centering prayer; untold thousands of people around the world today have found it to be a powerful tool for bringing them into a closer, deeper and stronger relationship with God.

3. You can also use your breath or what's known as the Sacred Gaze, but using a word is most common. I use the breath (deep breathing, in my case), but I sometimes use a word as well. The use of the word is not constantly repetitive like a mantra; if this bothers you, see footnote 9 below. The word used is generally God, Jesus, Spirit, or some other name of God; some use "love" or some other word that symbolizes God to them. Think of this as a one-word prayer, and in that one word is contained all the words of all the prayers, and all the thoughts and feelings behind them, that you've ever prayed or ever will pray. You don't need to try to put all that meaning into the God-word you use; it's already there. You just let go of all your efforts and call on God. He knows your heart and mind, so just surrender and rest in him as you lay on the altar before him every thought and feeling and memory that comes, until there's nothing but God and you. Sometimes you completely forget yourself, lose yourself in him, so there's nothing but God. There are times, also, when you don't feel God's presence at all. We walk by faith, not by sight. Not feeling he's there doesn't mean God has left you or that you've done something wrong; his peace is still there, all around you, like the air you breathe. If you don't feel it, that just means you're accessing a new level of faith—you know that you know that you know God is there for you whether you feel him or not, and you're able to keep going just fine without having a crisis.

4. Eckhart Tolle, in his book *A New Earth* (Plume Books/The Penguin Group, © 2005), calls the ego "the voice in your head that pretends to be you." Though Tolle is not a Christian, he recognizes many of the same issues one encounters through Christian contemplative spirituality. As stated in the Preface, contemplation is a bridge to other religious and spiritual traditions because it allows us to speak of what the Christian faith has in common with non-Christian forms of spirituality, making it easier to then communicate the gospel of Christ with others involved in similar kinds of spirituality in their own traditions—many of which recognize Christ's teachings as contemplative in nature.

5. A reference to *The Strange Case of Dr. Jekyll and Mr. Hyde* by Robert Louis Stevenson, first published in 1886. It's the story of a man with a split personality—one a fine upstanding citizen, the other a dark, violent and evil man. The book is considered one of the very first "psychological" novels, perhaps the first to examine the dark side of the human psyche.

6. Thomas Merton, *New Seeds of Contemplation,* © 1961 by the Abbey of Gethsemani Inc./New Directions Books, p. 34.

7. It's interesting that the way you open each doll is to remove its head! That's symbolic of silencing the thoughts through centering prayer. It's also interesting, and maybe not a coincidence, that these dolls come from the Russian culture, where contemplation has been such a normal part of the Orthodox Christian faith—and, indeed, of everyday life—for a millennium or more. (That's been somewhat less true in the past century due to persecution and suppression of Christianity under the Communist regime. Since the end of Communism, Russian Orthodox Christianity, and also Protestant and Catholic Christianity, have been gaining ground).

8. It's hard to prove definitively from Scripture that what Peter and the other disciples were doing was contemplation; as a form of prayer, it wasn't clearly expressed in writing until the third century. But the roots of contemplation are recognizable in the words of Christ and the writings of the Apostles; based on Paul's letters and the information about him in Acts, during his three years in the desert as a young Christian he certainly appears to have been led in a contemplative direction. The contemplative attitude is clearly evident throughout the New Testament

if you know what to look for. Many Christian mystics even believe Moses experienced the highest degrees of contemplative spirituality when he ascended Mt. Sinai and communed with God in the silence. Others in the Old Testament, especially Isaiah, also seem to echo the contemplative viewpoint. For more on the ancient historical roots of mystical Christianity, see Appendix 4.

9. Does this mean we shouldn't use our minds? Of course not. The paradoxes and parables of Jesus are to me the strongest evidence there is that God wants us to think—but where do those paradoxes and parables lead? To serious outside-the-box thinking. That's one of the main reasons Jesus taught the way he did: to get us thinking, not just with our minds, but with our hearts as well. This will lead, if we follow it far enough, to calling on God for answers and understanding, and then—to silence as we wait on God. The idea of emptying the mind evokes fear in many people, mainly because of repeated warnings that this practice can lead to demonic possession. Under some circumstances perhaps that's possible, but as part of Christ-focused and Holy Spirit-led centering prayer, that won't happen; what happens is Holy Spirit possession. See footnote 12 below, and also Chapter 2, for more on this modern misunderstanding within the Church.

10. "Who Is Like Our God?" by Brian Duane, Brian Doerksen & Brian Thiessen, © 1995 Mercy/Vineyard Publishing.

11. Thomas Keating, *Invitation to Love,* ©1992 Element Inc./Element Books Limited.

12. See note on 2 Cor. 3:18, NIV. A similar verse in the Old Testament is Psalm 27:4—"One thing I have desired of the LORD, that will I seek...To behold the beauty of the Lord, and to inquire in his temple." The word "inquire" in this passage is rendered, in many translations, "meditate" or "contemplate." Since the first part of that verse speaks of reducing the focus of one's desire down to one thing—knowing the Lord more deeply, forsaking everything else but that—I'd have to consider this a very contemplative verse. In the whole context of Psalm 27, that fits: David starts out talking about God's protection from his enemies, but what if the "enemies" he speaks of are the thoughts in his head that make

war against his relationship with God? Verse 5 speaks of being hidden in the secret place of God's tabernacle, which would be the Holy of Holies (though David couldn't literally go there because he was not the high priest, he understands that in contemplative prayer he can enter in there). Then, verse 8, which to me is the key to the whole psalm: "When you said, "Seek my face," my heart said to you, "Your face, Lord, I will seek." Not just his blessings, his attributes, or answers to prayer, but his face—his intimate presence. Face to face with God, the Divine Lover: that's contemplation.

13. For a more thorough description of Lectio Divina scripture meditation, see Appendix 3.

14. Many have been warned against repetitive prayer, based on the King James translation of Matthew 6:7. Jesus was saying that God hears your prayer every time you ask; he's not deaf. He wasn't warning against repetition, per se, but vain repetition. If there's vain repetition, that means there is also meaningful repetition—a repetitive prayer that's not in vain; if that wasn't true, Jesus would have said just "repetition," not "vain repetition." If mere repetition is a problem to God, then the writer of Psalm 136 and the four living creatures in Revelation 4:8—and Jesus in Gethsemane—didn't get the memo. Carrying this idea to its ridiculous extreme, a certain well-known word-of-faith preacher said he never prayed for his children when they were growing up, because he had prayed for God's full blessings on them when they were born, and he didn't want to offend God by being repetitive and praying for them again! More on this subject in Chapter 2, including footnote 11.

15. Though in the early 21st century we tend to ignore paradoxes (another sad legacy of the Age of Reason), they are in my opinion a vitally important part of contemplation: an apparent impossibility that nevertheless is true. Paradox is an indication of the upside-down-ness of our world, the right-side-up-ness of the way God sees and wants us to see, and what Eugene Peterson often refers to as God's "setting-things-right"—his Message Bible version of "being made righteous." For more paradoxes on Christ and the Christian life, see Appendix 4.

16. The term "union with God" really bothered me at first. I'm not God and never will be; neither are you, neither is anyone else who ever lived, except Jesus Christ. We must never forget this fact. Speaking of "union with God" is not meant to suggest that we are God or can become God, only that God lives in us and transforms us to become more and more like him. John 17:21 is probably the primary passage in the Bible on divine union. Just as with individual spiritual giftings (I Cor. 12-14), the contemplative gifts—including union with God—are "so that the body of Christ may be built up until we all reach unity in the faith and in the knowledge of the Son of God and become mature, attaining to the whole measure of the fullness of Christ" (Eph. 4:12b-13.) The Book of Privy Counseling (by the anonymous author of The Cloud of Unknowing) addresses this subject: "God is your being, and what you are, you are in God. But you are not God's being." For more information, see chapter 8, and also the quote from Cynthia Bourgeault in Chapter 2, from her book *Centering Prayer and Inner Awakening*.)

17. Where does the Bible say that if you empty your mind you'll get demon possessed? Many would point to Luke 11:24-26, but here Jesus was speaking in the context of having been accused of casting out demons by Beelzebub, the prince of demons. First he shows how irrational that idea is; then he goes on to speak authoritatively about various issues having to do with demons and casting them out. In this context he says that for someone who has a demon cast out, it's important to then be filled with God, so the demon can't come back and bring his friends. The teaching has nothing to do with emptying the mind of the thoughts one's false self feeds on to build its own kingdom. On the contrary, Isaiah 26:3 makes it clear that we need to keep our minds on God, which entails getting rid of every thought that comes to us and focusing only on God. If Christian music or teachings help you do that, great. It has never enabled me to stay totally God-focused.

What really works is what Paul recommended in 2 Cor. 10:1,4-5—"...by the gentleness and kindness of Christ himself...the very weapons we use are not human, but powerful in God's warfare for the destruction of the enemy's strongholds [including our own minds]. Our battle is to break down every deceptive argument and every imposing defense that men erect against the true knowledge of God. We fight to capture every thought until it acknowledges the authority of Christ"

(J.B. Phillips translation). Of course, Christian music can be helpful for keeping one's mind on God, but let's take heed to what some of these songs say: "In the secret, in the quiet place/In the stillness you are there/ In the secret, in the quiet hour I wait only for you/'cause I want to know you, Lord." (In The Secret by Andy Park, © 1995 Mercy/Vineyard Music). Worship music is great, but there are times when the Spirit calls us to let go of even that and surrender to God in silence, wordlessly loving God and doing absolutely nothing else. If your heart is right toward God, there's no way you're going to get demon possessed doing that, but you will get God-possessed. (More on this issue in Chapter 2).

18. Be the Center, by Michael Frye, © 1999 Vineyard Songs (UK/Eire). Administered by Mercy/Vineyard Publishing in North America. To me, this song expresses perfectly what centering prayer is all about: Jesus being the center of our lives, "The reason that I live: Jesus, Jesus."

19. The Heart of Worship, by Matt Redman, Copyright © 1999 Thankyou Music (Admin. by EMI Christian Music Publishing).

20. The breath is a beautiful symbol of God, who breathes the breath of life into us (Gen. 2:7). Every time you see the word "Spirit" in the Bible, it's the same word as "breath." So the Holy Spirit is God's breath; our breath is a symbol of our physical life and our spiritual life; both come from God. For more on the spirituality of breathing, see Appendix 7.

Chapter 2: Objections to Contemplative Spirituality

1. Luke 14:10. This parable of Jesus (Luke 14:8-11) is a perfect illustration of the call to centering prayer, or just deeper spirituality with God in general. You can take the parable at face value—i.e., be humble in social situations and wait for God to raise you up—which is perfectly valid; sticking to "the main and plain things of Scripture" (John Wimber) is a good thing. But, if you feel led to a deeper kind of spirituality— Mary's "better part" (Luke 10:38-42)—you can see in Christ's words a deeper application. From that point of view, it's the false self that tries to claim the best for itself—"I'm a mighty prayer warrior, I can kick the devil's butt," etc.—and it's the true self that chooses to get rid of all

boasting, to take a place of lowliness in the presence of God. Only the true self knows what it means to humble yourself in the sight of the Lord, knowing he will lift you up (1 Peter 5:6). The true self is willing to wait for God to say, "friend, move up here to a better place" (Luke 14:10), to a place of knowing and walking with God in a greater depth of spirituality and abundant life. How does that work? How do you do it? Sit in silence with God, allowing your self no concessions or favors; give all you are, even the very thoughts you think, to God. Stay there until there's nothing left of you that isn't handed over to God, until you're completely empty, completely humbled, until the false self is bowed low, in fact brought down to death. Then God will fill you with himself, his grace, his life; he will resurrect you (your true self) with Christ. Do that every day, and you'll begin to experience the infilling of God in ways you don't often see with regular prayer.

2. See footnote 16 of chapter 1 on this subject. The hypocritical other side of the coin is that, in some churches, when a rule is introduced that you don't believe is of God, you may be asked—or told—to, ironically, just "turn off your mind" and "accept it by faith"—in other words, just go with it, even if it goes against your conscience.

3. In 2006, the Catholic Church published a study on the New Age Movement called *Jesus Christ, the Bearer of the Water of Life: A Christian Reflection on the New Age.* Their intent was to leave no doubt that New Age thinking is incompatible with and contrary to Christianity's core beliefs, saying that New Age ideas blur the distinction between good and evil. For decades, most Protestants have been in general agreement that there are irreconcilable differences between Christianity and the New Age approach to spirituality. At the same time, however, some within Christian contemplative circles—Catholic, Orthodox and Protestant— feel it is appropriate to pursue open dialog with those in other contemplative traditions, for purposes of mutual understanding as well as to allow the light of Christ to shine into the lives of Buddhists, Hindus, Muslims, etc. (see footnote 6 below). How should we as Christians act toward and interact with people of other religions? I personally believe everything in contemplation must remain Christ-centered, bearing in mind that Christian contemplatives down through the ages (including me) have felt led by the Holy Spirit at times to explore meditation and

also things like breath control—things more commonly associated with Eastern religions, at least among American believers. For more on this issue, see Appendix 1.

4. This may sound familiar. Most likely, if you've been a Christian for very long, your relationship with God has taken you into places of deep hunger like this in worship or prayer or Bible reading. In other words, I'm not saying contemplatives have something no one else in the church experiences; I'm saying there are millions of contemplatives in churches around the world who don't know they're contemplatives. Many people would like to go deeper with God into these places (which are actually doorways, invitations from God), but they don't know how or they are afraid. If this sounds like you, read on.

5. The phrase "the face you had before you had a face" is borrowed and adapted from Cynthia Bourgeault, *Centering Prayer and Inner Awakening*. Saying that "Christ in you, the hope of glory" is our true self can be misleading. We are not Christ, but we are cells in his Body, so his blood and his life—his Spirit—flow through us. I picture the true self as the resurrected self, or for an unbeliever, the self that has been in the grave with Christ awaiting resurrection ever since conception. It has always been in the presence of God and is always open to God's voice and love, but the false self covers it over with the dirt of normal everyday thoughts. Even for believers, the dirt must be dug away so the true self can rise up and take its rightful place as the head servant standing before Christ who is on the throne of our lives. Most of us—including Christians, to an extent—go through life unaware that we are hindering the true self by covering it with the dirt of the daily mind/daily grind.

6. This paragraph is addressed to Christ-followers. If someone who is not a believer does this type of meditational prayer, Christ is not in them, according to Christian doctrine accepted by most churches. *But*—they still have a true self, and their true self was made in the image of God, and God can still speak to them and change them; they can still recognize the false self and learn to deny it. This is why there is room for discussion between Christian and non-Christian contemplatives. Contrary to some Christian "us-and-them" teachings, there is much in the Bible about God's grace and mercy toward those who have never heard of or yielded

to Christ. Examples: Romans 5:6; John 11:52; 1 Peter 1:12; Hebrews 11:4-10; John 8:1-11; Ps. 68:18 & 32; Acts 10:34-35; Acts 17:24-28, especially verses 25 and 27; 1 John 2:2.

Note that in Matthew 9:2 (the account of Jesus healing the paralytic lowered by his friends through a hole in the roof), Jesus's first words to the paralytic were, "Take heart, son; your sins are forgiven." He hadn't even asked for forgiveness! And he didn't even come to Jesus on his own; his friends brought him. The point is, the paralytic who got healed did nothing at all in the way of jumping through the hoops we tend to insist people have to jump through to become Christians or receive God's grace, yet he received a colossal dose of it. God's mercy is greater than we can even imagine. Is this true only for Jews? Of course not. It's for everyone. Can someone who has never heard of Jesus or has not "accepted Christ" receive grace and truth from God? Yes. Will that keep some "unbelievers" out of hell? That's the way I read many of the verses listed in this footnote, especially Acts 10:34-5. Mercy triumphs over judgment! (James 2:13b). See also Hosea 6:6 and Matthew 9:13.

7. Origen, Irenaeus, and Clement of Alexandria are probably the three main early Church Fathers whose writings include a mystical point of view. See footnote 9 of this chapter for more.

8. See, for example, I Cor. 4:1; Eph. 6:19; Col. 2:2. The word "mystery" in Greek comes from a root word which means "to shut the mouth" and refers to the idea of silence as part of the initiation into religious rites. So contemplation goes back to ancient Greece as well as to Moses and other Hebrew prophets; similar ideas can be found in all the world's religions. Christ has set us apart, but that doesn't mean we don't pray just because other religions include prayer as part of their worship. And it also doesn't mean we have to bar the prayer of silence (contemplation) from our worship, just because other religions practice the same thing. Prayer—with and without words—is universal throughout human history; it reflects the universal longing to know God. Christ has made the way to God open to all through his broken body on the Cross and the torn veil of the Temple. There's no reason to think he excluded silent prayer in the process.

9. For a fuller treatment of these issues, see William Johnston, *Mystical Theology: the Science of Love*, HarperCollins Publishers, 1995, pages 29-42. Orthodox Christianity has always been more contemplative— more accepting of the mystical aspects of the faith—than their counterparts in the West. I found this quote in the preface to a modern translation of one of the classics of early Christianity, Fourth century Church Father Gregory of Nyssa's *Life of Moses:*

> "...Gregory...was... inclined to...what is usually called "mysticism"...To the Western mind, mysticism is associated with forms of subjective, individual and necessarily esoteric knowledge, which, by definition, cannot be communicated to all. In early Christian and Byzantine Greek [the language in which Gregory wrote]...the term "mystical" is applied to forms of perception related to the Christian "mystery;" the text of the Eucharistic Prayer, for example, is frequently described as "mystical." Whereas [in the view of Gregory and many early believers, as well as the Orthodox Church] saints possess this "mystical" perception in an eminent way because they have attuned themselves to the gift of grace, all Christians are equally the recipients of the grace itself and are therefore called, by imitating the saints, to acquire and develop the "mystical knowledge.""

So, in other words, there are aspects of Christian belief and worship that Christians in America might view as mystical, but which Gregory (and many others throughout Christian history) would have viewed as a normal, natural part of following Christ. (From John Meyendorff, preface, *The Life of Moses* by Gregory of Nyssa, Paulist Press, 1978, pp. xii-xiii.)

10. The question is, what spirit or spirits are guiding such transformation? Are they of God and his kingdom or of Satan's kingdom? There are satanic counterfeits of the things of God, but I don't believe contemplation practices are counterfeits. They are the real deal, and if you study Chapter 3 to see what the Bible says about it, I think you'll become convinced.

11. Cynthia Bourgeault, *Centering Prayer and Inner Awakening*, © Cowley Publications, 2004, p 13.

12. One argument against Transcendental Meditation (TM) goes like this: in TM, you're assigned a phrase in Sanskrit (the ancient language of India, no longer spoken in everyday life) to use as your mantra. Unless you've studied ancient Hindu theology, it's not likely you'd know what the mantra means. It's often a prayer to one of the Hindu gods, and though you don't know what you're saying, the spirit that masquerades as that particular god could still begin influencing you if you use it.

13. There are Christian forms of repetitive prayer, such as the Jesus Prayer used by Russian Orthodox believers: "Lord Jesus Christ, Son of God, have mercy on me, a sinner" (a combination of Psalm 51:1, Luke 18:9-14 and 35-43, and various other prayers and pleas in the Bible). That prayer, along with "GodhelpmeGodhelpmeGodhelpme," have accompanied major turning points in my life. The idea that repetition in prayer is wrong is a misunderstanding, based on the King James translation of Matthew 6:7. The word translated "vain repetition" in that verse is probably better translated "babbling like pagans;" the Greek word means "to stammer." Pagans would chant incantations as a form of prayer to a specific god in charge of, say, the rain, or luck—thus, a form of prayer that has nothing to do with relationship with God, which is what Christian prayer is all about.

Jesus's point in the passage (v. 6-13) is that God knows our hearts and our needs much better than we do, so to a degree, talk is superfluous. He is also echoing Elijah's mockery of the prophets of Baal (1 Kings 18:25-29) and comparing the Pharisees' prayers to theirs. The point of repetition in prayer—a sacred word in centering prayer, the Jesus prayer, or others—isn't to keep saying it until God hears it. It's to keep us in the presence of God until the Spirit can complete a work of transformation in us. Christian prayer—petitionary, conversational, repetitive, meditational, or silent—is all about transformation. The Jesus prayer, repeating the Lord's Prayer, and similar prayers can be very powerful tools of transformation. Let's not be too quick to dismiss the power of such prayers.

14. We think of prayer today as "asking God for stuff," or just having a conversation with God. But that is the modern era's twist on prayer, influenced by the Age of Reason that said just sitting in silence and waiting for God, or using repetitive prayers, was worthless because the rational mind can't make sense of it. For most of Christian history, however, the term "prayer" has meant just calling on God, opening to God, waiting on God—with words, or with silent waiting and eager longing. "As a servant waits for his master...so our eyes are on you, oh God" (Psalm 123:2)

15. Even when what goes on in our heads isn't overtly selfish, it's almost always coming from the perspective of self and is ultimately (if subtly) self-serving. We have the mind of Christ, Paul says, but we have to learn how to use it. The first step in that process is learning how to get out of our own mind. That's what centering prayer is for. So, yes, I'll admit that centering prayer is a way of going out of your mind. But that's a good thing.

16. T. S. Eliot, *The Four Quartets*. (Need permission).

17. This is a wonderful book; I highly recommend it, especially Kitty Muggeridge's translation entitled *The Sacrament of the Present Moment*, a title I prefer. It wasn't that Mr. de Caussade couldn't make up his mind about the title. He didn't actually write a book; he just wrote lots of letters. Others after him read the letters, recognized the deeply mystical nature of his love for Christ, put them together in book form and published them. Others later republished them under other titles. That's why there are different titles.

18. When I emailed Bear to ask if I could use this quote, along with granting permission he said, "We make our relationship with the Lord too complicated. I'm asking Him to make me childlike in everything I do." (He also sent me a photo of him weightlifting. Nine hundred pounds, I kid you not. Wow.)

Chapter 3: What the Bible Says about Contemplative Spirituality

1. Let me say again that contemplation and mystical spirituality are not the special province of some elite group; there are many ordinary people who are contemplatives but don't know it. If, on a regular basis, you explore with God the mysteries of his Word to the point of experiencing supernatural revelation—which sounds ponderous, but can just be hearing that "still small voice" or sensing a deep closeness to God—you may be one of them. If you let these times of prayer and Word treasure-hunting extend into being in inner silence as you rest in God, or if you often see God's hand in the little things of everyday life, you can be considered a contemplative.

2. In the context of the entirety of Psalm 46, I fully believe verse 10 refers to contemplation, or at least to resting in and communing with God in silence. After comparing various translations and doing some Hebrew word studies, my brief paraphrase of Psalm 46 is this: God is our hope, our help, our everything (v. 1). Though we are often fearful, because of God there's nothing to fear (v. 2-3). His river of life, the Holy Spirit (and our place of connection to God, our inner, true self) are within us, giving joy (vs. 4). His very presence brings the stillness and peace of dawn to our hearts (v. 5). His voice brings to silence both our false-self kingdom within and the world's raging without (v. 6). Though we are weak, God is our strength (v. 7). We are encouraged to behold with awe the wonders of God; they show the world its own desolation, but to his people, God's wonders bring a worshipful sense of awe and reverence (v. 8). By such awe and reverence, God breaks down our defenses—and those of the whole world (v. 9). When we rest in the stillness of death in God, we come to truly know him and see his glory in the whole world (v. 10; be still: see Strong's, Hebrew dictionary entry 7503 with reference to 7495/7496). God is truly with us, our strength, our hope, our everything (v. 11).

3. Appendix 5 explores the subject of contemplation in early Christianity.

4. Unfortunately, this form of Christianity bears a striking resemblance to what we see in much of American Christianity today. There's a parallel there: one of the great blossomings of Christian contemplative spirituality

began at that point; there have been a few more, also beginning at times when the Church was at its worst; another appears to be starting in our day.

5. My own paraphrase. For those who feel this passage is being taken out of context, much of Scripture lends itself to deeper levels of meaning as well as the basic, simple meaning. And all of Psalm 23 has contemplative overtones. For instance, the "valley of the shadow of death" sounds a lot like John of the Cross's "Dark Night of the Soul."

6. Open the Eyes of My Heart lyrics ©1997, Integrity's Hosanna! Music, lyrics by Paul Baloche.

7. Behold Now the Kingdom, © 1980 by John Michael Talbot, Birdwing Music.

8. I suppose you could say revealing to people the inexpressible mystery of the life, death and resurrection of Christ brings him greater delight. I agree, but that's revealed by God in nature and everyday life too. For instance, my wife recently brought home three long, beautiful gladiolus flower stalks, each with a dozen or more blossoms on the verge of opening. They were gorgeous; one had violet blooms, another peach, and the third white. The first thing Diane did when she got them home was to cut off the top blossom of each stalk. She told me that the lady at the farmer's market where she bought them had explained to her that if you cut off the top blossom, the others will fully open; otherwise they won't. I immediately saw in this a picture of Christ, the Top Blossom of all humanity, cut off for us so we can live the abundant life—and a picture of the Christian life, with much of what we would have called "best" in our lives sacrificed to God, so that the rest of our lives can be lived in his presence and under his blessings. The gladiolus plant, it turns out, is a living illustration of a glorious truth: that only the crucified are truly alive. The world around us is stuffed full to bursting with little things like this. God made it that way for the edification and grace-ification of all those who learn to behold his making all things new every moment.

9. I think this is at least partly why, in Rev. 20, after Satan is loosed from the Abyss at the end of the Millennium, he is able to deceive people on

such a grand scale. He raises an army "from the four corners of the earth," "like the sand on the seashore" (v. 7-9a). Even during the Millennium, when Christ will be the Ruler of the earth, there will still be unbelievers. Satan will be locked away and unable to influence people as he does now, but people will still have a sinful nature. Knowing God's Word then won't be just a matter of memorizing scriptures; it will require knowing God himself, knowing him intimately and knowing his voice.

Chapter 4: True Self, False Self, and Crucifying the Ego

1. "Ego-trip" is a 1960's/70's term for being controlled by the ego in a prideful way, or a particular pet project of such an ego.

2. *Turn Your Eyes Upon Jesus*, by Helen Howarth Lemmel, 1922. Public domain.

3. Much of what the Bible is about is non-attachment to things in order to be attached fully to God. Non-attachment is all about dying to self. The term itself is more familiar to practitioners of eastern religions, but not unknown in Christianity; the more common term among Christians is detachment. Mother Teresa said this about detachment: "Once we take our eyes away from ourselves, from our interests, from our own rights, privileges, ambitions - then they will become clear to see Jesus around us." A few scriptures to think about on this subject: the parable of the prodigal son (Luke 15:11-32; for more on this, see the last section of chapter 8 of this book), Jesus's conversation with the rich young man (Luke 18:18-30), Jesus's temptations in the wilderness (Matthew 4:1-11), Mark 10:17-31, 1 Timothy 6:10/Hebrews 13:5, and the entire Sermon on the Mount (Matthew 5:1-7:29). Also, see Appendix 8 for the contemplative/non-attachment version of the Ten Commandments.

4. Another thing that helps, and helps with your centering prayer practice too, is fasting. It's also a good way to find out where you stand on the matter of attachment. In the Bible, fasting is usually spoken of in connection with food: not eating. Fasting helps show us our attachment to food and helps weaken that attachment; it can do the same for you with other attachments as well. Fasting helps put things in perspective:

God first; everything else in our lives must be submitted to him and his will. Centering prayer is, in fact, a short fast from thinking normal thoughts; like centering prayer, fasting is usually done for the purpose of focusing on God (although it has excellent health benefits as well). I highly recommend fasting as a way to help strengthen your centering prayer practice. (WARNING: Until you know how your body responds to fasting, be careful about driving or working, especially doing hard physical work, while fasting. Check with your doctor to make sure fasting won't cause problems with any physical conditions you have or any medications you are taking.)

Be aware that fasting isn't easy. If you do a water-only fast, you'll feel like you're dying, and actually, during that time, you sort of are. That's the point: dying to self. Juice fasts are easier and almost as effective. If you've never fasted before, start simply, just a one-meal juice fast on a day when you don't have to work or drive. Your mind may play tricks on you, but try to stick it out through whatever period of time you've chosen to fast. If you do okay with one meal, try two meals, then a whole day. During the time you choose to fast, drink only juice and herbal teas, no solid foods. Organic strawberry lemonade, raspberry lemonade or just plain old lemonade, work best; detox teas also are helpful because they help the body get rid of toxins (chemicals that have built up in the body, which can cause problems).

If fasting works for you, try getting in the habit of doing a juice fast one day a week. Try doing at least one extra centering prayer session while fasting; you will often find that fasting helps you to be more focused on and sensitive to God than usual. If one-day juice fasting works well for you, try a two or three day fast; if you're able to do that with no serious problems, try doing a three-day juice fast once a month, and even a ten-day juice fast once a year. (The third day is usually the worst; after that it gets easier.) If juice fasting doesn't cause any problems (other than the normal stuff that happens when you don't eat!), try fasting with water only, but remember, it will be harder! Also, you can fast anything, not just food; ask God about helping you to do centering prayer, intercessory prayer, Bible study, etc., during the time you would normally watch TV or play video games, for example. Things like this aren't wrong in themselves, but they do tend to lead us away from God; too much of any good thing is no longer good. (God is the exception to that rule; there's no such thing as too much of him!) It will also be helpful to meditate on what the Bible says about fasting: Isaiah 58:1-12, especially verses 6-7; Jesus's comment about fasting in Matthew 6:16-18; his 40-day fast in the desert (Matthew 4:1-11); Moses and Elijah's 40-day fasts, etc.

Chapter 5: Being Alone with God

1. And I Love Her, Lennon & McCartney, © 1965 Northern Songs Ltd.

2. This is true unless you live in Flagstaff, Arizona, the world's first International Dark Sky City, of which there are very few. Another place is the isolated village of Santa Rosa, New Mexico, a place I passed through a few years ago and found myself in deep awe, wonder and worship upon viewing the sky as I hadn't seen it since I was in grade school at Boy Scout Camp in the Rockies. Sadly, there are fewer and fewer places in our country, outside Alaska, where you can see the stars in all their glory in a fully dark sky.

3. The title of the Beatles' famous paean to LSD.

4. "The Lord is Gracious and Compassionate," by Graham Ord, ©1998 Vineyard Songs (UK/Eire).

5. Only the Blood of Jesus, by Brian Doerksen, © 1990 Mercy/Vineyard Publishing. The line "Mercy triumphs over judgment" is not a regular part of the song, but a spontaneous add-on repeated several times in the original recording of a worship service led by Doerksen on Vineyard's Winds of Worship CD #1, which first presented the song to the world. I first heard the song in 1993; to this day, it's one of my favorite worship songs.

6. Examples of the value God places on mercy: Exodus 20:6 and 33:18-20; 2 Sam. 24:14; Nehemiah 9:31; Psalms 5:7, 31:22, 51:1, 57:1, 116:1; Is. 55:7, 63:9; Dan. 9:18; Hosea 6:6; Micah 6:8, 7:18; Hab. 3:2; Matt. 5:7, 23:23; Luke 1:78, 10:30-37; John 8:1-11; Rom. 11:32, 12:1; Eph. 2:3-5; Heb. 4:16; James 2:13, 3:17; 1 Peter 1:3.

7. Lyrics from "To Be With You" by Danny Daniels, © 1989 Mercy / Vineyard Publishing, used by permission.

8. Hieromonk Damascene.

9. A couple of quotes from Einstein: "My religion consists of a humble admiration of the illimitable superior spirit who reveals himself in the slight details we are able to perceive with our frail and feeble mind." And, "Everyone who is seriously involved in the pursuit of science becomes convinced that a spirit is manifest in the laws of the Universe-a spirit vastly superior to that of man, and one in the face of which we with our modest powers must feel humble."

10. Everett Fox, The Five Books of Moses, Schocken Books, 1995, p. 92.

11. The fact that this is the first mention of love in the Bible is highly significant, according to many theologians. "The Law of First Mention may be said to be the principle that requires one to go to that portion of the Scriptures where a doctrine is mentioned for the first time and to study the first occurrence of the same in order to get the fundamental inherent meaning of that doctrine." This is rule four of the seven rules of interpretation of Scripture according to the Biblical Research Studies Group; the quote is taken from their website, http://www. biblicalresearch.info/page7.html. In other words, since Genesis 22 marks the first occurrence of the subject of love in the Bible, this passage— about Abraham's love for Isaac and his willingness to sacrifice him because of his greater love for God—tells us, from God's point of view, the basic meaning of what real love is all about.

Chapter 6: For Those who have Ears to Hear and Eyes to See

1. Richard Rohr, *Falling Upward: A Spirituality for the Two Halves of Life*. Taken from Goodreads Rohr quotes, chapter 7.

2. Richard Rohr and John Fiester, *Things Hidden: Scripture as Spirituality*, St. Anthony Messenger Press, © 2008.

3. This is a reference to one of the classics of Christian mysticism, compiled from letters written by Jean Pierre de Caussade, an 18th century French Jesuit priest. More than a century after he died, some of his letters were collected and published under the title *Abandonment to Divine Providence*, and also as *Self-Abandonment to Divine Providence*. An expanded version was republished decades later; it included some of his writings that had been edited out in the original publication. It was retranslated by Kitty Muggeridge, wife of writer Malcolm Muggeridge, and published again in 1966 under the title, *The Sacrament of the Present Moment*, a title I prefer. As with the writings of the 14th century German mystic Meister Eckhart, some writers have likened de Caussade's writings to Zen and other forms of Buddhism, but from a thoroughly Christ-centered viewpoint.

4. *Remember: Be Here Now*, © 1971 by Ram Dass, originally published by the Lama Foundation/Hanuman Foundation, now by Three Rivers Press. Ram Dass's original name was Richard Alpert, and he was Timothy Leary's partner in the experiments at Harvard with psychedelic drugs in the 1960's. Afterward, he traveled to India and eventually became a Hindu mystic. *Be Here Now* is one of the many teachings, from all ages of history and all religions, which explain the importance of learning to find God in the present moment. Jesus is among the greatest teachers of this worldwide doctrine (see Matt. 6:25-34, as noted in this chapter, for example).

5. Proverbs 11:2.

6. This doesn't mean they aren't real.

7. I am indebted to Carl McColman for his excellent insights into Biblical dualism. The following quote is from a question-and-answer page on his contemplative website, carlmccolman.com: "...many [Christian] mystics (for example, Isaac of Syria) proclaim that the fires of hell are actually the fires of God's love, which is experienced as "hellish" by those who reject such love. It's a beautiful way of seeing eternity that deconstructs the punitive idea of God tormenting the damned in the lake of fire: when we die, we all spend eternity immersed in the love of God; it is up to us whether we experience that love as radiant light or as burning

flame. Put another way: God is nondual (God loves all people equally),
but in this life it is us humans who filter the love of God dualistically,
dividing ourselves into the worthy "sheep" and the reprobate "goats.""" Of
course, at the final judgment, he will have to choose between those who
choose him and those who don't. But until then, his love for all of us is
the bottom line. Concerning going beyond seeing good-vs.-evil, the point
is that love resolves the two: both are in God's hands, so at some point,
even this most powerful of dichotomies disappears. C.S. Lewis's book *The
Great Divorce* deals with this issue in a similar way.

Chapter 7: The Mystical Christ

1. *From Eternity to Here* by Frank Viola, © 2009, David C. Cook,
publisher, p. 210; italics mine.

2. We tend to think the word "myth" means something that's not true.
Myth, however, is the basic belief system and point of view of any
culture, including Christian and American cultures. Jewish writer and
holocaust survivor Elie Wiesel said that some things are true whether
they happened or not. For Christians, whether the Adam and Eve story
happened literally or not, the truths expressed in it are beyond question;
that's why social scientists say the story is part of Christian mythology,
though many Christians object to that term. As American Christians,
our mythology is about little white country churches, God Bless America
bumper stickers, and the idea that God gave us this land. (Actually, our
white forefathers forcefully, violently and illegally took it away from the
hundreds of native tribal nations living here.) As a nation, our myths
have to do with George Washington and the cherry tree, "Honest" Abe
Lincoln, the idea that we are the greatest nation on earth, that God loves
Americans more than anyone else. Unfortunately, most nations have a
similar idea about their country, culture and people group. Jesus, on the
other hand, said "my kingdom is not of this world." That tells me that
fervent nationalism isn't on God's list of values. Christ loves the Chinese,
Polish, Saudis, Quechuas, Sudanese, and Brazilians just as much as
Americans. And yes, we are every bit as much under the sway of our own
mythology as the ancient Greeks, Romans or any other people group who
ever lived.

267

3. Lorraine Kisly, editor, quoting Father Thomas Hopko, Orthodox priest, quoted in *The Inner Journey: Views from the Christian Tradition*, Parabola Anthology Series, © 2006 Morning Light Press, page xiv. Hopko is quoting 1 Cor. 1:23.

4. 1 Peter 3:3-4.

5. As with the "Two Trees in Eden" section, I am also indebted to Frank Viola and his book *From Eternity to Here* (see footnote 1) for some of the insights in the "Bride of Christ" section.

6. Joseph Campbell with Bill Moyers, *The Power of Myth*, Doubleday, 1988, pp. 90-94.

Chapter 8: Transformation

1. Taken from *Invictus*, a poem by William Ernest Henley.

2. Like the Outback Steakhouse slogan: no rules, just right.

3. Lyrics from "How He Loves" by John Mark MacMillan, copyright 2005.

4. Luke 6:38 and Matthew 5:7.

5. Galatians 6:7.

6. This does not negate grace; without grace there would be no mercy, and every time we broke any of God's laws, retribution would be harsh and immediate. For a comparison of this and three other ways of looking at the Ten Commandments, see Appendix 8.

7. Also referred to sometimes in Christian mystical texts as theosis or divinization. This is NOT the same as the Mormon doctrine of theosis. The Mormons believe what Joseph Smith taught: that God was once a man, still is an exalted man with a physical body, that men can become Gods just like the God of the Bible, and that that's what Jesus

did—contrary to what the Bible says (see John 1:1-5, Hebrews 13:8, John 8:56-59, Revelation 1:5-8, etc.). This doctrine is patently false, false in many ways and easily refuted by those who know their Bible well. Rather than get into that discussion here, I will simply refer you to the following resources: the 4truth.net Comparison Chart: Mormonism and Christianity; So What's the Difference? by Fritz Ridenour, © 1967 and 2001, Gospel Light Publications; The Godmakers by Ed Decker and Dave Hunt, © 1997 Harvest House Publishers; contenderministries.org/mormonism/comparison.php.

8. "Waterlogging" article by Julie Wakefield, Smithsonian Magazine, September 2000.

9. A similar analogy God showed me concerning divine union has to do with the air in our bodies. Every living being in the animal kingdom breathes in air (or at least oxygen, in the case of marine creatures). The oxygen we take in ends up in every single one of our cells, even bone, to the point that it merges with the carbon, calcium, and all the other dozens of chemical elements that make up our bodies. What was once pure oxygen in a breath you inhaled at some point, has combined in hundreds of ways with other elements to make up your skin, muscle, hair, bone—everything from the cartilage in your ears and nose all the way down to your toenails. Is it still oxygen? As I understand it, at the atomic or sub-molecular level, scientists can separate out what is oxygen and what is, say, sulfur, or boron, or any other element. But at the molecular level, they are truly merged—in union.

10. The Augustine of Hippo quote is from the Psalm 50 commentary of his *Exposition on the Book of Psalms*. On the other hand, Augustine also said, "This is the very perfection of a man, to find out his own imperfections" (Sermon on Philippians 3:14, 15 Sermon CLXX). He couldn't have said that of God; of men, Jesus is the exception, though even he, in order to reach perfection, "learned obedience through the things he suffered" (Hebrews 5:8-9).

11. Thomas Aquinas, Summa Theologiae 3.1.2.

12. In case you got lost, the last 2 paragraphs are based on 2 Peter 1:4-9.

13. Note: the writings of John of the Cross aren't light reading. Much of his writings consist of meditations on Bible passages, and like many parts of scripture, John of the Cross can be difficult to understand, but the effort is well worth the time invested. Of the many translations, probably the best is his Collected Works translated by Kieran Kavanaugh and Otilio Rodriguez (these include John's original poetry in Spanish next to the English translations, which can be helpful even if you don't know Spanish). There are numerous commentaries on his works as well, available in print, online, and in e-book form as well.

14. Thomas Keating, *Invitation to Love*, © 1992 St. Benedict's Monastery.

15. "Love is the Hard Part," by Michael Anderson, © 1996 Up in the Mix Music (a division of the Forefront Communications Group, Inc.) (BMI) All Rights Reserved.

16. William Johnston, *Mystical Theology*, © 1995 Orbis Books.

17. Many of the cross-cultural and other insights into this parable came from Richard Clinton, senior pastor of the Springs Vineyard, Colorado Springs, Colorado, Nov. 14 and 21, 2012, and from Hurschel Hendrix, pastor emeritus, and Dieter Rademacher, pastor, of Community Fellowship of Christians Church in Lake George, Colorado, July 6, 2013.

18. With rare and questionable exceptions, whenever Jesus used the term "sinner," it was in reference to the Pharisees' use of the word to categorize those they didn't want to be associated with. It appears to me that in these instances, rather than referring to people as sinners, Jesus was mocking the Pharisees for their attitudes toward those God passionately loves, no matter how "sinful." The passage which is the subject of this section, Luke 15, is all about the contrast between how men see other men, and how God sees all men, even the worst of "sinners" (see verses 7 and 10).

Epilogue

(No endnotes)

Appendix 1: FAQ'S

(No endnotes)

Appendix 2: Paradoxes I Have Known and Loved

1. Singer-songwriter Michael Card, "God's Own Fool" © 1986 Birdwing Music and Mole End Music.

2. From Alister E. McGrath, *Surprised by Meaning*, © 2011 by Westminster John Knox Press, P. 55-56.

3. These last two examples are from Lao Tzu's Tao te Ching of ancient China, the "bible" of Taoism.

4. Deuteronomy 6:4, the central core of the Jewish faith: "Shema Yisrael Adonai Elohenu, Adonai Echad": Hear, O Israel, the Lord our God, the Lord is one"—a powerful paradox in itself.

5. From *Jewish Meditation* by Aryeh Kaplan, Schocken Books, 1985, p. 126-7.

6. From James R. Newby in www.mentoring-disciples.org/Dancing.html; Reprinted from *Quarterly Yoke Letter*, Vol. 39, No. 3, September, 1996.

Appendix 3: Lectio Divina

1. "The Gift of the Call" by Christopher Bamford, from The Inner Journey: Views from the Christian Tradition (Parabola Anthology Series, Morning Light Press, 2006, p. 7.

Appendix 4: Contemplation and Early Christian History

1. According to Jewish sources, various forms of meditation, including silent meditation, were practiced in ancient Israel (Isaac meditated, Gen.

24:63); the Hebrew word for one type of meditation, *hitbonenut*, means "being alone" or "isolating oneself"—which sounds exactly like what Christ was often known to do (e.g., Mark 1:35; Luke 5:16). *Hitbonenut* meditation is known to often lead to a deeper form of meditation or contemplation called *dveikus*, which means "cleaving to God." Other forms of Jewish meditation include meditation on God's presence to the point of forgetting all else, including oneself. (Aryeh Kaplan, *Jewish Meditation: A Practical Guide*, © 1985, Schocken Books, p. 49). The little-known (to Christians at least) subject of Jewish meditation and mystical practices was thoroughly explored by Kaplan in this and in his other books. In this footnote and the next I am providing a very brief overview of the subject with examples of types of Jewish meditational forms. Though I would love to include a larger section on this subject, space does not allow us to delve into this fascinating and rich tradition here. Suffice it to say that entire books could be written on the connection between the ancient Jewish mystical tradition and Christian contemplative practices.

One example of the numerous Old Testament mystical writings is found in Isaiah 55. There we are bid to "come to the water," water that is also wine, milk, and the richest of foods—but it's the thirsty and the poor who receive this living water. How do you get it? "Come to me with your ears wide open. Listen, for the life of your soul is at stake" (Is. 55:3, Living Bible). The words of God we are to listen for in silence, are words that accomplish God's purposes as rain brings life; for those who learn to listen closely to God, the mountains burst into song. Compare Psalm 63: "…earnestly I seek you; my soul thirsts for you in a dry and weary land where there is no water…my soul will be satisfied with the richest of foods…I sing in the shadow of your wings. My soul clings to you…" And of course, let's not forget the "Beside still waters" of Psalm 23 and "Be still and know that I am God" of Psalm 46. Christians since at least the second century have called these writings mystical.

2. Kaplan, *Jewish Meditation*; quotes are from p. 40-45. Why is the subject of Jewish meditation so little known in our day? The Jews seem to have been even more strongly affected by the Enlightenment's emphasis on the mind and rationalism than the rest of Western civilization, as evidenced perhaps by the predominance of Jewish people in the psychology and psychiatry professions and among writers in that field,

at least in the twentieth century. Kaplan explains how, as with Christian contemplative practices, the effect of the so-called Enlightenment/Age of Reason on the Jewish mystical tradition was to encourage people to ignore anything considered mystical. Kaplan says of this period of history, "Anything that touched upon the mystical was denigrated as superstition and occultism and was deemed unworthy of serious study." This same attitude toward contemplation and mysticism continues into our time, though the limitations of the rationalistic view and the value of meditation are again beginning to be recognized within the past generation or two.

Kaplan also discusses how, because of the difficulty of keeping Jewish religious practices from veering off into idolatry once the Jews were no longer together in their homeland, beginning with the Jewish Diaspora meditational practices came to gradually be observed only by elite groups of spiritual leaders, not by the average person in Jewish society. "…Around this time [beginning of the Diaspora], the more advanced forms of meditation were hidden from the masses and made part of a secret teaching" (Jewish Meditation, p. 43). In addition, because mystical terminology was couched in symbolism, it was not easily understood or even recognizable as such by those outside its system. For example, the "discipline of the chariot" (*maaseh merkavah*) mentioned in various Jewish religious texts refers to the study of the first chapter of Ezekiel, believed by Jewish mystics to hold "the keys to prophetic meditation" (p. 43); "…since meditation had become a secret doctrine within Judaism by Talmudic times, everything is couched in allusion and allegory. Only to one who is aware of the methods do the accounts even begin to make sense" (p. 46). In any case, the fact that all of the common Jewish terms for meditation are in Hebrew shows how ancient the practice is; Aramaic started becoming the common language of the Jewish people in the Second Temple period, several centuries before Christ and Christianity.

One interesting type of Jewish meditation Kaplan speaks of is based on a phrase in Proverbs 3:6, "In all your ways know him," which the Talmud says "contains the entire essence of the Torah" (*Jewish Meditation*, p. 141ff.) "It [the Talmud] teaches that no matter what a person does, he can dedicate it to God and make it into an act of worship. Even the most mundane act can serve as a link to the Divine…When a person has such a love for God, then even an act as mundane as washing dishes becomes an expression of this love…It is as if God's love is on one side, our love is on the other, and the act is in the middle." (*Jewish Meditation*, p. 141-142). This is easily comparable to the teaching expressed in the great 17th century Christian contemplative classic, *The Practice of the Presence of God* by Brother Lawrence.

Another interesting type of Jewish meditation involves meditating on God's commands. Kaplan writes, "When you keep a commandment, try meditating on the fact that God's will is in the commandment. In a deep meditative state, you will actually be able to feel God's will in the action and the fact that God and His will are one." (*Jewish Meditation*, p. 149-150). From these examples we can begin to get a taste of the depth and richness of the Jewish mystical and meditational traditions.

3. The church in the Kerala region of India, along the southwest coast near the southern tip of India, is believed to have been started by the Apostle Thomas. In the first two or three centuries, while still trying to gain footholds in Europe, Christianity was thriving in the Middle East—which is western Asia, the real center of Christianity in those centuries—and expanding eastward as far as Persia (Iran), Afghanistan, India and China. For more on this subject, see Philip Jenkins's excellent book, *The Lost History of Christianity: The Thousand-Year Golden Age of the Church in the Middle East, Africa and Asia—and How it Died*, © 2008 HarperOne (HarperCollins Publishers).

4. Christianity in Asia mainly was a form known as Nestorianism, named for Nestorius, a Christian leader of the 5th century. He was eventually condemned as heretical by the Catholic Church for refusing to call Mary the "Mother of God" and for saying Christ's human and divine natures were separate and distinct but loosely joined; in other words, he emphasized the humanity of Christ without denying his divinity. Although certain aspects of Asian Christianity were condemned by the Western Church, what the two had in common was always much greater than their differences and, in retrospect, hardly worth fighting about.

5. Jenkins, *The Lost History of Christianity*, p. 9.

6. *Ibid.*, p. 74. "The quest for divinity" refers to the practice of *theosis*, or attaining union with God, not efforts to become God; the idea that one could actually become God or a god was considered heretical among

the Eastern churches as well as in European Christianity. Union with God means becoming one with God as man and woman are physically united in marriage yet remaining separate entities, not becoming God as some of the new-age prophets claim (and it certainly doesn't refer to the blasphemous notion of having sex with God). For more, see chapter 8, the Union with God section.

7. *Ibid.*, p. 93-95. Jenkins's account of this Chinese monk, Markos, and his traveling partner Bar Sauma (also a monk), is truly fascinating. Bar Sauma ended up in the royal courts of Europe; Markos, who became Patriarch of the Eastern Church, with authority over churches from Jerusalem to China, ""exercised ecclesiastical sovereignty over more of the earth's surface than even the pontiff in Rome"" (p. 94, quoting Samuel Hugh Moffett, *History of Christianity in Asia*, © 1998 Orbis Books, 1:434.

8. Aramaic and its descendant languages, such as Hebrew and Arabic, are even written right-to-left like Chinese, rather than left-to-right like European languages. For more on the Aramaic roots of Christianity, see *Prayers of the Cosmos: Meditations on the Aramaic Words of Jesus,* by Neil Douglas-Klotz, HarperSanFrancisco, © 1990. Although not written from a perspective modern American Christians would identify with, the book does provide valuable information on the Aramaic language and associated culture in which Jesus grew up.

9. See footnotes 1 and 2.

10. "Although scholars debate the origins of Sufism, some of the parallels to Eastern Christianity are overwhelming, particularly in terms of practices of mystical prayer and devotion. *From the earliest Christian ages*, Egypt and the Near East had flourishing mystical and ascetic traditions..." Jenkins, p. 198, italics mine.

11. Jenkins, *The Lost History of Christianity*, p. 38. We tend to think of the Middle East, or western and central Asian countries, as 100 percent Muslim, but there have been significant Christian communities in Iraq and other Middle Eastern countries up to our time. In 1980 there were over a million Christians in Iraq, 7% of the Iraqi population. One

negative and underreported effect of the American invasions of Iraq in 1991 and 2003 was increased persecution of Christians; in 2005, the Christian population of Iraq was down to just 3 percent of Iraqis. Many fled to other countries; others were killed by Saddam Hussein's regime and by Muslim tribal groups. In Iran, there has been a Christian presence since the days of the Book of Acts (see Acts 2:9; Parthians and Medes were the ancient people groups of Persia—today's Iran—at the time of Christ.) In Afghanistan, there was a large Christian population for many centuries, but Christianity was nearly eradicated there under the persecutions of Timur, commonly known to history as Tamerlane, who "was responsible for the effective destruction of the Christian Church in much of Asia." (Sources: http://en.wikipedia.org/wiki/Christianity_in_Iraq; http://en.wikipedia.org/wiki/Christianity_in_Iran; http://en.wikipedia.org/wiki/Timur.

12. For more on this subject, see *The Wisdom Jesus* by Cynthia Bourgeault, Shambhala Publications, 2008, and *Lost Christianities: The Battles for Scripture and the Faiths we Never Knew,* by Bart D. Ehrman, Oxford University Press, 2003 (written when Ehrman still considered himself a practicing Christian, though he now says he's an agnostic).

13. Taken from Princeton Theological Seminary professor Samuel Hugh Moffett's *A History of Christianity in Asia,* ©1992, Harper San Francisco, p. xiii. See also http://www.religion-online.org/showchapter. asp?title=1553&C=1360, and The Christian History Timeline website, http://www.christianhistorytimeline.com/GLIMPSEF/Glimpses/ glmps043.shtml. This website also notes that King Tiridates of Armenia was led to Christ about 301 AD by an evangelist known as Gregory the Illuminator and that Armenia is considered to have been the first nation in the world to officially accept Christianity, in 301.

14. (Concerning modern Western theology's separation of spirituality from theology): "...in the [Church] Fathers, there is no divorce between dogmatic and mystical theology...their mysticism...is at the heart of their theology, the issues raised in their dogmatic theology being... resolved at the level of their mystical theology." The Origins of the Christian Mystical Tradition: From Plato to Denys, © 1983 by Andrew Louth, Oxford University Press, p. xi.

15. R. P. Lawson, ed., Origen's *Commentary on the Song of Songs*, Westminster, MD, 1957, p. 265, quoted in William Johnston, *Mystical Theology*, ©1995 Orbis Books, p. 13.

16. Bernard McGinn, *The Essential Writings of Christian Mysticism*, ©2006 The Modern Library (Random House), p. 6. Also, this note on Origen from the same book: "Origen…was the first to see in some paired figures of the Old and New Testaments biblical proof for the superiority of contemplation over action. The most important of these twinned figures were the sisters Mary and Martha visited by Jesus in Luke 10:38-42. Origen identified Mary with contemplation and Martha, who was "busy about many things," with action, so Jesus' statement that Mary "has chosen the best part which shall not be taken from her" proved the superiority of contemplation. Many later mystics followed Origen's view, but by no means all." The author goes on to say that Gregory the Great, three and a half centuries later, spoke of the merits of the active life and said contemplation should yield to action when another's need calls for it. (Gregory was also a contemplative who "insisted that all Christians, even the active laity, were called to some measure of contemplation.") *Ibid.,* p. 521.

17. Origen's New Testament Canon was the same as our New Testament today with the exclusion of the Books of James, 2 Peter and 2 and 3 John, and with the inclusion of the Shepherd of Hermas. This is similar to and consistent with what most other Christian leaders of the first four centuries of Christianity considered Scripture; until after the Council of Hippo, many Christian leaders were unwilling to accept some of the letters of Paul, John, Peter, James, Jude, and John's Apocalypse (the Book of Revelation) and believed books we now consider apocryphal to be the sacred Word of God.

Appendix 5: The Spirituality of Breathing

1. © 1995 Mercy/Vineyard Publishing. Words and Music by Marie Barnett.

2. The "sacred word" is one of the common factors of centering prayer; most practitioners use a short word such as Love, or Way, or God. When

I first started doing centering prayer, God made it clear to me that, rather than using a word to return my attention to him when it starts drifting, like most practitioners of centering prayer, he wanted me to use my own breath. I found out later that in centering prayer circles this is called the "sacred breath." (The only thing sacred about my breath is that I use it to help me return my attention to God. Other than being used for that purpose, it's just plain old breathing.) There are also people who use what is known as the "sacred gaze," as if seeing God when closing your eyes. Go with whichever method God leads you to.

Appendix 6: The Ten Commandments: Four Perspectives

1. For this splendid bit of wisdom I am indebted to Grace K. at http://uk.answers.yahoo.com/question/index?qid= 20090608110408AA8AYSC

Bibliography

Benson, Robert, *The Body Broken*, © 2003 Doubleday.

Bourgeault, Cynthia, *Centering Prayer and Inner Awakening*,© 2004 Cowley Publications.

DeCaussade, Jean Pierre; Muggeridge, Kitty, translator, *The Sacrament of the Present Moment*, English translation © 1981 William Collins Sons & Co. Ltd.,
HarperCollins Publishers.

Finley, James, *Christian Meditation*, © 2004 HarperSanFrancisco.

---------------, *Merton's Palace of Nowhere*, © 1978 Ave Maria Press.

Foster, Richard, *Celebration of Discipline*, © 1998 HarperSanFrancisco.

Hagberg, Janet O. and Guelich, Robert A., *The Critical Journey: Stages in the Life of Faith*, © 1995 Sheffield Publishing Company.

Hall, Thelma, *Too Deep for Words: Rediscovering Lectio Divina*, ©1988 Paulist Press.

Johnston, William, *Mystical Theology*, © 1995 Orbis Books.

---------------, ed. (author anonymous), *The Cloud of Unknowing*, © 1973 Image Books.

Keating, Thomas, *Intimacy with God*, © 1994 St. Benedict's Monastery, Snowmass, CO.

---------------, *Invitation to Love*, ©1992 Element Inc./Element Books Limited.

---------------, *Open Mind, Open Heart*, © 1986 Element Books.

---------------, The Mystery of Christ

Kisly, Lorraine, ed., *The Inner Journey: Views from the Christian Tradition*, Parabola Anthology Series, © 2006 Morning Light Press.

Laird, Martin, *Into the Silent Land*, © 2006 Darton, Longman and Todd Ltd.

McGinn, Bernard, *The Essential Writings of Christian Mysticism*, © 2006 The Modern Library.

--------------, *The Foundations of Mysticism* (Volume I of *The Presence of God: A History of Western Christian Mysticism*), © 1995 The Crossroad Publishing Company.

Merton, Thomas, *New Seeds of Contemplation*, © 1961 The Abbey of Gethsemani/New Directions Books.

Pennington, M. Basil, *Lectio Divina*, © 1998 Crossroad Publishing.

Reininger, Gustave, ed., *Centering Prayer in Daily Life and Ministry*, © 1998 Continuum.

Rohr, Richard, *The Naked Now*, © 2009 Crossroad Publishing Company.

Smith, Cyprian, *The Way of Paradox*, © 1987 Darton, Longman and Todd Ltd.

Wiederkehr, Macrina, *Seven Sacred Pauses*, © 2008 Sorin Books.

About the Author

A third-generation Colorado native, the author studied the Bible at Faith Bible College, Arvada, Colorado, in the late 1970's. He received his Bachelor of Arts degree in Writing at the University of Colorado at Denver, 1988. Gary has been a practicing Christian since 1974 and involved in worship ministry since that time. He has been absorbed in the study and practice of contemplative prayer since 2002. When not engaged in contemplative prayer and writing, Gary enjoys hiking, drumming, playing guitar, and reading. He is currently working on a contemplative devotional. He is available for speaking engagements and retreats.

Website: coloradicalwriter.com
Email: coloradical-writing@hotmail.com

www.ingramcontent.com/pod-product-compliance
Lightning Source LLC
Chambersburg PA
CBHW020847090426
42736CB00008B/277